Human Relations

HUMAN RELATIONS

Ann Ellenson

Moorhead Area Vocational-Technical Institute
Moorhead, Minnesota

Prentice-Hall, Inc., Englewood Cliffs, New Jersey

Library of Congress Cataloging in Publication Data

Ellenson, Ann.
 Human relations.

 Includes bibliographies.
 1. Social psychology. 2. Human behavior.
I. Title
HM251.E436 301.1 72-10458
ISBN 0-13-445643-2

Printed in the United States of America

10 9 8 7 6 5 4 3

Prentice-Hall International, Inc., *London*
Prentice-Hall of Australia, Pty. Ltd., *Sydney*
Prentice-Hall of Canada, Ltd., *Toronto*
Prentice-Hall of India Private Limited, *New Delhi*
Prentice-Hall of Japan, Inc., *Tokyo*

With Love to

Ed,
Betsy, and Becky

For Their Understanding

Contents

Preface

You have always been faced with the problem of building meaningful human relationships – first as a child, then as an adolescent, and now as an adult. What is meant by "meaningful" will vary with each individual, just as it has varied with each different age. Before you can determine what is meaningful for you as an individual, you must learn to understand yourself in relation to others and the society in which you live.

The study of human behavior can be fascinating and rewarding. As individuals living and working together, it is necessary to see our own behavior in light of the behavior of our own culture and society. Perhaps the speed with which change is occurring in our world today is one of the most important factors to consider in the study of human relationships. *Change* is one of the few certainties that we can count on. Personalities change, job requirements change, technology changes, laws change, customs change, and relationships change. When you are able to see yourself as a changing person in a changing society, you will be better able to understand your own behavior and that of others.

This book is designed and written to provide resource material for students and teachers for classroom discussion regarding the establishment of meaningful human relationships. You will find that it will raise questions rather than supply "easy answers." It is hoped that after reading each chapter, you will be able to have the type of classroom conversations that will help you to begin arriving at your own answers to your own questions in your own way. You will need to make decisions in these areas:

1. Who is this person I call ME? Why do I feel the way I do? How do I react to problems?
2. What do I believe in? What is of value to me? Can I formulate realistic goals in the midst of accelerating change?
3. How do I fit into the world of work? Will I be able to find a job that will both support me and provide me with enjoyment? Or will I be trapped in a job I hate?
4. Why is there so much misunderstanding? Can I learn to communicate more effectively? Do I "read" the messages of others correctly?
5. How do I feel about my sexuality? Am I comfortable with members of both sexes? The rest of my life is a long time — do I want to share it with someone else?
6. Do I want marriage or do I have any alternatives? Am I ready to face the responsibilities involved in marriage? Is there more involved in marriage than love? How do I feel about raising children of my own?
7. What does the future hold for me? What can I contribute to the future? Do I have any responsibilities to the future?

Building meaningful human relationships requires time, interaction, and people. If more people took the time to be loving human beings, relationships would be more satisfying. Do you want to *take time to be human*?

Taking time to be human connotes a decision or choice. It means sharing and receiving, helping and being helped. It also means responsibility; it means making a decision and accepting the consequences of that personal decision.

Taking *time* to be human connotes a personal involvement; it means reaching out to others and building bridges of understanding. It also means giving; in a busy world, time carries a high value for most of us. Giving and involvement are personal commitments, with immediate satisfaction often delayed in favor of more lasting, long-range goals.

Taking time to be *human* involves the feeling and caring side of life; it means concern for others as well as self. Humanness also involves risk: daring to take a chance on human relationships; trusting in self and others; probing the unknown for answers; and realizing that humans can be the most destructive as well as most constructive of all creatures.

Perhaps *taking time to be human* can best be summed up in the words written by a student who took a course based upon the ideas presented in this book:

> I'm beginning to be *me*! This is happiness. I feel myself growing and I'm satisfied. I think *I* know me – but can I tell *you*?
>
> This class has been great for me because it has stimulated me to relate! *People* have become more important to me. Life is exciting because of chances with people.
>
> I have a *good* family. I only appreciate them now when we're all separated. My mom and dad are alone for the first time in twenty years – they need me now. I don't know if I want to be needed. Yes, I do – but love can't be *demanded*. I want my parents to *want* to let me go.
>
> I feel free. Uninhibited. No strings. This is great. Something I couldn't have till I left home. Not freedom in an irresponsible manner, but free to grow within myself.
>
> Reaching out to people is my philosophy: I never want to be too busy to listen or talk. *People* are lasting and rewarding.

It is for students like this that I have written this book, students who are questioning, searching, and reaching out for meaningful *human relationships*. Teaching such students can be very rewarding and I hope that this book will help other teachers and students share in the mutual experience of establishing meaningful personal relationships.

Many individuals and companies were very helpful to me in the preparation of the "work-oriented" chapters, 8–10. I am especially indebted to the following for their candid and enlightening correspondence:

American Motors, K. G. Pelkey
Dow Chemical Company, Stephen H. Phillips and J. H. Hanes
Johnson & Johnson, Robert V. Moore

Lincoln National Life Insurance Company, R. J. Bade
National Cash Register Company, R. E. Ludwig
Sherwin-Williams Company, E. B. Stadler

To M. J. Warnock, President of Armstrong Cork Company, for his speech, "The Importance of People"; to J. M. Ewell, of Procter & Gamble, for his speech, "The Effect of Change on Organization"; to Eastman Kodak Company for their booklet, "What Industry Looks for in the High School Graduate"; to Richardson-Merrell, Inc., for the report, "The Ideal Vick Executive," original outline by Richard D. Waters; to B. F. Goodrich Company; to Burroughs Corporation; and to an industrial relations manager in the pulp and paper industry who wished to remain anonymous.

I would like to express my appreciation to my family and the many friends who have assisted and supported me during the writing of this book; to list them all would involve another whole chapter, so I will merely say thank you.

Specifically, I would like to thank my colleagues at Moorhead Tech, especially in the Business Department, for their understanding and encouragement; and to my students who, over the years, helped me formulate the outline for this book.

Thanks, also, to my friends at Concordia College, Moorhead, MN., especially in the library, for their encouragement and help; to all my editors at Prentice-Hall, for their advice and coordination; to Reed Carlson for his imaginative photographs; and to my typists, Darlene Geiszler and Virginia Seed, for making readable copy out of the scribbled notes and rough draft of this manuscript. Very special thanks to Reed Merrill for his inspired illustrations; his characters have become an integral part of many chapters.

This book would never have been a reality without the love, faith, and reassurance of my husband Ed and our daughters Betsy and Becky. They shared this experience totally, adapting their life style to meet my needs, and they were my constant source of encouragement. If there is an atmosphere of love and understanding present in this book, it is because of our relationship. Without them, this book would not have happened.

Ann Ellenson

Human Relations

Introduction:
What Does It Mean
To Be Human?

Ours is a world of contrasts. Although we still have abject poverty and want, never before have so many people enjoyed such luxury or so many opportunities for fulfilling their personal needs and desires. This exciting age of expanding technology propels us through life at ever increasing speed and provides us with increased abundance; yet in all our affluence, we seem to be no closer to a better understanding of ourselves, our neighbors, our co-workers, or other nations. We have seen tremendous polarization: "generation gap" has become a common phrase; racial strife continues; wars and conflict still rage; we are surrounded by much noise but little understanding.

There are no easy and simple solutions to this lack of understanding, but we can approach the problem by first establishing some basic foundation of concepts regarding the general nature of mankind. An understanding of the nature of man and of the individual as part of the human race are basic to any study of human relationships.

Nature of Man

It is difficult to establish a common ground which we can call the *basic nature of man;* there are many conflicting views regarding this concept. Three contradictory views need to be reconciled before we can come to a statement regarding the basic nature of man:

1. Is man basically *good* or *evil?*
2. Is man basically *able to reason* or *unable to reason?*
3. Is man's behavior *predetermined* or does he possess a *free will?*

Am I Good or Evil?

The debate regarding the "goodness" or "evilness" of mankind has raged for centuries. The French philosopher Pascal remarked in the seventeenth century that individuals and societies that try to become angels end up as beasts. The ideology at that time leaned toward the view that man was more inherently evil than good, but in more recent years the human desire for love and peace has been stressed as a part of man's basic nature.

Is there any evidence supporting these two points of view? On the one hand, we can review the record of war, violence, and man's inhumanity to man, and we conclude that man's basic nature is evil or destructive. Many would suggest that we require controls or "law and order" if we want an opportunity for good to be expressed.

On the other hand, we can look at the studies of anthropologists who have researched various peoples and have found an absence of aggressiveness. Psychologist Abraham Maslow writes, "This . . . was enough to convince me directly of the fundamental fact that the amount of destructiveness and aggression is largely culturally determined. . . . These are not weak people by any means. The Northern Blackfoot Indians were a prideful, strong, upstanding, self-valuing group. They were simply apt to regard aggression as wrong or pitiful or crazy" [Maslow, pp. 124-25]. Other psychologists and anthropologists have reported similar findings.

Gordon Allport states: "Normal men everywhere reject, in principle and by preference, the path of war and destruction. They like to live in peace and friendship with their neighbors; they prefer to love and be loved rather than to hate and be hated. . . . While wars rage, yet our desire is for peace, and while animosity prevails, the weight of mankind's approval is on the side of affiliation" [Allport, p. xiv].

If we look at our own lives, most of us will agree that we are happiest when we are being loving and "good" and unhappiest when we are being hostile and aggressive. Is such an emotional pattern unrealistic in a world that has such a record of betrayal, war, torture, destruction, and general inhumanity? Can we reconcile these two opposing points of view?

Any possible reconciliation would have to be based on the conclusion that man is a combination of both good and evil — that he has *potentialities* to develop in either direction. He is neither completely good nor completely bad by nature, but he is a highly educable and "shapeable" being; whether he becomes cruel, selfish, and warlike, or kind, loving, and peaceful will depend largely upon the culture and conditions in which he is reared.

Am I Reasonable or Unreasonable?

Is man governed by reason or by whim? Our whole system of social organization in this country is based upon the belief that man, with sufficient information and opportunity, can make responsible decisions to govern himself and to control the direction of his country and his own future. However, we sometimes question man's innate good sense and rationality.

When asked to describe mankind, we tend to think in terms of selfishness, cruelty, and aggression just as often as we think in terms of generosity, kindness, and gentleness; we think in terms of laziness, stupidity, and unreasonableness just as often as ambition, intelligence, and reasonableness. All too often we read in the newspapers or hear stories of so-called "reasonable" people who have acted very irrationally, or who have been completely misled by some scheme that a "reasonable" person should have seen through.

Our faith in man's rationality may be weakened from time to time, but it is never totally lost. Most modern psychologists believe that man's natural tendencies are toward reason and common sense, although these can be distorted by the influences of our environment. Sometimes we can be misled by false information, nearly hypnotized by repetitious stimuli from the mass communications media, overwhelmed by the complex situations of the day, or restricted by our cultural background. It is easy to lapse into believing only what we want to believe, blindly ignoring facts or past lessons.

But we also look at the continuing efforts on the part of man to help create a better world, to make sense out of his daily life, to probe the secrets of the unknown, to attempt to cure the incurable, to exercise reason and control for the long-range good, and to attempt to live in harmony with his fellowmen. Surely this is a sign of a potentially rational and reasonable people. Certainly, we are often irrational; we are often selfish and blind, seeking only immediate goals with no thoughts for others or the future. But man is also a builder, using simple objects to make more complex ones, striving to establish a workable order in both his physical surroundings and in his social relationships.

Am I Subject to Fate or Do I Have a Free Will?

Most of us operate in everyday life under the assumption that we have a free will and that we are able to make decisions and to choose our own course of action. Is this freedom "real" or an "illusion"? Are we at the hands of fate?

Belief in the irreversibility of fate has been held since the days of ancient Greece. Many people today strongly believe in strict determinism, that is, that all events have been predetermined and nothing we can do can change them. You have probably heard statements such as these: "It was supposed to be that way"; "What will be will be"; "There is a reason for everything; just accept it as fate." But our system of law and justice is predicated on the individual's ability to be responsible for his actions, and if all events are predetermined, how can anyone be held responsible for his actions?

There may be times when we feel forced into a decision or action, stating, "I had no choice." But in most instances we *do* have choices; we can exercise our free will and the decision we reach can be *our* decision, not necessarily that of "fate."

Of course, the debate between determinism and belief in free will is not simply a matter of black and white; there is also a lot of gray. This book holds the general view that man in our society *is* free to make choices and to evaluate issues with some degree of objectivity and rationality; he does not merely react in a completely conditioned or predetermined manner. Along with this freedom of choice goes responsibility for decisions.

Effect of Culture

The society or culture in which we live is one of the most important "shapers" and "molders" of our behavior. We are influenced not only by our individual "family culture" but also by the various subgroups to which we belong — religious, age, geographic, occupational, national.

Both knowingly and unknowingly we are taught the ideals, attitudes, customs, and types of behavior that are acceptable to our society. Through learning and experience, beginning in our infancy, we feel the effects of our society or culture. We experiment with types of behavior and soon learn to act in accordance with the basic beliefs, values, and norms of the culture in which we live.

We learn about our culture through a system of reward and punishment for specific actions or behavior, through habits of obedience and imitation, and through the trial-and-error process of getting along with others. The gestures, attitudes, and words used by children often exhibit a striking resemblance to those of their parents.

The social roles which we assume are largely the result of our culture. There is a strong relationship between our culture and our interpretation of the basic nature of man. What is "good," "evil," "reasonable," "unreasonable," or what constitutes "freedom" often differs in degree from one culture to another — even from one subculture to another. Today we are becoming more aware than ever of these "gray" areas, where conditions and events influence the "rightness or wrongness," the "reasonableness or unreasonableness" of behavior or action.

This book will not attempt to set down clear-cut solutions or answers. It will attempt to probe some of these "gray" areas so that *you* can seek your own answers, and in so doing live a happier and more productive life. As N. J. Berrill writes:

> I am a human being, whatever that may be. I speak for all of us who move and think and feel and whom time consumes. I speak as an individual unique in a universe beyond my understanding, and I speak

for man. I am hemmed in by limitations of sense and mind and body, of place and time and circumstance, some of which I know but most of which I do not. I am like a man journeying through a forest, aware of occasional glints of light overhead, with recollections of the long trail I have already traveled, and conscious of wider spaces ahead. I want to see more clearly where I have been and where I am going, and above all I want to know why I am where I am and why I am traveling at all. [Berrill, p. 1.]

Summary

We are aware of many contrasts in life; we have abundance, increased opportunity, and advanced technology, but we are no closer to better understanding. We seek guidelines and direction in our search for the "good life."

We need to understand the nature of our humanness. It seems that man has a potential for both good and evil, but which of the two tendencies is developed depends largely upon the culture and conditions under which he is raised. Man has the ability to reason, but he is often and easily misled; he often acts irrationally. Our behavior is somewhat conditioned, but as humans, we are uniquely endowed with awareness, imagination, and free will.

Culture and society affect the development of our behavior. The meaning of "good," "evil," "reasonable," "unreasonable," and "freedom" is influenced by the conditions of each culture.

Terms to Define

Potentiality   Anthropologist
Ability   Culture
Capacity   Heredity
Instinct   Environment
Conditioned

Questions:

1. What are some of the contrasts that exist in the world today?
2. What kinds of behavior might be classified as "predetermined"?

GROUP DISCUSSION

1. What type of behavior might be classified as "acceptable" in one society but not in another? Does this apply to subgroups also (ethnic, economic, occupational groups)? Why?
2. Why do people have a tendency to blame "bad luck" or "fate" for disappointments? What do you think about "luck" or "fate"?

BIBLIOGRAPHY

Allport, Gordon. *The Nature of Prejudice.* Reading, Mass.: Addison-Wesley Publishing Company, Inc., 1954.

Berrill, N. J. *Man's Emerging Mind.* New York: Dodd, Mead & Company, Inc., 1955.

Maslow, Abraham H. *Motivation and Personality.* 2nd ed. New York: Harper & Row, Publishers, Inc., 1970.

I

TIME TO LOOK AT ME

1

Who Is This Person
I Call Me?

Learning all you can about yourself and the world in which you live is one of the first steps in the study of human relations. This study involves your needs, emotions, wants and desires, potentialities, ability or inability to judge reasonably, and your total picture of yourself. Your view of yourself, whether accurate or inaccurate, provides the framework for your view of the rest of the world.

The first question to be considered, then, is: Who am I as a person? *Personality* will be discussed in general as well as in developmental terms.

Personality Viewpoints and Development

There are many schools of thought regarding the definition and study of personality. Some stress the functions of personality, with greatest emphasis placed upon *adjustment.* According to this view, your ability to adjust to your surroundings is the most important aspect of your personality.

Others stress personality *behavior* as such and tend to regard learning and conditioning as most important. People who hold this view point out that you usually react to a specific situation in a specific manner as a result of past experiences. Still another view stresses that personality has been *predetermined,* that nothing in your emotional or mental life results from chance, but rather from specific causes or forces which may be known or unknown.

The point of view developed in this book is one that has become more widely accepted in recent years. It is one that does not tend to compartmentalize personality, but rather views it *in totality* — stressing the whole human being with inherited qualities as well as acquired qualities. It stresses love and respect for both self and others as essential to a wholesome personality. Authors such as Frankl, Maslow, Rogers, May, Allport, and Fromm all have in common their belief in the free will of man which *helps* to direct his life. They stress the "human" aspects of personality, believing that human beings can use their capacity to learn, reason, evaluate, and make choices in the action that they take. A man is not like an animal, who only acts instinctively in his behavior; he is not like a machine that has been completely programmed and is merely waiting for someone to push a button which will activate a response. In most situations man is able to make a reasoned choice of action.

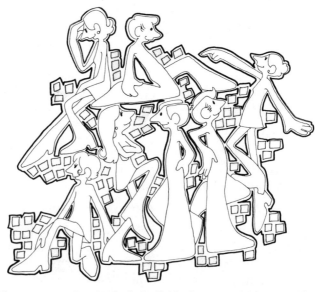

You are a unique, whole individual as you interact with others and become a vital part of your total surroundings.

This viewpoint also recognizes the *growing* aspect of personality, which is not a static unchanging set of characteristics, but a composite of ever-changing patterns. Human beings need to have a "meaning" or purpose for their lives, an ultimate goal for the sake of which they develop their individual potentialities to their fullest extent.

Let us examine personality in terms of *development, effect,* and *roles.*

How Is Personality Developed?

Personality differences stem from three major forces: heredity, environment, and experience. Working together, these three forces help to shape you into a unique human being.

Heredity.   At conception you received a genetic inheritance from your parents; this provided the potentialities for all of your behavior and development throughout your life. It included your physical attributes, which could be developed into certain specific skills and abilities. But, it did not determine or forecast what you would do with those potentialities or capacities. The inherited potentialities or capacities of human beings, are not such that we instinctively know how to build a house, raise children, or do any of the numerous tasks society expects us to be able to perform. For these learning is necessary.

It is important to understand and make a clear distinction between *ability* and *capacity.* *Capacity* is an inherited potentiality or possibility; *ability* is a developed skill or aptitude, based on our capacities.

For example, baseball *ability* is built upon certain capacities — good reflexes, manual dexterity, endurance, and so forth. But these capacities are also needed for participation in other activities, such as becoming an expert auto driver, a golfer, or a good keypunch operator. Whether one develops his *capacities* into baseball ability, racing ability, or keypunch ability is a result of individual choice and motivation. We do not have any reason to suppose that there are baseball genes, or golf genes, or keypunch genes, or even any specific combination of genes that determine these abilities. *Potential* (or capacity) is inherited; *ability* is learned or developed.

Environment.   An individual's personality will be influenced by the circumstances in which he lives. Whether he is raised in the United States or in Brazil, whether he lives in a metropolitan city, a small town, or on a farm, whether his family's social and economic status is lower, middle, or upper, whether his parents are divorced, unhappily married, or happily married, whether he is an only child or one of ten children – all of these and many other conditions form the environment in which he lives. We can call these influences cultural or subcultural factors.

> Culture largely determines the experiences a person has, the frustrations and adjustments he must deal with, and the standards of conduct required of him. Each culture has its distinctive values, morals, and ways of behaving. It lays down the rules for child training and the relationships within a family. Thus culture influences personality because it dictates many of the characteristics a person will acquire. *The process of acquiring the personality traits typical of members of a particular culture is called SOCIALIZATION.* [Morgan and King, p. 383.]

You *learn* appropriate and acceptable behavior, and how to interact with other human beings; you learn these patterns largely through your social and cultural environment. The newborn infant has no idea of "right" or "wrong," but very early in life he learns that he is either rewarded or punished for his behavior. Thus he develops an awareness of "good" and "bad," acceptable and unacceptable.

"It is safe to say that the nature of early social experiences will greatly influence later social success or failure," Justin Pikunas has written [Pikunas, p. 90]. Although the family is the main socializing agent in early childhood, peer groups become more influential as adolescence approaches. We have all felt the pressure exerted upon us to feel like we are "one of the group." The surroundings or environment of the individual is an important factor contributing to the development of his personality.

We tend to think that all United States citizens share certain general cultural values or attitudes. We talk about the "American dream" in general terms, we share a common respect for the ideals of our "founding fathers," and we discuss the "American way of life." Within the larger "American" culture, however, there are various *subcultures,* which may be divided along religious, racial, ethnic, geographic, or occupational lines. The "American" child growing up in the ghetto will have experienced different types of "environmental influences" than the "American" child growing up in a middle-class environment. Environmental characteristics, both cultural and sub-cultural, are important factors to consider when studying personality development.

Experience and Learning.   Environment is *where* you live; experience is *what happens* to you in your total surroundings. Your daily experiences, which are unique to you, help to mold your personality and your view of life.

You mentally file away the experiences you have had, and your reactions to those experiences help determine how you will react in the future. You tend to see your own experiences as *fact* and may tend to expect that others will have had those same factual experiences and therefore will tend to see things "your way."

However, your interpretation of past experiences might not be correct. It is sometimes difficult to recognize that you have made faulty interpretations. You sometimes may tend to screen out or fail to "see" the other side of an issue because that view does not agree with your view of the world.

This is somewhat like the case of the child who did not realize he needed glasses. He thought that everyone saw fuzzy trees or blurred signs until he stepped out into the world with corrected vision; he then realized how distorted his sight had been. Without an eye examination and the necessary correction, he would have continued viewing the world in a distorted fashion.

Your past experiences, your interpretations of those experiences, and all the assumptions which you have made about yourself and your world make up your frame of reference. This is the lens through which you view the rest of the world. *frame of Reference*

Your frame of reference changes constantly, as you revise your point of view. Often, your personal world of experience is the focal point for the only "reality" that you can understand. For example, every day you might be exposed to violence or evidences of hate via the news media, but you remain detached and distant from this "reality." You *know* it exists, but it does not exist *personally.* If, however, you were personally confronted with a violent or hateful situation, such as a robbery, a beating, or even a "verbal beating," you would then experience the *reality* of violence or hate. Previously, you were able to remain detached and relatively unaffected by these "realities," but this experience has now drawn it into sharp reality on a personal level. Your personal frame of reference now would be changed to include this experience.

Personality Roles

If someone asked you, "Who are you?" you could answer in many different ways. You might say, "I am Margaret Jones," "I am Mary's roommate," "I'm George Jones' daughter," "I am Dick's girlfriend," "I am a student at this school," or any of numerous other possible responses. All of these responses answer the question, and the circumstances would determine which one would be appropriate.

Every day you fulfill different "roles" as a person. You may think of yourself as playing the roles of student, roommate, daughter, son, mother, father, sister, brother, employee, – and many more. You are not a *different* person in each of these instances, but you *use* your personality differently or *show* different aspects of your personality in each case.

When sociologists talk about roles, they mean patterns of acting which are more or less standardized by the various social situations in which a person may find himself. This standardization is not very rigid in most cases; it merely sets down acceptable guidelines which establish the permissible limits of behavior. For example, the role of casual acquaintance is quite different from the role of intimate friend. If you were to sit down next to someone on the bus and begin telling him personal details about yourself or asking searching questions about his private life, he would quickly become offended. On the other hand, if you spend an evening with your closest friend talking only about the weather and other bits of small talk, he might begin to question the closeness of your friendship.

Clearly, some amount of role playing is necessary if we are to get along with all the countless people we meet in various situations. What is more, each person shapes the roles he plays to fit in with his own personality. Some people, for example, are naturally very outgoing; even with casual acquaintances they will talk more openly than other people would. Conversely, some people are naturally somewhat reticent and will tend to be less communicative even with their friends. But even the reticent person will tell his friends more than he tells strangers, and the outgoing type will behave with more restraint among strangers than among friends. Thus each person plays a number of roles, which are determined in general by social expectations but which are shaped in all their particular details by the individual personality of the role player.

There is nothing "phony" or artificial about playing such roles. This type of role playing involves only natural adjustments of your personality to each situation in which you find yourself. Phoniness is another matter entirely. For example, the role you play in a student-student relationship is different from the role you play in a student-teacher relationship. Almost every student sounds more serious about his studies when he is talking to the teacher than when he is talking to his friends. This is natural. But you all probably have run into the type of student who comes on to the teacher as though nothing were more important in his life than the subject the teacher is teaching. Such behavior is immediately recognizable as phony, for the person engaging in it is overplaying his role in an unnatural way.

Because your actions are based upon the expectations of the situation, they will differ from one time to the next; you will act differently as a student than as a roommate because each role calls for a different type of behavior. Thus people observing you in different situations may get completely different impressions of your "personality," or at least of your apparent personality. The person who sees you in only one role has no way of judging those deeper elements of your personality which remain constant despite changes in roles. His assessment of you is based on superficial aspects of your personality and on characteristics of physical or outward appearance. Although such a view of you tends to be rather simplistic and external, it is worth brief discussion here because these superficial qualities are also a part of the totality of personality — indeed, they are the parts that people first run into, before they have decided whether or not they want to get to know you better.

The most obvious apparent personality traits are such first impression qualities as physical factors, including body build, size, skin coloring, and bone structure, as well as facial expression, posture, and general appearance. The nonphysical aspect of apparent personality traits include attitude factors; these are intangible qualities that display a person's inner feelings. The more positive ones are described in such terms as "friendly," "warm," "sincere," "bubbly," "vibrant," "poised," "calm," or "intelligent." These descriptive words are used to express your evaluation of the effect of the other person's inner being — that person's personality.

Perhaps you have heard or said of someone that "He has no personality at all." This is a false statement. Every person has a personality; it is a personality that is unique to him alone. The personality in question here is perhaps not pleasing to you, but it *is* a personality; indeed, such a statement is the reflection of two personalities: yours and the other personality to which you are reacting.

You may also have said or heard, "She's completely different once you get to know her." The girl in question is not really "different," but the person who gets to know her is meeting her in a new role and is thus being exposed to new facets of her personality. It is important to recognize that a flexible attitude helps one to assume various roles and interact effectively. It is also important to realize that each of a person's roles is merely one different facet of his *total personality.*

As you mature and enter the world of business and industry, or the world of marriage and parenthood, you will be thrust into all kinds of new, strange, unfamiliar, and even peculiar situations where the ability to adapt and react positively might be the deciding factor regarding success or failure. In order to do this more effectively you must learn to understand yourself and others and to know why you act as you do.

Individuation of Personality

We have discussed the development of personality in this way: personality includes biological inheritance, environmental influences, experience, and learning. *Personality refers to you as a total person, how you act and react to all of life's situations; it is the expression of everything that you are and everything that you do; it is a continuing process. It is the core or center of your being, the product of all your responses as they are expressed in everyday living; it is your conception of your SELF — it is the image that you have of yourself as an individual.*

"The self," Rollo May* has written, "is not merely the sum of the various 'roles' one plays — it is the capacity by which one *knows* he plays these roles; it is the center from which one sees and is aware of these so called different 'sides' of himself" [May, p. 80]. There is often a difference between the way you view yourself and the way others view you. For example, a roommate may say, "Mary, you can make friends if you really want to; you are just like everyone else. Just be more outgoing." But if Mary does not *see herself* in this way, she will find it very difficult, if not impossible, to be the "outgoing" person her roommate wants her to be.

Self-Image

Unless you have adequate self-knowledge, you may merely think of maturity as simply reaching some magical age. With adequate self-knowledge, however, you will be able to recognize that maturity involves knowing what you want and taking the appropriate action to achieve that goal. Self-knowledge enables you to recognize yourself as you truly are. It means both owning up to your annoying habits and recognizing and building upon your positive features. "The self represents the individual's awareness or perception of his own personality" [Morgan and King, p. 372].

You are not born with a self-image; you acquire one. It is indeed a wonderful experience to watch a child discover the wonder of his fingers and toes — and the accompanying realization that they are a part of *him*! This is the first step in the development of his self-image, but self-identity, self-knowledge, and self-image involve more than the realization that one's physical attributes are a part of him. As a child grows, he learns that his *actions* also represent a part of him, he discovers that he reaps reward or punishment for such actions, and he learns to accept responsibility for his actions. The fact that a person is responsible for his actions is a part of his self-image. Because this is so, self-control and self-direction accompany a healthy self-concept. A mature individual does not view himself as the only consideration, the center of everyone else's world, as he did when he was a child.

---

*Reprinted from *Man's Search for Himself* by Rollo May. By permission of W. W. Norton & Company, Inc. Copyright 1953 by W. W. Norton & Company, Inc.

During adolescence, self-concept is in a state of constant motion, for many changes are taking place in the adolescent's life. "The uncertainties of the future make the formulation of definite goals a difficult task," Pikunas has written. "However, it is in the resolution of these adolescent problems and conflicts that the self-concept of the adult is born. The values and attitudes which are part of the self-concept at the end of adolescence are those which tend to remain as relatively permanent organizers of behavior" [Pikunas, p. 95].

An important aspect of your self-image is your frame of reference. If you have an unrealistic or defective frame of reference, your view of yourself will be distorted. You will find yourself presented over and over again with experiences which are inconsistent with your self-concept and you will therefore feel threatened. Unfortunately, many individuals with unrealistic frames of reference tend to respond to threatening situations by attempting to maintain their distorted view of themselves all the more rigidly. You probably can think of many examples of persons who have not been able to adjust their frame of reference to their changing situation.

Take the example of the small-town athletic star who had been the town hero for many years; he could do no wrong, and his self-image reflected this status. When he went away to college, he just couldn't make the grade in big-time athletics, but he somehow was not able to fit this realization into his frame of reference. It was not *his* fault, personally, that he couldn't make it; it was the coach's fault, or it was the result of a minor injury (which became a major injury in his frame of reference), or it was because of "school politics." At any rate, his "hero" frame of reference was still intact for him, and he constantly reinforced this image by recounting "past glories" and triumphs. "If it hadn't been for that injury, I would have been in pro ball by now." "You think *that* was a great play? Did I ever tell you about that game where I . . . ?" Thus he becomes dependent upon this vicious circle of warding off threats to his inappropriate image by clinging stubbornly to that image.

Perhaps the most unfortunate aspect of this type of unrealistic self-image and frame of reference is that others usually recognize the error and simply put up with his reinforcing stories rather than offend him. Thus his failure to adjust his frame of reference meets with little or no resistance. As a result he is unable to make a realistic self-appraisal, and so he becomes trapped in the world of "what might have been."

The development of a satisfactory self-image carries with it awareness of all facets of one's personality. In other words, you must be aware of yourself both as you see yourself and as you think others see you.

Is awareness of your self-image the final stage of personality development? What happens if that self-image is not acceptable? What if it seems to be unacceptable to others? Will your self-image remain the same?

A Process of Becoming

Personality and self-image are not static, rigid, unchanging patterns or traits. "Personality is less a finished product than a transitive process," Gordon Allport explains. "While it has some stable features, it is at the same time continually undergoing change. It is this course of change, *of becoming,* of individuation that is now our special concern" [Allport, p. 19].

Modification

The fact that personality is a transitional process means that personality is moving, active, flowing — passing from one state to another. This being the case, it follows that you *can* modify or change your personality and self-image if you desire to do so. If you do not "like" the image you become aware of, you can change it. This change may involve only the more superficial aspects of personality, such as the attitude you display when talking with others. If you become aware of the fact that what you say and how you say it offend people, you have several alternatives. You can dismiss the problem by saying, "They're just too touchy; they should have known I was just kidding." Or you could say, "That's just the way I am, and if they don't accept me as I am, then it's too bad for them." Or you could say, "Why do I always seem to put my foot in my mouth — clear up to my knee? Maybe I'd better think before I speak." There may be other alternatives also, but the point is: *it's up to you.* You can change aspects of your self-image and the effect of your personality *if you are aware* of these factors — and if you really *want* to make the modification.

Of course, sometimes the aspects of an unacceptable self-image that need changing may present more of a problem than changing merely the way one speaks to others. For example, learning to acknowledge responsibility for actions instead of blaming others may be a big step in the direction of personality modification. Redirection of goals or realistic appraisal of success or failure are other examples of modifications that may need to be made and may require considerable effort.

Much of the modification in your personality and self-image comes about gradually and without your actual awareness through the everyday process of living and experiencing. If you were asked to describe your personality and self-image one, two, three, or more years ago, then one week ago, and again today, you would probably find that many changes have taken place, both consciously and unconsciously. Outward changes may be recognized fairly easily. Just look at a photograph of yourself taken a few years ago and you will probably notice the outward changes quite readily. Such changes are rather superficial but quite apparent.

What about the *inner* person? Has that person changed also, just as the outward appearance has changed? Certainly you are physically the same person, but your self-image and personality have been affected by all of the experiences you have had — successes and failures, compliments and "put-downs," happy times and sad times, personal experiences and world experiences, people and places.

Dr. Thomas Harris, in his book *I'M OK — YOU'RE OK** discusses one's past experiences by making an analogy to a tape recorder: "Another conclusion we may make from these findings is that the brain functions as a high-fidelity recorder, putting on tape, as it were, every experience from the time of birth, possibly even before birth. . . . Perhaps oversimple, the tape recorder analogy nevertheless has proved useful in explaining the memory process. The important point is that, however the recording is done, the playback is high fidelity" [Harris, p. 9].

He goes on to explain that one has "recorded" not only past experiences but also the *feelings* associated with those experiences.

---

*Copyright © 1969 by Thomas A. Harris, M.D. By permission of Harper & Row Publishers, Inc.

All of these "recordings" affect your self-image, both unconsciously and consciously. They are one of the bases for your changing feelings about yourself.

Acceptance and Growth

When you are able to see yourself realistically, you may then be able to take two big steps: acceptance and growth. In the *acceptance* step you acknowledge that there may be certain aspects of your self that will need modification or change, but you also accept the unchangeable aspects of yourself. You will be able to accept past experiences as past, but will recognize the effect that those experiences have had on you. You will build upon those past experiences for *growth.*

Many unhappy people have not been able to accept themselves, not only *as they are* but also *as they can be.* In order for growth to occur, an "as-I-can-be" attitude must go hand in hand with the "as-I-am-right-now" attitude. If you stop with "as-I-am-now" you will become stagnant — you will not grow.

Sometimes the expectations of others can help you become all that you can be. The encouragement and reinforcement of others can be very positive factors when setting goals and continuing to grow as a person. However, if you feel *compelled* to live up to someone else's expectations, instead of setting up your own expectations on the basis of a healthy self-image, you are not necessarily growing. On the contrary, you may find yourself in the position of being set up for disappointment, because achievement of those goals may not coincide with your own goals.

Often, however, the expectations of others will coincide with your own, for in the total picture of human relations you cannot isolate yourself from others and remain mentally healthy. If there is this coincidence of your own expectations and those of others, you can grow and become your own person, not on a *have to* basis, but on a *want to* basis. You may want to live up to the expectations of others if those expectations are in harmony with your own.

Acceptance involves not only acceptance of your own image of yourself but also acceptance of other people in terms of their own personalities. True acceptance of others forms a bond that does not strangle and choke, but allows for individuality and personal expression. In true acceptance of others, you are not bound to agree with others; on the contrary, you make a step toward understanding them by allowing for differences of opinion. Acceptance of others is the opposite of manipulation of others — of *using* others for your own purposes.

Acceptance of self and others carries with it a feeling of worth and recognition. The word "stroking" has been used to describe these positive feelings of worth and recognition. When someone accepts you or genuinely shows concern for you, you *feel* it by direct physical contact, verbal expression, and nonverbal expression. When someone says, "You did a good job," "I love you," or when you have the feeling of acceptance, you are receiving positive *strokes.* The amount and type of "strokes" that you have received during your lifetime help to formulate your attitudes about yourself and others.

Outlook on Life

Harris has formulated four basic positions or outlooks that may be held with respect to yourself and others:

1. I'M NOT OK — YOU'RE OK
2. I'M NOT OK — YOU'RE NOT OK
3. I'M OK — YOU'RE NOT OK
4. I'M OK — YOU'RE OK

Which of these positions a person holds is determined largely by the amount and type of "stroking" he has received in the past. Dr. Harris states, " 'I'M NOT OK — YOU'RE OK' would be the universal position of early childhood, being the logical conclusion from the situation of birth and infancy" [Harris, p. 43]. During the first year of life, an infant needs to be cared for, picked up, fed, and clothed by someone else for his survival; he is being "stroked." The I'M NOT OK — YOU'RE OK person has a feeling of being dependent upon others, of needing approval and recognition from others. " 'Some of our best people' are where they are because of these efforts to gain approval. However, they are committed to a lifetime of mountain climbing, and when they reach the top of one mountain, they are confronted by still another mountain" [*ibid.*, p. 46].

The NOT OK person tends to feel that his efforts are never quite good enough, and he is aware of the vague, nagging feeling that no matter what he does, he is still NOT OK. Somehow, he feels that others are always better: "YOU'RE OK, but I'm not."

This position may change to I'M NOT OK – YOU'RE NOT OK if positive stroking ceases. For the average child, things begin to change after the first year of life. During their second year, most children are walking, climbing, getting into things, and they no longer constantly need to be picked up to be cared for. If parents are cold and unloving, this may mean that the child is pretty much on his own. "The stroking ceases entirely. . . . If this state of abandonment and difficulty continues without relief through the second year of life, the child concludes, 'I'M NOT OK – YOU'RE NOT OK.' . . . A person in this position gives up. There is no hope. He simply *gets through* life and ultimately may end up in a mental institution in a state of extreme withdrawal" [*ibid.,* p. 47].

The third position, I'M OK – YOU'RE NOT OK, may result from a situation where a child has been brutalized by parents. Harris considers this the "criminal" position. This person's sense of OKness does not come from the stroking of others, but from his own stroking. "I believe this self-stroking does in fact occur during the time that a little person is healing from major painful injuries," Harris writes. ". . . While this little individual is healing, in a sense 'lying there licking his wounds' he experiences a sense of comfort alone and by himself. . . . It is as if he senses, I'll be all right if you leave me alone. I'm OK by myself. . . . Such a little person has experienced brutality, but he has also experienced survival. . . . For this child the I'M OK – YOU'RE NOT OK position is a life-saving decision. The tragedy, for himself and for society, is that he goes through life refusing to look inward. He is unable to be objective about his own complicity in what happens to him. It is always 'their fault.' It's 'all them' " [*ibid.,* pp. 48–49].

The fourth position, I'M OK – YOU'RE OK, is the position of hope.

> There is a qualitative difference between the first three positions and the fourth position. The first three are unconscious, having been made early in life. I'M NOT OK – YOU'RE OK came first and persists for most people throughout life. *The first three positions are based on feelings. The fourth is based on thought, faith and the wager of action.* The first three have to do with WHY? The fourth has to do with WHY NOT? . . . *We do not drift into a new position. It is a decision we*

make. . . . Fortunate are the children who are helped early in life to find they are "OK" by repeated exposure to situations in which they can prove, to themselves, their own worth and the worth of others.

. . . Finally it is essential to understand that I'M OK — YOU'RE OK is a *position and not a feeling.* The NOT OK recordings in the Child are not erased by a decision in the present. The task at hand is how to start a collection of recordings which play OK outcomes. . . . The reason I'M OK — YOU'RE OK works is that instant joy or tranquility is NOT expected. . . . Personal or social storms are not going to subside immediately when we assume a new position. The Child wants immediate results — like instant coffee, thirty-second waffles, and immediate relief from acid indigestion. The Adult can comprehend that patience and faith are required. We cannot guarantee instant OK feelings by assuming of the I'M OK — YOU'RE OK position. We have to be sensitive to the presence of the old recordings but we can choose to turn them off when they replay in a way that undermines the faith we have in a new way to live, which IN TIME, will bring forth new results and new happiness in our living. [*ibid.,* pp. 50–53.]

What life position or outlook on life do you hold? Are you one of the "majority" people who hold the I'M NOT OK — YOU'RE OK position? Or have you reached the point in your life where you can honestly accept both yourself and others, by intelligently listening to the "recordings" of the past and adjusting to the NOT OK tapes? In order to feel that you are an OK person, you will need to have a realistic self-image as well as a relationship with other people in which you accept them as OK individuals, too.

If we want to be OK we must feel that we have self-worth. This healthy feeling of self-worth is necessary for an individual to feel confident and sure of himself. It is essential that you believe in yourself — in *you* as a person, in *your* abilities, and in your accepting relationships with others. But that is not enough by itself. You will also need to feel that others are OK, too; you do not exist by yourself. A healthy acceptance of others as worthwhile individuals — unique persons of value — is the other side of happy and meaningful relationships with others.

Summary

Personality viewpoints differ. Some people think of personality merely in superficial terms, stressing physical characteristics, popularity, or attractiveness. But personality involves the *total* person, with all his inherited qualities as well as his acquired qualities.

We are influenced by our heredity in the development of our personality. Our potentialities or capacities are inherited, whereas our abilities are developed. Another factor influencing the development of our personality is our environment; where we live, our surroundings, and our subculture are part of our environment. Experience and learning also help to mold our personality and our view of life.

Some of our more apparent personality traits affect the way we act in different situations — the different roles that we fulfill.

It is essential that each individual develop an acceptable self-image. Recognition of all aspects of oneself is part of a health self-image or self-concept.

Personality continues to change and grow; it is not a static and unchanging quality. Harris distinguishes between four positions of OKness that one may hold regarding his outlook on life: I'M NOT OK – YOU'RE OK; I'M NOT OK – YOU'RE NOT OK; I'M OK – YOU'RE NOT OK; I'M OK – YOU'RE OK. When a person is able to accept both himself as he is and others as they are, he will carry with him a sense of worth of both himself and others.

Terms to Define

Personality	Frame of Reference
Heredity	Roles
Environment	OKness
Self-Image	

Questions:

1. What are some of the hereditary factors which have helped to develop your personality? What are some of the environmental factors which have helped to develop your personality?
2. How have your experiences affected your personality development?
3. How has one's culture or subculture affected his personality?
4. What makes up one's frame of reference? Why is it different from another's frame of reference?

5. What is meant by the statement, "Your view depends upon your point of view"? Do you agree or disagree? Why or why not?

6. May some of the apparent personality traits be misleading? In what way?

7. List some of the "personality roles" you assume each day. How do these differ from each other? Are you more "real" in some situations than others? Explain.

8. What is meant by self-image? How do you become aware of your self-image?

9. What is meant by describing personality as a "process of becoming"?

10. What is the most common OKness outlook? What type of OKness should we strive for?

GROUP DISCUSSION. Break up into small groups and discuss these questions; be sure every member's opinion is included before you try to reach your consensus. Then present your consensus to the rest of the class.

1. Which, in your opinion, plays the most important role in determining personality: heredity, environment, or experience?

2. Each person has the power to either damage or enhance the self-image of others and of himself.

3. Why do so many people think of personality only in terms of the more superficial qualities (looks, voice, appearance, and so forth) or in terms of popularity? Do you feel that this view of "personality" is more important at one age than at another — for example, during teenage years as compared to middle age?

4. Why is it important to study human behavior and individual personality in terms of the society in which one lives? How will your personality and behavior affect you in different parts of society?

5. How do people show their OKness attitudes about themselves and others?

6. What do you think is meant by the statement, " 'I'M OK — YOU'RE OK' is a position and not a feeling"? How does this position differ from the first three positions?

BIBLIOGRAPHY

Allport, Gordon. *Becoming: Basic Considerations for a Psychology of Personality.* New Haven: Yale University Press, Inc., 1955. (Paperback: Colonial Press, Inc., 1960.)

Harris, Thomas A. *I'm O.K. – You're O.K.* New York: Harper & Row, Publishers, 1969.

May, Rollo. *Man's Search for Himself.* New York: W. W. Norton & Company, Inc., 1953. (Paperback: Signet Books, 1967.)

May, Rollo. *Man in Search for Himself.* London: George Allen and Unwin Ltd.

Morgan, Clifford T., and Richard A. King. *Introduction to Psychology.* New York: McGraw-Hill Book Company, 1971.

Pikunas, Justin. *Human Development: A Science of Growth.* New York: McGraw-Hill Book Company, 1969.

2

I Need and I Feel—
I Am Human

Emotions and needs are two separate yet interrelated areas which are major factors in determining human behavior. Each day you seek to satisfy the needs which arise and you experience many emotions. Those emotions and needs in turn affect your behavior.

In this chapter we will discuss emotions, their effect upon our body and behavior, and the difficulties associated with living with "problem" emotions. We also will discuss the various needs which we have, and their order of importance.

Emotions

We usually think of emotions as *feelings* which are experienced. Because many emotions also involve various chemical changes within the body, we can see their connection with biological functions. However, these body reactions are automatically called forth when an emotion is experienced, so we have relatively little control over the biological aspect of emotions. For example, you do not tell your heart to beat faster when you are angry – it just does. For this reason we will discuss emotions in this chapter mainly from the psychological point of view.

You may experience specific feelings or emotions, such as anger, joy, grief, fear, or disgust, but you also may experience a more general kind of emotion, which we call a "mood." These moods are often evident to others: "Watch out for Mr. Freeberg today – he's really grouchy," or "Let's try to talk Miss Strom out of that test today; she's in a good mood." Your moods are a general feeling tone and they have considerable influence on your emotions. If you are in a bad mood you may be still angry today about an insult you received yesterday, whereas a good mood probably would have helped dissipate that negative emotion.

Development of Emotions

Emotions may be either pleasant or unpleasant, likeable or disagreeable, annoying or happy. At a very early age the two most basic emotions of man – delight and distress – are evident. Babies come into this world crying, and they continue to show their excitement by crying periodically for many months. It is their only expression of emotion to begin with, but after a few weeks an infant's life expands in its emotional expression to include the emotion of delight – smiling, gurgling, and other babyish sounds of joy. From these two emotions, delight and distress, a variety of other additional emotional responses is developed. For example, a child may experience frustration or strong distress when he cannot reach a toy, have what he wants, get out of his crib, or find himself faced with any similar situation.

As the child's awareness of the world expands, he learns, both from copying and through his own experience, emotions such as fear, anger, or joy. Children soon learn what type of behavior will get results. For example, some employ the temper tantrum routine; if this succeeds, a pattern begins to develop and the stage is set for future tactics. He will probably continue this technique until he learns that this behavior pattern is unacceptable.

As he grows, his parents usually start to teach him to control some of his emotions and to display others freely. Punishment and reward are very big factors in the development of emotional behavior patterns. We all have learned to avoid or try to avoid displaying the emotions which will result in "punishment" of some sort, whether physical or social. Public displays of violent anger usually are very much frowned upon and we try to control this emotion or display it in acceptable ways.

Changes in Emotional Expression

Compare the emotional displays of children to those of adults. Usually children are much more open and free in their reactions. As children mature, methods of emotional expression are modified and changed so the child "fits in" with his social surroundings. We have been taught that "boys don't cry" or that we should "control" our outward expressions of joy, sorrow, or other "private" emotions. We carry this "training" into adulthood.

We certainly need to know the difference between acceptable and unacceptable methods of displaying emotions. As children grow older, their outbursts become less frequent, both because they want to "act" like mature adults and because they realize that adults do not approve of certain types of outbursts, especially crying and fighting.

A child who is upset usually gets over it in a hurry, but an adolescent experiencing the same emotion tends to react differently. Anger, frustration, and disappointment are often shown through the method of sulking and a general "bad mood," which can last for quite some time. This is also a period of increased brooding and "hurt pride," for the adolescent is caught in a bind between the various emotions he *feels,* such as fear, anger, doubt, or guilt, and the fact that he has been taught to restrain his emotions. As a result he is unsure of himself and his emotional competence. His increased intellectual ability and his awareness of others allow him to think about and question his self-identity and his relationships with others.

At this stage of life some individuals simply change their methods of expressing their emotions in an attempt to get what they want. For example, the temper tantrum becomes the "silent treatment" or the "Nobody-loves-me-around-here" syndrome, or a tendency to pouting. If you have been able to work out a pattern of emotional competency that achieves a balance between emotional expression and control, you should be able to feel free enough to express your strong emotions in a *constructive* manner while also being able to control those emotions or expressions which might be destructive or detrimental to yourself or others.

Emotions are a very real part of you.

Effects of Emotions

How do emotions affect you? How do you feel when you are angry, afraid, or nervous? When you experience these emotions, your body reactions contribute to your "feeling." With anger, your whole body is mobilized for action: you breathe faster, your heart beats faster, your muscles contract, and you often feel very warm as the blood rushes through your system. You may have said, "I felt like exploding!" or "My head was just pounding!"

You did not have to tell your body to get ready for a fight — it automatically was stimulated by nerve fibers leading to the heart. Your adrenal glands were stimulated so that they discharged adrenalin into the bloodstream, resulting in increased energy and alertness. This was your body's way of mobilizing you for action. This mobilization affected your "feeling" and contributed to the emotion of anger. Other emotions also involve bodily reactions. These are automatic and become part of the emotion you are feeling.

Building Emotional Competence

When you have a basic understanding of the emotions you are feeling, you can assume a healthy and accepting attitude toward them. You will live with your emotions rather than deny or fight them.

Much of the anxiety about emotional behavior can be avoided if you can anticipate how you will react to problem situations. There are many everyday situations as well as some emergency problems for which you can try to prepare. You are preparing yourself for a future job by learning specific skills. If you are contemplating marriage, you should be preparing for the adjustments and problems which might arise. This sort of preparation will help you cope with emotion-laden situations when they arise.

Sometimes, no matter how "prepared" you think you are, a new situation will arouse stressful emotions. For example, imagine that you are driving on an icy road for the first time; you approach a stop sign — perhaps a *little* too fast — and you apply the brakes. Instead of stopping, the car slides through the stop sign, barely avoiding a collision. As you recover, you experience several emotions: shock, fear, relief, perhaps even disgust. You have reacted to an unfamiliar situation (an icy road), and because of this learning experience with its resulting emotions you will react differently the next time a similar situation arises. You probably will drive more slowly and you will apply the brakes more calmly, gently pumping them as you were taught to do in driver education class.

Constructive Emotional Release

Emotions need to be expressed, especially very strong emotions. Sometimes circumstances require that one cannot express these emotions directly. You may feel like "telling off" someone or physically striking someone, but your social conditioning tells you that this is not acceptable behavior. It is essential that you learn constructive methods of expressing strong emotions.

1. *Physical Activity.* All of us have no doubt experienced the feeling of an intense emotional buildup. Sometimes the best way to work out such feelings is through physical activity. Some people find

sports activities good emotional outlets, whereas others release their pent-up emotions on creative projects. Still others find that their emotional energy is best released by some other activity, such as cleaning the house or washing the car; this way you can work out your frustrations and have the "bonus" of a clean closet, clean house, mowed lawn, or a washed car as the result of the constructive release of tensions through physical activity. Hobbies such as hunting, fishing, painting, woodworking, and sewing are good constructive releases.

2. *Talk It Out.* Sometimes the best "therapy" for releasing emotional tension is talking things out with a trusted friend, teacher, parent, or counselor. The experience of "getting it off your chest" rids you of some of the pressure. Often the other person can help you see alternatives you weren't aware of and can assist you in learning to understand your feelings more clearly.

3. *Sense of Humor.* The ability to retain a sense of humor is a big asset in the constructive expression of emotions. To be able to laugh at yourself and to laugh *with* others is a rare combination. What some people try to pass off as humor is sometimes really just a way of poking fun at others — to build up self-image — an attempt to feel superior at someone else's expense. The constructive sense of humor shows an appreciation for self and others; it is not cutting or hostile.

4. *Positive Thoughts and Action.* Constructive emotional expression also emphasizes the positive. It is easier to talk about positive attitudes than it is to cultivate them. Cultivation of positive attitudes begins with a healthy self-image, acknowledgment rather than denial of problems, and a conscious effort to build habits that will contribute to positive personal growth. You can resolve to "think positively" but if you have not established a healthy personal attitude as a foundation, "positive thinking" becomes an empty phrase.

Painful Scars

You might be hampered in your attempt to attain emotional competency by certain sensitive or vulnerable areas. You probably are able to recognize these touchy spots and have learned to deal effectively with them. No one has escaped some minor crises which at the time seemed major: it may have been a social blunder (saying the wrong thing at the wrong time), an embarrassing situation (slipping and falling down when you wanted to be "so cool"), or a similar experience. Or you may have felt the effects of rejection, humiliation, and perhaps discrimination; these experiences have left their marks.

Many of these weak spots have been caused by experiences during very impressionable younger years. You may bear the emotional scars of "crisis" experiences for a long time. Although you usually forget many of these experiences consciously, you carry with you the emotional reactions that you felt. They have been recorded and are played back when a new situation refreshes that particular memory. If you learn to recognize these situations and to become conscious of the sources of your emotional reactions, you will be much better able to control them. When you understand the causes for some of your reactions, you usually will be better equipped to make your reactions more appropriate to the present situation and less tied to the past. In this way you can help the scars to heal.

Living With Problem Emotions

Some emotions cause more difficulties than others: fear, anxiety, anger and hostility, and love are such emotions which are experienced often and with mixed reactions.

Fear

Everyone has experienced the emotion of fear; it can take many forms, serve many purposes, and evoke many responses. It is important to distinguish *fear* from *anxiety*. "Fear is the feeling associated with expectancies of unpleasantness. This may involve an expectancy of actual pain or it may involve an expectancy of distress of another sort, like a fear of failure or a fear of loneliness. Sometimes the basis of a fear is not understood by the person. Then we call the fear an anxiety" [McKeachie and Doyle, p. 211].

Fear

You may feel the emotion of fear as a type of warning that danger is near. This warning may take the form of an external "cue" or it may reflect your learning. For example, you might feel very frightened if you were confronted by a burglar carrying a gun. This feeling of fear was caused by an external force. Or you might feel fearful when you see a fire because someone you know once was badly burned in a fife. In this case you are experiencing fear as the result of a past experience. Sometimes fears have to be unlearned. For example, a young child may be afraid of being left alone or of the dark, but as he grows older he should try to leave those fears behind.

As a child reaches adolescence, types of threatening or fearful situations tend to take on a more social character — fear of being left out of the crowd, fear of rejection, or fear of ridicule. As we grow older, it seems that more of our "fears" are associated with social situations and fewer with simple physical dangers.

Fear reactions may be learned not only through experience but also by example or association. You might be afraid of thunderstorms because you have watched the reactions of older brothers, sisters, or even parents. You may have witnessed the humiliation or rejection of another person and vowed that you would never let that happen to you. You may have watched the punishment of another for some action, and your fear of that punishment makes you avoid similar action and similar punishment.

Fear can be constructive: inasmuch as everyone is subject to dangers and risks, you can avoid some destructive consequences if you know how to react in fearful situations and what the results of your action might be. For example, running around in circles waving your arms when your clothing is on fire will not put out the fire, but will only spread it. Most people know this, but many are unable to apply this knowledge when the situation demands it.

You certainly cannot plan ahead to prepare for every situation which might occur, but a general knowledge of causes and reactions to your particular "fear situations" will help you to develop a constructive approach to handling them without panic. There will always be some situations that may prove overwhelming for you, but in most cases if you are able to recognize fear, to know what to expect, and what action to take, you should be able to respond constructively.

Anxiety

We have said that when the basis for our fear is not understood, we are experiencing anxiety. Rollo May, in his book, *Man's Search for Himself,* * states:

> Anxiety is the feeling of being "caught," "overwhelmed," and instead of becoming sharper, our perceptions generally become blurred or vague. Anxiety may occur in slight or great intensity. It may be a mild tension before meeting some important person; or it may be apprehension before an examination when one's future is at stake and one is uncertain whether one is prepared to pass the exam. Or it may be the stark terror, when the beads of sweat appear on one's forehead, in waiting to hear whether a loved one is lost in a plane wreck, or whether one's child is drowned or gets back safely after the storm on the lake. People experience anxiety in all sorts of ways: a "gnawing" within, a constriction of the chest, a general bewilderment; or they may describe it as a feeling as though all the world around were dark grey or black, or as though a heavy weight were upon them, or a feeling like the terror which a small child experiences when he realizes he is lost.
>
> Indeed, anxiety may take all forms and intensities, for it is the human being's basic *reaction to a danger to his existence, or to some*

*Reprinted from *Man's Search for Himself* by Rollo May. By permission of W. W. Norton & Company, Inc. Copyright 1953 by W. W. Norton & Company, Inc.

value he identifies with his existence. . . . It is the quality of an experience which makes it anxiety rather than the quantity. [May, pp. 34–35.]

Sometimes mild anxiety can be constructive; it can warn us that something is wrong. Anxiety about passing a test could prompt you to study harder; anxiety about the job market might cause you to reevaluate your choice of occupation. In these cases, you may be able to turn anxiety into a working tool for your benefit. We might say that these are "normal" anxieties; they are real and, if confronted realistically, they usually can be handled without too much difficulty.

It may be a feeling of being trapped.

It may be vague or it may be terrifying.

It may be a continued gnawing feeling.

I often can't explain it ——

Anxiety

But all too often anxiety hampers our general emotional competency. You may feel vaguely unsure of some danger or threat — you *might* not get the job; that "special" person *might* not call; you *might* have an automobile accident; we may all be faced with extinction because of the ecological condition of the world. Many of these anxieties are based upon a sense that one is not in control of the situation, a general feeling of inability to understand or take action.

We might say that "neurotic anxiety" is when the *quality* of the threatening experience is blown way out of proportion to the actual danger posed. Because the "danger" is not assessed realistically, it tends to block out everything else. The mother who is on the point of nervous exhaustion because her son is half an hour late ("I just *know* he's had an accident") and the student who gets completely "shook" over a test ("I *can't* do it; — I just *know* I'm going to flunk") are two examples of neurotic anxiety. It is sometimes difficult to distinguish between "normal" anxiety and "neurotic" anxiety. The difference can be expressed in terms on one's ability to handle the anxiety-producing situation: does this anxiety rule your life, or are you in control?

Anger and Hostility

There are many other terms which are related to anger and hostility: resentment, hate, or aggression all denote *degrees* of anger or hostility. Anger is a very normal emotion; to deny one's feelings of anger would be to deny one's humanness. When you have been irritated, threatened, or unfairly treated, you often become angry and hostile; you want to strike out and defend yourself against your real or imagined foe.

Anger is often the result of frustration. When a child is unable to reach a toy or is prevented from achieving some goal, he expresses his frustration through different methods: he may cry, he may throw a temper tantrum, or he may strike out aggressively at the source of his frustration. As he grows older, he normally learns to control his aggressive urge to solve problems by physical force.

Anger

As people mature they must learn to control their anger, or at least to express it in "acceptable" ways. Unless you understand the emotion of anger, you might merely substitute destructive words for destructive force in releasing your anger. You have probably had many insulting, degrading, or humiliating experiences as the result of words spoken in anger. It would be misleading to think that destructive anger can only be displayed through physical force; words are very powerful and can be destructive.

It is difficult to consider the emotion of anger from a purely objective point of view. Most of us have a difficult time discussing our feelings of anger without lashing into a retaliatory or judgmental attitude. Instead of simply stating, "I am very angry" or "That makes me just furious," we tend to say things like "You really love to pick on me don't you; you're not perfect either, you know," or "See what you've done to me! How could you do this to me?" Quite naturally, we are concerned about our personal feelings, but learning to recognize feelings of anger so that you can avoid attaching "hurt" or "get even" feelings is a step toward emotional competency in the area of anger.

Anger can be used constructively. You may become so angry about poverty, discrimination, pollution, or some other inequality or condition that you take action to correct it. From a personal standpoint, realizing that anger is a normal emotion and that it need not be destructive can allow you to recognize this emotion when you feel it and to express it constructively.

Anger becomes a major problem when it becomes unreasonable. In that case, hostile feelings are out of control and the person lashes out in retaliation – usually at the nearest person. This type of angry reaction may become habitual, for it provides the individual with temporary release from his tension. This type of individual tends to overreact to minor disappointments, upset plans, or the misfortunes of everyday life. Everything becomes a crisis to him, and woe unto anyone who gets in his way when he's angry! He becomes *furious* if the bus is five minutes late, if his football team loses a game, or if someone cuts in front of him during heavy traffic. This type of anger is very detrimental, both to the individual displaying it and to those around him. Co-workers, spouse, children, or friends become the scapegoats for his frustration, and he is a very unreasonable and unhappy person.

Just as you must learn to understand and successfully express anger within yourself, you also must learn to accept and understand the anger of others. If you allow yourself to get caught up in the cat-and-mouse game of "I'll hurt you just as much as you hurt me," *you* are the loser.

Understanding the reasons behind the emotion of anger is very important if you want to express this feeling constructively. Do you feel a personal threat? Are you really more hurt than angry? Do you automatically feel the need to defend yourself – right or wrong? The causes of anger are complex and not easily understood. Often you cannot really understand all the reasons for your anger, but if you include anger and your reaction to it in your self-image, you will be better prepared to accept anger and display it constructively.

Love

The past few years might be appropriately called the "love age": we have seen the word *love* plastered all over the sides of cars and busses in all shapes and various colors; "love beads" were very "in"; clothing, sweatshirts, pins, jewelry proclaimed LOVE; protest signs read "Make love, not war." Perhaps no other word has been used so many times by so many people with so many different variations of meaning.

Just what do we mean by love? *The Art of Loving,* by Erich Fromm, is strongly recommended for your reading; this powerful little book deals with love, not as a sentiment, but as an involvement of the total person. Fromm feels that love is the mature answer to our problem of existence.

> Love is an active power in man; a power which breaks through the walls which separate man from his fellow men, which unites him with others; love makes him overcome the sense of isolation and separateness, yet it permits him to be himself, to retain his integrity. In love, the paradox occurs that two beings become one and yet remain two. [Fromm, p. 17.]

You probably would agree that the ability to give and receive love is one of the most important qualities you can possess. A relationship in which one of the partners is able only to give or only to receive is not a truly mature love relationship. The mature love relationship does not call for submission or domination of one party by the other; if this happens, one person has surrendered his individuality. A mature love relationship does not involve loss of individuality or integrity for either party. Love, as we think of it, usually involves a relationship between two people. We will discuss love in the dating, premarriage, and marriage relationships in part four.

Five different types of love relationships or attitudes are outlined by Fromm:

1. *Brotherly love.* This is the love of equals and is perhaps the most universal and basic type of love. Fromm states that this type of love entails "the sense of responsibility, care, respect, knowledge of any other human being, the wish to further his life. . . . Brotherly love is love between equals: but, indeed, even as equals we are not always 'equal'; inasmuch as we are human, we are all in need of help. Today I, tomorrow you" [ibid., pp. 39–40]. This type of love is not exclusive but is universal. It is the type of love that is shown by one human being to another simply because the other is a human being.

2. *Motherly love.* Fromm emphasizes the *unconditional* quality of this type of love. Motherly love involves care and responsibility for the sustaining and growth in a child's life, but it also involves the conveying of a feeling – the sense that it is good to be alive! The quality or attitude of motherly love is contagious: if the mother loves life and is happy giving love to her child, this feeling is conveyed to the child.

This type of love is different from brotherly love in that it is love of *unequals*: – mother gives all the help and the child receives it. The most difficult problem for true motherly love is to recognize and accept the inevitable point of separation from the child. For "the child must grow. It must emerge from mother's womb, from mother's breast; it must eventually become a completely separate human being. The very essence of motherly love is to care for the child's growth, and that means to want the child's separation from herself" [ibid., p. 43].

The desire to see another person happy, with no strings attached, is true motherly love. Many find it very difficult to want their child to separate from them. Yet the ability to let go, so that the child can continue to grow and become a separate being is the epitome of motherly love.

3. *Erotic love.* This type of love is often exclusive. "It is the craving for complete fusion, for union with one other person,"

Fromm writes. "It is by its very nature exclusive and not universal; it is also perhaps the most deceptive form of love there is" [ibid., p. 44].

Erotic love implies sexual union and often finds its culmination in the marriage relationship. It involves commitment and a willingness to share experiences. But physical union is just one of the shared experiences that is involved in erotic love, for unless the desire for physical union is motivated by love, it is no more than a biological release.

Erotic love involves *will*. "To love somebody is not just a strong feeling — it is a decision, it is a judgment, it is a promise. If love were only a feeling, there would be no basis for the promise to love each other forever. A feeling comes and it may go. How can I judge that it will stay forever, when my act does not involve judgment and decision?" [ibid., p. 47].

Erotic love is exclusive, but not possessive; it involves commitment and shared experiences; physical expression is based upon love; and it involves a decision — a will, not just a feeling.

4. *Self-Love.*   People often assume that loving others is a virtue and that loving oneself is evil. We have long associated self-love with selfishness and conceit. When we discussed self-image, however, we pointed out that one must have a healthy respect for oneself. Is this contradictory? No.

> The idea expressed in the Biblical "Love thy neighbor as thyself,"
> implies that respect for one's own integrity and uniqueness, love for
> and understanding of one's own self, cannot be separated from respect
> and love and understanding for another individual. The love for my
> own self is inseparably connected with the love for any other being.
> [ibid., p. 49.]

We do not have to choose between loving ourself and loving others; these are compatible attitudes. Indeed, it seems necessary that one have a love for self in order to be capable of love for others. Conversely, if we are able to love others, we should be able to love ourselves as well.

What about selfishness? If we correctly understand the meaning of love for self (happiness in one's own life, rooted in care, respect, responsibility and knowledge), then we can see that love of self and selfishness are opposites. The selfish person is concerned only about himself, lacks true feeling for others, and desires to judge everything on the basis of its usefulness to him. "It is true that selfish persons are incapable of loving others, but they are not capable of loving themselves either," Fromm explains [ibid., p. 51]. The truly loving person loves both himself and others.

5. *Love of God.* We stated previously that our basis for love stemmed from our need to overcome the anxiety of separateness. Religious love springs from this need to overcome separateness also.

> In the dominant Western religious system, the love of God is essentially the same as the belief in God, in God's existence, God's justice, God's love. The love of God is essentially a thought experience. In the Eastern religions and in mysticism, the love of God is an intense feeling experience of oneness, inseparably linked with the expression of this love in every act of living. [ibid., p. 67.]

People in all ages and places have tried to understand the universe and bring meaning to their lives through religious love. The love of God allows many people to bring more meaning into their lives.

If these are the five basic types of love relationships, why do we list love as a "problem emotion"? The answer is that in each of these brief descriptions of love, we have discussed the *ideal* conditions under which these types of love would be shown. But "love" is not always manifested in these ways. We have many examples of destructive, neurotic, and "pseudo" love. If mother love turns into "smother" love, overpossessiveness, or an inability to "let go" of the loved one, it becomes a problem relationship; if love is used as the policeman or control agent in a relationship, it is distorted and becomes a problem emotion.

Neurotic love is more concerned about "being loved" than about loving. It is the "gimme" type of attitude, concerned only with self-enhancement. This demanding type of love is difficult, if not impossible, to satisfy, for new demands are being set forth constantly; disappointment and bitterness often are the end result of "neurotic love." Pseudo love might best be described as the "sentimental" or "romantic" love that is thought of in terms of moonlight, roses, and eternal bliss. This fantasy type of so-called love may be sought through the vicarious experience of movies, love songs, or "love magazines." Lovers in this type of relationship share a fantasized "dream world" and miss out on the reality of person-to-person contact.

Countless volumes have been written about the subject of love. This brief discussion is by no means meant to be a thorough analysis; rather, it is meant to introduce the reader to some of the different realities of love. Loving and being loved is very personal; each individual must experience it for himself. It is not merely a matter of finding the "right object" to love, for love is a capacity as well as an activity. Constructive, powerful love takes practice and patience; it is not merely a matter of "falling head over heels" *into* something. It means becoming sensitive to the commitment of a relationship.

Needs

Emotions are the feelings expressed in your life. Basic needs are closely related to emotions, inasmuch as feelings will play a role in determining how those needs are satisfied. If you were asked to answer the question, "What do you need most right now?" your answer would be influenced by many factors — your mood, your immediate situation, as well as your emotions at the moment.

A. H. Maslow has established a widely accepted "Hierarchy of Needs." The five needs listed below are ranked in order of basic importance. The "higher" needs arise as the "lower" needs are satisfied. The five categories are *physiological needs, safety needs, belongingness and love needs, esteem needs,* and *self-actualization* [Maslow, pp. 35-46].

Physiological Needs

Your body requires many substances or conditions to maintain its delicate physical and chemical balances. You must meet these biological needs in order to survive. These are the most basic of all needs: if you were in a position where everything was lacking — food and water, safety, love and esteem — you would no doubt desire food and water more than anything else. All other needs would become less important than the satisfaction of that one need which would keep you alive.

When you experience hunger, your body lets you know that this need is not being fulfilled; you do not have to tell youself "I am hungry or thirsty." Sometimes the smell or sight of food can stimulate this need; this is an automatic bodily reaction. Most of the time, though, when you say, "I am hungry," you are expressing *appetite* more than *hunger,* desire more than need. If you were in a position where satisfaction of hunger was your primary goal, that need would fill your mind and you would not be concerned about a job, social popularity, or similar less important needs.

When this need is satisfied, other higher needs take over in importance. And when those needs have been satisfied, still other needs emerge. This is what is meant by the "hierarchy" of needs; needs arrange themselves in order of importance, and once a lower need has been satisfied, a higher need assumes immediate importance. When a need or want has been satisfied, it is no longer a need; in this sense, we are motivated by our *unsatisfied* wants or needs.

Safety Needs

When biological needs have been satisfied, the safety needs take over as primary in importance. These safety needs display themselves at an early age – for example, the child who reacts in a frightened manner to rough handling, loud noises, or other unusual circumstances is exhibiting a need for safety.

The category of safety needs includes a desire for orderliness and a reasonably predictable way of life. This certainly will vary with individuals. A strict and rigid routine is hardly necessary or even desirable, but most of us do like to have some kind of schedule, a routine of sorts, so that we basically know what to expect. We would not be happy if our lives were overorganized and overstructured, but, as Maslow reports, "it has been found that most children prefer some limits, rather than complete permissiveness; that a *reasonably* orderly, predictable, and structured world represents a *safe* world in the eyes of a child" [Maslow, pp. 85–87].

As an adult, you probably have found your safety needs satisfied in your personal life; if you have been able to provide your life with reasonable order and structure, you should be able to function effectively. However, you still will feel outside threats to your safety occasionally, and when such a threat occurs it takes precedence over any other need. For example, if you feared that an earthquake would occur any minute, or if you suddenly discovered that your building was on fire – right down the hall from you – your need to be safe from this danger would be uppermost in your mind.

The newspapers a few years ago reported the story of a coal miner trapped underground after an explosion. It was determined that he was still alive and the necessary work was accomplished to rescue him. Of course, we cannot know what went on in his mind while he was trapped, but imagine what *you* would have felt. Would you have been concerned about the payments on your car, or living in the "right" neighborhood, or getting a date for Saturday night? Probably not. You would have been concerned with only one thing – rescue. After the miner was rescued and brought to the surface, however, reporters crowded around him and asked him how he felt: the caption under his grinning picture read, "Boy, do I need a shower!" Do you suppose that thought even crossed his mind underground? Once the rescue was completed, however, his safety need was fulfilled and he could move on to other needs. The same is true in our lives; when our safety needs have been fulfilled reasonably, we can move on to other needs.

Belongingness and Love Needs

After your basic biological and safety needs have been satisfied, "socialization" and learning come to play an increasing role in shaping your needs. Needs for love, affection, and belonging assume greater importance. Meaningful relationships with people become the central goal for you.

You need to feel that you belong, to establish social relationships, and to delight in the warmth and approval of others. You satisfy these needs in different ways as you grow older. As a small child, your sense of belonging stemmed mainly from the family circle, with your life pretty much dependent upon this relationship. During your "growing up" years, you still felt the ties of the family, but you reached out to those outside of the immediate family in an attempt to satisfy these needs.

Being "one of the crowd" and feeling the acceptance of the peer group usually play a major role in the development of most teenagers. Conformity, in various degrees, is influential during adolescence and carries over into adulthood – again in varying degrees. The companionship and associations involved in clubs and organizations provide part of the satisfaction of this need.

Friendship plays a very important part in satisfying this need. There are many different categories of friendship, from the trusted and loyal confidant to the more casual "group" friendship. Your definition of friendship probably will change as you grow older. Many students have expressed the opinion that as they grew out of adolescence they found that they would rather have fewer *close* friends than many casual friends.

As you grow older, your circle of friends probably will expand to include people of varying ages; the strictly peer group friendships of childhood become a thing of the past. Age no longer seems to be the main criterion of friendship, as quality or similar interest become more important. Many friends would be classified as loved ones. The giving and receiving of love, affection, and friendship are tremendously significant in achieving the fulfillment of the need for belongingness and love.

Esteem Needs

As we saw in Chapter I, most people have a strong need for a healthy self-image. We satisfy this need in many ways. We might say that self-confidence is an offshoot of the esteem need. When you feel sure of your ability or talents, your self-esteem is strengthened. Edgar Z. Friedenberg states in *The Vanishing Adolescent*:

> What we must decide is perhaps *how we are valuable* rather than *how valuable we are*; the question is more qualitative than quantitative. We learn as we grow older what our specific qualities and defects are; what we can expect of ourselves, what we are good for as human beings. We learn how we affect other people and what kinds of responses to expect of them. We learn fairly accurately how we look through their eyes, but if we are at all wise we learn not to see ourselves through their eyes, but rather to accept their image of us as *one* guide to be considered in establishing our conception of ourselves. [Friedenberg, p. 64.]

In other words, you need to know what you can do well – to experience some degree of success, to feel that you have achieved something worthwhile – in order for self-worth to really take on meaning. It is unfortunate to see young people who say, by their attitude, "I'm no good, I can't do *anything.* So why try?" They exemplify *not OK* feelings, and this affects their outlook on life. One step toward changing this attitude involves recognizing that the attitude is a *learned* one – one that could be *unlearned* through the experience of success. When one's need to feel self-worth is not fulfilled, the end result is an individual who feels inferior, weak, and worthless.

Self-esteem is important in the adult world also; we think in terms of status, prestige, reputation, titles, and, in the extreme case, domination. Self-esteem and self-worth are necessary to sound mental health; they are the opposite of false pride, conceit, and vanity. Just as lack of self-esteem is detrimental, so is *false* self-esteem, the hallmark of the "phony."

Self-Actualization

The term *self-actualization* was coined by Kurt Goldstein and has been used by many writers to define the need for self-fulfillment – *the need to become all that one is capable of becoming.* It is the *becoming* aspect of personality, the continual changing and developing of one's self.

Satisfaction of this need is achieved in different ways by different people. To one person, complete fulfillment might mean being the ideal mother; to another, it would involve creative expression through a hobby, such as painting, art, or woodworking; another might achieve this by setting an occupational goal and reaching it.

The emphasis in this concept is on the uniqueness of self; the self-actualizing person desires to be accepted, admired, loved, recognized, and understood *for his own true worth,* for the person he or she is, regardless of age, sex, or race. [Maslow, pp. 36–37.]

Women seem to struggle with problems of fulfillment more than men because of traditional views that "a woman's place is in the home" and similar ideas. In 1963, Betty Friedan published *The Feminine Mystique* and pointed out the "emptiness" that was being experienced by many suburban housewives. Some married women feel that they are merely extensions of their husbands or children – "Bob's wife" or "Tommy's mother" – and that they have surrendered part of their individuality. Being a wife and mother is one very important aspect of their total personality but it is not the *only* aspect; they want to be taken as individuals in their own right, becoming all that they are capable of becoming. For some, this may involve being wife and mother as well as pursuing personal goals.

Self-actualization is a matter of individual interpretation; what constitutes self-fulfillment to one might be enslavement to another. Staying home and taking care of the house after the children are in school, working full- or part-time, participation in service clubs, involvement with civic or volunteer groups, as well as choice of hobbies should be a matter of personal choice. Each person should have the right to decide what constitutes a self-fulfilling activity for himself or herself. Note that this need is placed at the top of the hierarchy of needs because it usually is not felt strongly until the other needs have been staisfied.

Variations in Basic Needs

The needs as we have listed them are not in a rigid order. Most people feel these needs in this order, but there are many exceptions. Some people may feel that self-esteem is more important than love; others may consider creativeness more important than belonging and love.

Most of us do not stay at one level of need. We move around while satisfying our needs. Sometimes we feel several needs together. We may seek to achieve a sense of belonging and status by membership in a certain club. When we do work that we like, we gain self-fulfillment from it and at the same time help to satisfy our biological and safety needs.

Let us refer again to the question mentioned earlier: "What do you need most right now?" Can you see the relationship between various stages of needs? Perhaps you thought, "What I need right now is some sleep!" or "What I need right now is a job," or "I need a date." Your "short-term" immediate answer undoubtedly will differ from your long-range needs. By carefully analyzing your basic emotions and needs, you can gain a better understanding of both your immediate and your long-range goals.

Summary

Emotions are very strong feelings which we experience. They affect our bodies through automatic biological reactions. We may experience many kinds of emotions, all of which have in common the fact that they develop out of our basic feelings of delight and distress. As we grow and mature we show our emotions differently than we did as children. Because emotions may be so strong, it is essential that we learn to assume a healthy attitude toward them. We also must learn constructive means of displaying emotions.

Some emotions may be more difficult for us to handle than others. These include fear, anxiety, anger, and love, which we have called the "problem emotions." We experience these emotions often, and with mixed reactions.

Our basic needs are closely related to emotions. A. H. Maslow has developed a "Hierarchy of Needs" in which he ranks our needs in their order of basic importance. These are survival needs, safety needs, belongingness and love needs, esteem needs, and self-actualization needs. When we have satisfied one of our "lower" needs, we then can move on to one of the "higher" needs. Although most of us satisfy our needs in this order, there are many variations in the importance individuals assign to them.

Terms to Define

Emotions	"Hierarchy of Needs"
Fear	Survival Needs
Anger	Safety Needs
Joy	Belonging Needs
Love	Esteem Needs
Anxiety	Self-Actualizing Needs

Questions:

1. How do the following emotions affect your body: fear, anger, anxiety, joy.
2. Why do our emotions often "color" our point of view and affect our opinions?
3. How can love be both destructive *and* constructive? What about fear?

4. Which of Maslow's five basic needs seems most important for you to satisfy right now? How might this change?
5. How can your emotions affect your needs?

GROUP DISCUSSION

1. Answer these three questions individually: "What do you hold most near and dear?" "About what do you have very serious doubts?" "What would you *never* change?" After you have done this individually, compare your answers to those of the others in your group. How are they similar? How are they different? What does this tell you about your feelings and needs?
2. Discuss the different ways of showing anger, joy, or fear. How has your emotional expression changed over the last ten years? Compare your methods of showing emotions with those of the others in your group. Are there similarities or differences?
3. Discuss the statement: "Males and females show emotions differently." Do you agree or disagree? Why?
4. Discuss Maslow's five basic needs in terms of where you are on the scale. Do you tend to stay in the same place (satisfying the belonging need, for example) or do you move around? What determines your needs at any moment? Compare with your group.
5. Discuss some of the ways that adults throw "temper tantrums."
6. Discuss what is meant by "emotionally colored" experiences. How do emotions affect your judgment?

BIBLIOGRAPHY

Friedenberg, Edgar Z. *The Vanishing Adolescent.* Boston: Beacon Press, 1959. (Paperback: Dell Publishing Co., Inc.)

Fromm, Erich. *The Art of Loving.* New York: Harper & Row, Publishers, Inc., 1956. (Paperback: Bantam Books, 1963–70.)

Maslow, Abraham H. *Motivation and Personality,* 2nd ed. New York: Harper & Row, Publishers, Inc., 1970.

May, Rollo. *Man's Search for Himself.* New York: W. W. Norton & Company, Inc., 1953. (Paperback: Signet Books, 1967.)

McKeachie, Wilbert James, and Charlotte Lockner Doyle. *Psychology,* 2nd ed. Reading, Mass.: Addison-Wesley Publishing Company, Inc., 1970.

3

Confusion and Problems—
Now What Do I Do?

What we want to happen and what really happens are often not the same. Sometimes everything works out so perfectly, but other times anything from minor disappointment to utter catastrophe can occur. When this happens it is somewhat like buying a garment that doesn't fit: it needs alteration or adjustment.

Most of us can handle everyday situations quite easily. Other situations are more difficult to deal with. Adjustment is involved in almost all cases.

What is meant by *adjustment*? Is it always quietly giving in to avoid trouble or making a scene? Is it forcing others to give in to our wishes — never being able to compromise but having the other person do the adjusting? In short, do we adjust to please others — or ourselves?

There are many ways of adjusting to situations, but with all of them we still have to ask how we can make the best adjustment for each situation.

"We only think when we
are confronted with a problem." — John Dewey

Types of Problems

Generally speaking, we can classify problem areas into two broad
categories: *frustration* and *conflict*. We will deal only with the
everyday types of problems and will not discuss the more serious
types of problems which might require professional help.

Frustration

When we are not able to proceed toward the satisfaction of some
desired goal, we experience *frustration*. In most cases, an obstacle
presents itself which blocks achievement of our goal. For example, if

you get a flat tire on the way to work, or if you have to wait while a long freight train passes, or if you're stuck in a five-mile traffic jam, you experience frustration.

Frustrating experiences stem from many causes. There may be situations which are caused by *outside forces* over which you have little or no control. The traffic jam mentioned above would be a good example of this – you feel caught with nowhere to turn. *Personal qualities* also may be the cause of frustration. Another person's habit of sarcasm may place you in the frustrating position of feeling uncomfortable, wanting to retaliate, and being unable to, either because you know he will get the better of you if you try or because you believe it's wrong to match rudeness with rudeness. Or your own personal inadequacies, real or imagined, may hinder the accomplishment of some goals and thus frustrate you.

Our *social structure* itself may be another source of frustration. The emphasis upon time – rushing, hurrying, and scheduling – gets everyone down occasionally. *Waiting* can be frustrating: waiting in line, waiting for class, waiting for work to be over, and waiting for a bus or cab all produce stress.

Our *affluence* seemingly has had the effect of transforming luxuries into necessities. Many people feel frustrated if they don't have color televison, the newest gadgets, not only a new car, but one with stereo. Frustration is a very real part of our daily lives.

Conflict

Conflict arises when we have to choose between alternatives. Conflict is closely related to frustration and one affects the other. The choice made in settling a conflict is usually determined by the strength of various alternatives.

One type of conflict presents alternatives which are all desirable. For example, both Brad and Tom have asked Mary to go out on the same evening; she likes them both, but her choice will be determined by weighing the merits of a date with each and then choosing the *most* desirable alternative.

Another type of conflict often seems to take the form of a desirable alternative in competition with an undesirable one. At first glance, one would think there would be no contest – the desirable choice would win. But undesirable alternatives often have a way of

Conflict presents us with various choices.

linking themselves up with positive values, such as helping a friend, doing a favor, fulfilling a duty, and so on. Consider this example. Mr. Johnson comes home and says, "Honey, I have great news. Jerry said we can use his tent and go camping for our vacation. How about it?" His wife has made reservations at a resort and was going to surprise him; she dislikes camping, but she also knows he loves to camp out, and she realizes it would be less expensive. Although she knows *she* would enjoy the resort more, the undesirable alternative – camping – is associated with the positive (desirable) values of pleasing her husband and saving money. The decision will be based on relative strength of two choices.

Some conflicts present two undesirable choices. Judy's father says, "You be home on time tonight or you're not going out for two weeks!" Both are undesirable alternatives, but a choice will have to be made.

Methods of Adjustment

Frustration and conflict as well as pressure and stress are real everyday occurrences. How do you handle them, or do they handle you? No one answer can be put forth as the invariably correct way to handle all situations because there are so many variable factors involved. However, there are some broad patterns which we all follow in making adjustments to conflictual situations.

Figure A.

When a person confronts frustration or conflict, some action must follow. In the following example, we can see the four main ways that people handle frustration and conflict. In Figure A, we see someone who has come upon a problem which presents an obstacle in his way. What types of reactions follow? Most of the reactions described are defense mechanisms and are used to protect pride, save face, ease failure, and justify actions. Many reactions overlap into different classifications.

Figure B.

Retreat.   Figure B depicts the type of person who would rather *retreat* than tangle with the obstacle. This type of behavior ranges all the way from the person who will never defend his point of view ("peace at any price") to the more serious type of behavior characterized by withdrawal from society, severe regression, isolation, or escapism. Loss of a loved one might have the effect of causing one to retreat in fear of future loss, rejection, or loneliness. In extreme examples, reality is too painful to face, so one retreats.

Less severe forms of this type of behavior are manifested in running away from problems, refusing to "see" that a problem exists, giving up without trying ("I can't do it"), or refusing to admit fault by blaming others — e.g., parents, teachers, or society.

Figure C.

Stand Still.   Figure C represents that type of behavior where a person *blocks* out the problem and more or less *stands still,* rather than facing and meeting it. There are many types of "blocking" techniques, some of which overlap into other areas. They include rationalization (illogical thinking), projection, daydreaming, forgetting, and various forms of regression.

Rationalization is perhaps the most widely used defense mechanism, and all of us use this type of "reasoning" at one time or another in order to justify something that we did, are doing, or propose to do. The bald man states, "Well, you can't have both brains and hair," while the secretary who decides to use one of her "sick days" to go shopping reasons, "The company allows us these days, and I really don't feel too well. Anyway, I have it coming; I've worked so hard I deserve it." We tell ourselves we *deserve* a new car, or a new coat, or a bigger home, or that going to the movies will really provide a well-deserved break from studies. We should begin to suspect that we are rationalizing when we have to *find* reasons to justify our behavior or beliefs, when others recognize our inconsistencies and we do not, and when we become sensitive and defensive when people question our reasons for our behavior.

We often see some *regressive* behavior pattern at work by immature persons: crying to get one's way, throwing a temper tantrum, engaging in baby talk, and similar behavior. Unfortunately, many of these behavior patterns become habits and are carried over into adulthood, when the temper tantrum evolves into the "silent treatment" or pouting; crying may be used with little modification to gain sympathy or to avoid facing a problem.

Another type of "standstill" behavior is *projection,* where we place the blame on others for our failure. In this type of behavior, the student fails a test "Because the teacher doesn't like me," the employee fails to get promoted "Because the boss favors someone else," the dishonest person steals "Because you can't trust anybody nowadays, so I'm going to get my share while I can." Usually projections center around covering up for feelings of inferiority and are most prevalent in those individuals with rigid conscience development and unrealistic personal standards.

Daydreaming and *forgetting* are similar in that by means of them we attempt to screen out unpleasant problems or reality by thinking more pleasant thoughts. In daydreaming, we find it possible to do that which is impossible in daily life. (Daydreaming can be very harmless, and most individuals engage in daydreaming from time to time, especially when their present circumstances do not hold their interest.)

Another blocking defense is one which may be called *denial.* This is used by those who cannot or do not want to get involved with faults, failure, or unpleasantness. By refusing to "see" the problem, they can go on, blissfully unaware of it. This can be done by putting things off (procrastinating), getting sick headaches, or even by being so busy with other things that one "doesn't have time" for real problems. Thus a student in scholastic trouble may let himself get so caught up in the social activities of his school that he never finds the time to study. He runs away from his problem until it is too late and he learns that he cannot graduate. Denial, you may note, not only serves to protect its practitioner from having to face an unpleasant situation (the scholastic trouble) but also provides a ready excuse after the fact ("I was so busy that year I just didn't do well in my schoolwork").

Some find another way of standing still in front of conflict; they would rather stay in one place and feel safe and secure than risk the danger of defeat or rejection. The student with great potential who takes the easiest course, so that he doesn't have to work up to his full capacity but can just coast along; or the adult fighting against some change with this argument, "It was good enough for my parents and for me, so why change now?" are both examples of this way of avoiding potentially disturbing situations.

Figure D.

Detour. Figure D depicts the *detour* type of defense mechanism. The person who uses this type of behavior pattern often feels that he is meeting the conflict, but in reality he is merely avoiding it by evasive tactics. Here again, all of us employ this type of action sometimes. But the person who constantly evades the issue is in dire difficulty.

When rationalization becomes a habit it amounts to a type of detour. It doesn't solve any problems but allows one to ease himself around the problem — until the next one arises. The student who has gotten into the *habit* of rationalizing may detour around facing up to his own problems in school by saying "Fred's just getting good marks because he's the teacher's pet."

Displacement is another evasive or detour type of defense mechanism. In this case, an individual "takes out" his feelings on someone or something else. Most of us have used this device. If you have had a bad day, you tend to take it out on those around you – spouse, roommate, brothers and sisters, parents. Instead of recognizing the cause of the emotional problem at the time, you deal with the *effect* that this emotion is having on you. We see this most often in the form of displaced anger, when one person "blows up" at someone totally unrelated to the cause of that anger.

We often "take out" our feelings on someone who cannot or will not "take it out" on us in return. Examination will easily show that problems are not solved in this way, and that human relationships often suffer as a result. We hope inwardly that the other person will understand us and let us blow off steam. Sometimes this works, but most of us realize that when we displace or "take out" our hostility on others, the result is often unhappiness, not understanding.

Compensation is another pattern that may be classified as evasive. As the term suggests, it involves substituting traits or attributes that will give us a more pleasant picture of ourselves for inferior or inadequate traits (these may be either real or imagined). The rejected or insecure person may show off, be sarcastic, or misbehave just to get attention and the "approval" he desires; overeating may compensate for feelings of rejection; a slightly built boy may assume a very aggressive attitude to make up for his feelings of physical inadequacy. It must be pointed out that in some cases compensation results in favorable behavior patterns; for example, a frail young man who compensates for the fact that he will never become a football player by trying to excel in another area is doing himself a real service.

Uninvolvement is another type of conflict avoidance by evasion. Here an individual emotionally withdraws from situations of stress or conflict by refusing to get involved. If he does not get involved, he reasons, he will not "get hurt." The boy who refuses to get involved with girls so that he won't get turned down when he asks for a date or the girl who won't try out for the play because she is afraid she won't get the part are both defending themselves by uninvolvement. Up to a certain point, we all must draw the line on involvement or we run the risk of unnecessary disappointment or hurt. But we must run the risk of failure and disappointment from time to time if we are ever to succeed in getting or accomplishing something we want.

Some people suffer so badly from rejection, hurt, or disappointment that they react by declaring, "I'll never let myself get hurt like that again." Broken love affairs often result in this type of reaction, and some young people find it very difficult to form close relationships of trust after an experience of rejection. When persons have been hurt and disappointed over and over again, they tend to form a type of shell of uninvolvement and detachment around themselves. It is very difficult for such a person to give or receive love, so that a full measure of happiness in life is difficult for this person to achieve.

Figure E.

Encounter

Figure E depicts the healthiest way to handle frustrations, conflicts, stress, and pressure. No one solution will fit all circumstances, but the person who faces his problems realistically stands a far better chance of solving them than the person who avoids, evades, or ignores them.

Of course, it is easy to advise others to face their problems, but when it is your own problem it is a different story. How can you handle problem situations in a way that will lead to a positive solution? Let us set up some guidelines to help in solving problem situations:

1. *Define the Problem.*   Let's start with an example. Three people have been assigned to work together on a school project. Mary and Sue work diligently on their portion, but Liz fails to follow through on her part and talks Mary into doing it for her. "You always do such a good job, and I just don't have time to get it done right. You're a doll, Mary." When they turn in the project, Liz takes over and infers to the teacher that she did most of the work. When they leave the room, Mary is both hurt and angry. She feels used. Sue doesn't help much, adding, "You're such a sucker, Mary. Liz can always talk you into anything. You should have told the teacher the truth." If Mary is to overcome her feelings of hostility here, how should she define her problem: Is it one of seeking revenge for being taken advantage of — being used? Is it simply a matter of rectifying the situation — by telling the teacher the whole story? (Why might Mary hesitate to do this? How might the teacher react?) Is the problem Mary's feeling that there was a lack of loyalty on the part of Sue? Does Mary perhaps feel that Sue should have helped by telling the teacher? Is it a problem of defining "friendship" and coopera-tion? Is it a problem of possible rejection of friendship if Mary confronts Liz with her feelings? Is it a problem in Mary's character that makes her, as Sue said, "a sucker"? Is it a combination problem consisting of many of the "problems" just mentioned? Or is it some other problem? Whatever it is, the problem must be recognized if it is to be dealt with, and the first step in recognizing it is to list the possibilities. Once you have done this you are a good way toward getting a handle on what is bothering you. Besides, the intellectual effort involved in examining the situation and defining the possibil-ities may serve to cool you down, so that you can approach the problem more objectively and with less emotional distortion.

2. *State the Facts.*   What is the difference between a fact and an opinion? In the previous example, it would be a fact to state that Liz has not cooperated in the agreed upon manner. It would *not* be a fact to state that Mary had it coming and that she should have expected the results. Perhaps we may think that she really should have expected it, especially if such a situation had occurred in the past, but this is still a *conclusion,* not a *fact.* State the *facts*: there is a disagreement between the girls; feelings are involved; the paper was completed, but not under the conditions originally set forth. Can you state any other facts?

3. *Talk About It with the Persons Involved.* There are differing opinions regarding the feasibility of discussing a problem when you are angry. Some say, talk it over right away; don't harbor anger. Others say, write it all down, wait a day, read it over, and then throw it away; if it still bothers you, then you should talk about it, but at least you will have cooled off enough to be a little more objective. The old adage "count to ten" could be good advice, but often talking over a problem with the people involved serves several purposes. It allows you to get it off your chest and release the tension. It may also help with the next step.

4. *Set up Alternative Solutions.* You may think that everything is very grim and dark, and that there is no possible answer. Talking it over with a friend may very well present you with an alternative that you hadn't thought of. Try to anticipate the unexpected, as well as the results of your alternative solutions. This will help you to make the right choice.

5. *Make Your Decision.* Indecision often causes a great deal of tension. Although you will want to avoid making snap decisions, you will not solve your problem by continuous procrastination. When you have determined all the alternatives, you must choose one of them as your course of action.

Try to anticipate the outcome of your decision: Will it adequately solve your problem, or will it be a temporary measure allowing some breathing time before the same problem occurs again? Is this the result you want?

If a feeling of uneasiness accompanies your decision, you may be wise to review both your facts and your feelings regarding this problem. Each problem will have to be considered individually, and your decision in each case will usually reflect your personal principles. Finally, and perhaps most important:

6. *Don't Expect 100 Percent Accuracy in Your Decision Making.* The perfectionist invites ulcers! No one makes the right decision all the time. You won't always make the right decision. On the other hand, this doesn't mean you should *expect* that your decisions will turn out wrong. It simply means you should not be afraid of failure. Failure can be one of the best teachers we can have;

we can learn from our occasional mistakes, and try not to repeat them.

Summary

We have talked about adjustment in this chapter. We live in a society where we must learn to compromise and adjust to those around us, for we interact with others every day.

Our society confronts us with frustration and conflict every day. In order to function in this society, we must learn to meet those frustrations and conflicts. People have various ways of handling these difficulties. They may retreat. They may block the difficulty in such a way that they stand still and the problem remains. They may detour around the problem — a method that works sometimes but poses the danger that detouring around problems rather than confronting them may become habitual. The healthiest method of handling problems is the confrontation or encounter method, where a person faces conflict and frustration head on and reaches a satisfactory solution.

Terms to Define

Frustration	Regression
Conflict	Projection
Adjustment	Daydreaming
Rationalization	Displacement
Uninvolvement	Compensation

Questions:

1. How do frustration and conflict differ? How does one affect the other?
2. What types of situations do you find most frustrating? How do you react to frustration?
3. What is the most recent conflict you had to settle? What determined your choice?
4. Why do you think so many people "detour" rather than confront their problems?

5. How do you feel when you have confronted a problem and solved it? Compare that feeling to the one you get when you merely evade the issue.

GROUP DISCUSSION

1. Discuss the methods of handling problems. Why is it sometimes very difficult to meet problems head on and try to solve them? Why do we often try to avoid, detour around, or ignore our problems?
2. Discuss some of the methods used by some of today's youth as an attempt to avoid or ignore problems. How do they compare with some of the "adult" methods of ignoring or avoiding problems?
3. Discuss the steps in problem solving. Are these steps realistic? Why is it sometimes difficult to follow these steps?
4. What types of situations are most frustrating to you? Discuss these with your group. Do you find any similarities? Is there anything you can do about these feelings?

Supplementary Readings

Coleman, James C. *Personality Dynamics and Effective Behavior.* Chicago: Scott, Foresman and Company, 1960.

Maslow, A. H. *Motivation and Personality.* 2nd ed., New York: Harper & Row, Publishers, Inc., 1970.

Morgan, Clifford T., and Richard A. King. *Introduction to Psychology.* 4th ed., New York: McGraw-Hill Book Company, 1971.

Russon, Allien R. *Business Behavior.* 3rd ed., Cincinnati: South-Western Publishing Company, 1964.

Sferra, Adam, Mary Elizabeth Wright, Louis A. Rice. *Personality and Human Relations.* New York: McGraw-Hill Book Company (Gregg Division,), 1961.

Steiner, Heiri, and Jean Gebser. *Anxiety: A Condition of Modern Man.* New York: Dell Publishing Co., Inc., 1962.

II

TIME TO UNDERSTAND OTHERS

4

What's the Message?

"Teen-Adult Forum." "Student-Faculty Liaison Committee." "Inter-Generational Discussion Group." "Labor-Management Review Board." "Producer-Consumer Protection Panel." What do all of these groups have in common? They all share the common cause of trying to combat the problem of communication breakdown. Theirs is a problem involving credibility and understanding. Of course, this problem is not unique to these five groups; it is *shared by all of us* in many various situations.

The ability to communicate real meaning and understanding is one of the biggest concerns confronting people today. In this chapter we want to discuss some of the techniques involved in building bridges of communication. We will discuss: the means of communication, the built-in roadblocks, the types of gaps to be bridged, building bridges, and ground rules for communicating.

"Culture is communication and communication is culture." — Edward T. Hall

Means of Communication

Communication is the process of transmitting feelings, attitudes, facts, beliefs and ideas between living beings. While language is the primary means of communication, it is by no means the only one. Non-verbal communication encompasses facial expression, silences, gestures, touch, hearing, vision, and all the other non-language symbols and clues used by persons in giving and receiving meaning. In short, interpersonal communication may include all the means by which individuals influence and understand one another. [Bienvenu, p. 3.]

Purpose of Communication

The purpose of communication is to provide channels for sending and receiving messages. Perhaps many of the difficulties which arise in communication stem from the fact that we often fail to remember that *communication is a two-way street.* Communication involves both the sending and receiving of messages: if our message is *sent* and not received, it is wasted. To be sure, we may sometimes be in a position where we only receive messages and are not permitted to send a message in return. For example, some teachers never allow two-way communication in a classroom; they lecture and that's it. Students have no opportunity to react or question; if they try to do so, they are quickly discouraged. "Look it up in the book," they are told. "You can read, can't you?"

At the other extreme are the situations where one blocks out the message that is being sent: "What was today's lecture about?" "Oh, I don't know; I just tune him out."

These two types of communication breakdown are repeated in different forms in many types of situations — parent-child, employer-employee, boyfriend-girlfriend, or similar combinations. The purpose of communication is being thwarted here, for messages are being transmitted only one way. The channels of communication have become plugged, making real communication — two-way communication — impossible.

Verbal Communication

When we think of communication, the first method that comes to mind is *verbal communication* — words and language. The words we use are important, but perhaps even more important is *how* words are used to convey our messages. Take a simple phrase like, "You know, I really enjoyed that program." Depending upon the emphasis and inflection in your voice, the meaning would vary. It could mean, "You *know* I enjoyed it — so why did you even ask?" It could mean, "*I* enjoyed it even if you didn't." It could mean, "I *enjoyed* it — I didn't think I would." It could mean, "I enjoyed *that* particular program." And it could even mean, sarcastically, "That was the worst program I've ever attended." Repeat the sentence yourself several times. Can you hear the different meanings that are implied?

You would have a difficult time communicating without words, but in verbal communication words are only a small part of meaning. The emphasis, inflection, tone of voice, — the *way* words are used — convey more meaning. The simple word "Oh" can convey anger, joy, sorrow, surprise, shock, sarcasm, embarrassment, and many other reactions. When you become angry, you may communicate this by the use of words, but the degree of your anger is shown by *how* you use the words. You may feel that you are concealing your anger, but your tone of voice gives you away. Try to recall the last time you heard someone who was angry; how did he communicate this to you with and without words?

A clerk in a store may ask, "May I help you?" but you might *hear* "I really don't want to help you," "I'm not concerned about you," "I wish you hadn't come in."

You and a friend are standing in the hallway talking. "Yes, go on," she says, but she's telling you by the *way* she expresses this that she's not really interested. Your advisor says, "What's your problem" but he is arranging papers and you feel that his actions speak louder than his words. He doesn't *mean* what his words said.

Words are a very important part of communicating, but they also can be very misleading. We will discuss this further when we come to examine the roadblocks to communication.

Nonverbal Communication

We have just seen the effect that nonverbal communication has upon words. Nonverbal communication includes all of the methods used independently of words to convey messages: facial expression, silences, gestures, touch, hearing, vision, and symbols.

Facial expression. "Something is bothering Mary, you can just tell by looking at her." You often express your feelings quite vividly without realizing it just by your facial expression. Facial expressions communicate questioning, shock, sadness, anger, boredom, or happiness. Consider the young girl who has just become engaged — her whole face radiates her happiness.

When one is deep in thought, his thoughts often are reflected on his face. You can tell just from looking at someone whether he is sad, angry, worried, cross, or puzzled.

Silence. This technique is used to convey meaning either consciously or unconsciously. "She's mad at me — I'm getting the silent treatment again." Often this trick is used by immature people for manipulative purposes. Silence also is used by the unaccepting, unapproving, uninvolved, or apathetic person. His silence says, "If I don't say anything, I won't get into trouble," "That's someone else's problem," "You don't belong to our group," or "You don't really count."

Sometimes silence can convey positive messages: "Yes, I understand," "I enjoy being with you," or "It's nice to be alone."

Gestures. Most of us use our hands when we talk. Words don't seem adequate sometimes: we feel that we must use our hands to describe something, to add emphasis, or to illustrate our meaning.

Certain universally understood gestures do not require words. The policeman directing traffic gets his point across very well without words. People visiting in different countries sometimes have to rely on gestures almost exclusively if they run into a language problem. In recent years we have found other gestures that have assumed universal meaning — the "peace" sign, for example.

The small gestures that a person makes convey a lot of meaning. For example, a teacher usually can tell if the class is "with him" by their facial expression and their gestures. The pencil tapper, the clock-watcher, and the doodler convey their uncaptivated attention without a word. ("The clock-watcher doesn't bother me too much," one teacher said. "You usually have at least one in every class. But what really does bother me is when a student takes off his watch, shakes it, and looks up in disbelief. Then I *know* it's time to quit!")

Touching and looking.   When someone reaches out to you or looks at you in a certain manner, no words are necessary — you understand the meaning. In a time of sorrow, the physical contact involved in comforting another person is extremely meaningful. Somehow, when one reaches out and touches another at a time of happiness or sorrow, that contact says more than words could express.

The eye contact between two people "tells" a lot. When a teacher glares at a student, his eyes clearly transmit the message, "Stop whispering or I'll kick you out." When your eyes fasten on someone's face as he talks, they tell him you are listening; when they drop to his necktie or move about the room they tell him you have tuned him out.

Symbols.   Advertisers often pick out a symbol to represent their product and repeated use of that symbol imprints a message on the mind of the viewer or listener. We are decoding symbols every time we recognize a trademark.

Some symbols are universally accepted; for example, red and green traffic signals indicate flow of traffic practically anywhere in the world. Some symbols, however, can be interpreted differently by different viewers. The display of a flag was an easily interpretable symbol in the past, but today we have to look at the "displayer" before we can interpret the meaning. The long-haired youth with a shirt of red, white, and blue stars and stripes is not necessarily saying the same thing with his display as the marcher in an American Legion parade.

Built-in Roadblocks

We already have mentioned some of the hazards involved in communicating real meaning, but the roadblocks that interfere can be overcome. The various types of roadblocks are closely related and overlap, but for the sake of clarity we will classify them in terms of semantics, experience, social structure, and defensive self-image.

Semantics

Semantics is the study of meaning and changes of meaning in words. Often, your meaning for a word might differ totally from that of the person you are talking with. It is very difficult to communicate effectively if both parties do not understand the same terminology, or if they hold different meanings for the same word. (For example, when is a steak "well done"?)

The concept of time is one area where many of the words have many different meanings. What is "a little while"? To a mother it might mean anywhere from a few minutes to a year or more. ("Bobby will be going to college in a little while," may mean that he is a junior in high school.) To a child, though, time is much more fleeting; "a little while" is rarely longer than a few moments. When we say, "Just a minute," that "minute" might be anywhere from a minute to half an hour to eternity — that is, many things we are going to do in "just a minute" never get done.

There are many examples of words that are misunderstood because of semantic difficulties. For example, consider the different meanings of "pride," "natural," "normal," "good," "bad," "hippie," "grass," "cool," "tough." This list could go on and on.

In a sense, communications problems involving semantics arise from a vocabulary within a vocabulary. Unless people share a common understanding of the meaning of terms, they will not communicate effectively.

Experience

Past experiences sometimes set up some roadblocks that interfere with effective communications. (They also can be a big help in providing a background or basis for evaluation.) In effect, we have to learn to interpret messages on the basis of our feelings and past experience.

In the book, *Games People Play,* Eric Berne discusses the way we tend to "play games" in our interpersonal relationships. He suggests that each person communicates on three different levels — as a Parent, as an Adult, and as a Child.

Describing the Parent level, Berne writes, "You are now in the same state of mind as one of your parents (or a parental substitute) used to be, and you are responding as he would, with the same posture, gestures, vocabulary, feelings, etc." The Adult response means: "You have just made an independent, objective appraisal of the situation and are stating these thought-processes, or the problems you see, or the conclusions you have come to, in a nonprejudicial manner." The Child reaction means: "The manner and intent of your reaction is the same as it would have been when you were a very little boy or girl" [Berne,* p. 24].

None of us communicate on only one level all the time. Because we communicate with others who also carry with them Parent-Adult-Child experiences, we can communicate on many different levels. For example, our Parent reaction might address the Parent level in another person in this way: "Isn't it terrible about the condition of the world today?" The corresponding Parent response would be, "Yes, it certainly is terrible that we're in such a mess."

An Adult to Adult conversation might go like this: "I can't find my math book; have you seen it?" "Yes, it's over on the table." In contrast, "Let's cut class today, it's so beautiful outside" – "Hey, that's a great idea" is a typical Child-Child exchange.

Berne goes on to explain that problems arise when lines of communication become crossed. (pp. 30–31) For example, Adult says to Adult, "I can't find my Math book; have you seen it?" But Parent replies to Child, "Why can't you look after your own books – it's no one's fault but your own!" Or Child says to Parent, "Will you help me clean my room? I've got so much to do." But Child replies to Parent, "I don't want to. That's not fun." As long as lines don't cross, problems usually do not occur. For example, Child says to Parent, "I feel so sick today; get me a glass of water please," and Parent replies to Child, "Sure, you just rest easy and I'll take care of you."

Sometimes we play games with our communications and don't really mean what we say. For example, Adult boy says to Adult girl, "Let's go out by the lake and look for the Big Dipper." "Oh, that's a good idea; I've always liked astrology," the girl replies. The psychological meaning of this exchange, however, is on the Child-Child (Let's play) level: "Let's go out and neck." – "Hey, that's a great idea. You really turn me on!"

It is especially important for us to recognize the extent to which we play games with our communication, saying one thing but meaning another. This "gamesmanship" can be harmless fun, but it also can be a huge roadblock. It is because of this tendency to play games that experience is so important in decoding messages. Experience may

_____
*Copyright © 1964 by Eric Berne. Reprinted by permission of Grove Press, Inc.

have taught us that what we mean or want to say is not "proper," is threatening to our security, or will not achieve our purposes, so we disguise it into an "acceptable" form. The listener then has to have sufficient experience to understand what we really mean.

For example, an experience that we have had during the day may cause us to react with words that we do not really mean. Nancy spent the whole day registering for classes; her schedule was all fouled up, the bookstore was out of books, and her bill for the books that were available was much more than she had expected. At home, meanwhile, her mother had inadvertently shrunk Nancy's favorite sweater and was just sick about her error. Nancy walked in the door, saw the sweater, and exploded, "Well, I see you shrunk my sweater!" Her mother's response depends upon her feelings at the time and could range from "Yes, and I'm sorry; we'll have to replace it," to "Listen, smarty, I was only trying to help. Where do you get off talking to *me* like that?" Psychologically, Nancy was probably saying, "Oh, no, that's the last straw. I've had a *terrible* day and now this! Please reassure me." Psychologically, her mother was probably saying either "I feel sick about this, please understand!" or "Listen, I've had a hard day too."

We need to become skilled at recognizing what others are saying and at letting them know what we have understood by their words. Awareness of the feelings and needs of the other person is essential to good understanding. We do not want to fall into the trap of manipulating others with our words. Bob and Joan are having an argument and Bob says, in response to some statement of Joan's, "Boy, of all the stupid things to say." Joan bursts into tears: "Oh, so now I'm stupid, too!" she wails. On a psychological level Bob perhaps meant, "I don't understand you at all and I wish this stupid argument were over." Joan's reply means, "You really hurt my feelings and I want you to apologize." Yet these two people are not *aware* of their own true feelings or of the feelings of each other. They are communicating only at a surface level and are using communication to manipulate one another rather than to understand each other.

It is important to understand the role and importance of experience in our communication process, for such understanding will help us turn experience into a bridge-builder for spanning the communication gaps that occur.

Social Structure

Sometimes the structure of our society seems to encourage communication breakdowns. Labor and management are *supposed* to be at odds; so are teachers and students, parents and children, old and young, and all the other stereotyped opposing groups. Young people and old people do have separate "languages" of their own, but there are also many similarities. Unfortunately, we sometimes tend to emphasize the differences rather than the likenesses.

Our "always on the go – don't waste my time" type of life seems to foster a dehumanized communication system in which we cannot take the time to concern ourselves and really listen to the needs of others. The emphasis is upon keeping up appearances while not getting involved.

The story has been told of the couple who were discussing the "listening" ability of one of their friends. Susan said their friend always was the "perfect hostess" and seemed to say and do all the right things; Dave said it was all a false front and that she didn't really hear what anyone said. They decided to try an experiment to determine who was right. They were due at a party in her apartment at eight-thirty, but didn't arrive until a little after nine. When their hostess met them at the door, Dave announced, "I'm so sorry we're late, but we had to stop and rob a gas station on the way." The "perfect" hostess replied, "Oh, that's perfectly all right – do come in!"

Good communications involve more than merely saying what you think you are "supposed" to say. It involves listening.

Defensive Self-Image

Many times we have taken a perfectly innocent remark and reacted with, "What did you mean by that?" We have felt that our self-image was being threatened and our defenses immediately are aroused. This is especially true in circumstances where we feel insecure or unsafe. We tend to guard our conversation and closely examine the conversation of others.

The "put-down" is in this category. We don't like to feel cut down or embarrassed by others, and if we have been, one of our first reactions is to react defensively and retaliate with a similar remark.

Some people almost automatically respond to a threatening situation by putting down someone else. The cynical attitude displayed by some students (or faculty) is an example of this defense mechanism when it has become habitual. The cynic has an attitude that says, in effect, "I'll put you down before you can put *me* down!"

Types of Gaps to be Bridged

Age

It is misleading to think that age gaps are to be found only between generations. The polarity seems to occur more because of lack of understanding or the inability to communicate honest feelings, rather than merely the difference in ages, for there may be large gaps between people relatively close in age and small gaps between people widely separated chronologically. What, after all, do "old" or "maturity" or "immaturity" mean? There may be many eighteen-year-olds who are "older" in their thinking than some fifty-year-olds, and some sixty-year olds who are "younger" in thought and ideas than some teenagers.

Nevertheless, age is a factor that may cause some breakdown in communication. The older generation has had to adjust to events and attitudes which are part of modern youth's everyday life. As Margaret Mead has pointed out, "Even recently, the elders could say, 'You know, I have been young and *you* never have been old.' But today's young people can reply: 'You never have been young in the world I am young in, and you never can be' " [Mead,* p. 63].

The fact that the "when-I-was-young" response of elders is no longer terribly relevant to today's youth comes as a very difficult revelation for parents and elders. The older generation won't see repeated in the lives of their children the experiences that they have had — and have had to adjust to. Today's youth — the "older generation" of tomorrow — will experience the same shock when they realize that *they* can never be young as *their* children will be young.

---

*From *Culture and Commitment* by Margaret Mead. Copyright © 1970 by Margaret Mead. Reprinted by permission of Doubleday & Company, Inc.

Peer Group

Just as there often is a break in the communication lines between generations, so there may be a break between members of a peer group. To assume that everyone over thirty holds the same point of view is certainly a faulty assumption. Young people do not understand and communicate with each other perfectly either. For example, roommates may run into difficulty when they discover that "keeping the apartment clean" means extremely different things to the various people involved. Brothers and sisters also are prime examples of similar agemates disagreeing. It would be a rare sibling relationship that did not have a few arguments or disagreements – usually over a misunderstanding or misinterpretation in communication.

Occupation

Scientists have a language all their own; so do carpenters, computer programmers, and workers in any other occupation. The "specialty" of their particular occupation sets them apart in a certain way, creating the possibility of communication breakdowns between members of different occupational groups. Most of us have had the experience of feeling like, "I just didn't belong – I didn't know what to say." We tend to feel most comfortable around those people who share a similar occupation, hobby, or interest with us. Occupational interests may or may not be a problem area for you.

Social

"We are so different; we have nothing in common." Social background can be a problem to some people, but it does not have to be. The mobility of people in modern times has tended to decrease the importance of social "class." Yet, some *feel* that there is a distinction and this *feeling* can cause some communication difficulties.

Perhaps the biggest problem presented in this area is by the person who is trying to *impress* others by his real or imagined social position. Often people who are "on the way up" (but feel rather insecure about it) feel the need to enhance their position by putting other people down — to more or less look down their noses at others, to make themselves feel that they are important. They communicate this feeling to others.

The truly great person does not put others down; he does not need to enhance his own position at the expense of others. Although others may look upon him as somewhat unapproachable, this type of truly great person — a person with "real class" — is in reality an ordinary, honest, *real* person. Social "class" is often in the eye of the beholder.

Building Bridges

What can we do to knock down the roadblocks and bridge the gaps or breaks that occur in communication.

Understanding

Before we can build any bridges of communications, we must be able to understand the problems that have to be bridged. We have to recognize the roadblocks and the gaps that are present, and also recognize that they *are* bridgeable.

We are all different; no two people are alike. This is really a blessing, for it is the differences that make life more interesting. I received a birthday card that read, "If all the sisters in the world were like you, what a different place this would be." Then I opened the card and it continued, "Not necessarily better — just different!"

Without these differences the world would be like scrambled eggs without salt or pepper — rather bland. It is the "difference" of salt and pepper that makes the eggs enjoyable. If we all had to think alike, talk alike, dress alike, and *be* alike, life would be rather bland and uninteresting.

To have understanding we have to recognize that differences exist, and then say, "That's okay. I accept you as you are." We do not have to agree with people who are different from us, but we will be much happier if we try to understand others.

Understanding does not mean coercing someone to your point of view. The manipulator tries to do this. He sees understanding as having someone else come around to *his* point of view. Then *he* is being understood. This is faulty thinking.

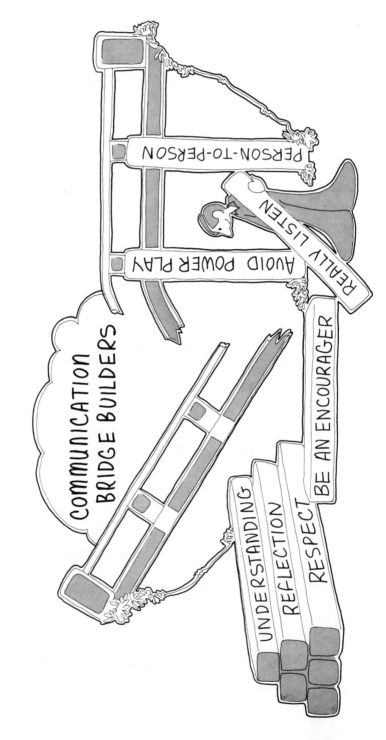

The understanding person communicates verbally and nonverbally that he accepts and understands, even if he does not agree; if there happens to be agreement, that is great. But the understanding communicator does not insist on agreement.

Reflection

If you are not sure that you understand the intent or meaning of another person, ask. You can ask reflectively, saying, "Do I understand you correctly . . ." and then go on to state your sense of what the other person was trying to say. Or you might say, "Are you saying that you feel . . ." and then state your understanding of his intent.

In this way, both parties work their way together to the point of understanding. One party is not jumping to some conclusion or misinterpreting the other's intention. Interpretations are "tried out" for size, to see if the message is being received clearly.

Respect

Gaps can be bridged if communicators will treat each other with mutual respect, on a personal one-to-one level. The instructor who replies to a student's question, "That's a good question, Mary; let's look at that," demonstrates respect for another's point of view.

Respect means that communicators approach each other with genuine and sincere acceptance. "I feel that you are worthwhile and I will listen to what you have to say," is the *feeling* transmitted. One feels free to bring up topics of concern, knowing that the other person will accept them as worthy of discussion. He knows that the reaction will not be "What a dumb thing to say" or "You must be kidding."

Really Listen

Sometimes you may feel like saying, "What's the use? Talking to my Dad is just like talking to a fence." You want people to *really* listen, not just to sit like a stone wall, letting your statements bounce off him. If one really listens, he will be able to reflect what he feels the other person is saying, and communication lines will remain open.

A student was discussing counselors. He said, "Nobody wants to talk to Mr. Smith. Why? Because he doesn't really listen — he doesn't care about *you* — he's more concerned about his precious files. If you go in to see him, he *says,* 'Yes, go on, I'm listening,' but he's looking through some papers, or doodling, or something else and you just want to get out of there. But Mr. Jones' office is completely different — I guess that's why it's harder to get in to see him. He always has students there! And you *know* that he cares and that he is really listening. Even the way his office is arranged gives you that feeling. There's no desk right in the way like some big barrier; his desk is over against the wall, and he stops what he's doing and concentrates on *you* when you come in."

We can learn a lot from this story about our own habits when we are "listening" to others. What feeling do we convey? Who is most important? Do we *really* care?

Be an Encourager

Accepting another person *as he is* encourages communication. The encourager operates in an atmosphere of loving acceptance. If you make a mistake you are still accepted as the person that you are.

The encourager does not "put down" others; we all have had the experience of being put down. It's not fun! The "put-down" is interpreted as blame, rejection, criticism, or ridicule; it makes its victim feel a sense of shame or unworthiness.

"How could you be so stupid?" "If you think you're so smart, why don't you do it youself?" "If it weren't for you we would have won that game. I hope you're proud of yourself." Messages of this kind do not build bridges — they tear them down. They often set up a chain reaction response of a similar nature, like, "Well, you're not so great either" or "It wasn't *my* fault."

The encourager communicates messages of acceptance instead of rejection: "I guess I haven't gotten my point across to you. Let me put it this way. . . ." The encouraging message gets the point across without destroying the other person's sense of self-worth.

Avoid the Power Play

Sometimes people in authority feel that their position gives them the right to use their power in any way they like. The argument that "Father knows best" or the statement that "I'm the boss and we'll do it *my* way" are power plays. Certainly those in positions of responsibility need the authority to make decisions, but the question is *how* they use that power.

One student remarked, "My parents have *all* the answers — at least they think they do. If they don't, they try to fake it, or give me that old line, 'When you're older, you'll realize that we knew what was best for you. This is for your own good.' "

Certainly there will be many instances where authority figures really do know what is best. If they are skillful communicators they will help others to arrive at the best decision, rather than using their power to control and manipulate others. They do not play Junior God; they don't have all the answers and they admit it.

A person's "power" may lie in the eyes of the other person; we see this in interpersonal relationships where people rely upon each other for support and reassurance. It would be wise to avoid the tendency by some to set up "conditions" for receiving this support. "If you love me, you wouldn't act like that." "Do as I say and I'll help you." "If you don't stop that, you will really be in trouble." In these instances, power is being used wrongly; the other person is not taken into consideration. Relationships of trust and understanding are not based upon the power of the individuals, but upon their trustworthiness and credibility.

Person-to-Person

A person-to-person relationship is the element in communication bridge-building that ties everything together. When we deal with others on a personal basis, conveying a sincere "I care" attitude, the channels of communication will remain open. This feeling can occur between two people or between the members of a large group. Even the teacher who conducts a large class can convey the feeling "You are important — *you* individually." A member of a family can feel strong group membership, but also can know that as a person, as an individual, he is unique and important.

Communication on a person-to-person basis is not a simple and easy task. It requires that a person be open and honest to the needs of another, and this involves some risk – primarily the risk of rejection. But there is also the chance that you will achieve a deep and meaningful relationship. There is the risk that you might be misunderstood, but there is also the chance that you will be able to work your way to a point of understanding.

Ground Rules for Communicating

Effective communication is a two-way process. In order to keep the channels open both ways, both participants need to cooperate. Following are a few basic ground rules that might help you to establish and continue communications on an understanding level.

1. As much as possible, remove the stereotyped barriers that may be blocking good communication. Perhaps the most obvious barrier in this category is age. Don't assume that communication is not possible just because of a separation in ages. A willingness to communicate is the first step.
2. Remember that understanding goes both ways; if you want to be understood, it seems only fair that you try to understand the other party as well. Both communicating parties have wants and feelings that need to be expressed if two-way communication is going to occur.
3. Try to listen with an open mind; do not enter into the communication process with preformed judgments. Try to see the situation from the other person's point of view. This is what you expect in return.
4. Share your thoughts and experiences; take a chance. You often may find yourself holding back on your ideas or feelings because you think the other person will disapprove or even laugh at you. But your thoughts and experiences may be just the key to unlocking the door to understanding.
5. Take the initiative in trying to clear up cloudy issues. Some topics are very difficult to discuss, but discussion may be the only way to work through the cloudiness.

6. If you look for trust and confidence in others, you must be a trustworthy person in return. This will mean taking responsibility for actions and living up to the confidence placed in you. Whenever you wish to confide in someone, you seek someone you know you can trust. You must be that kind of person, too.

7. Practice courtesy and consideration for others and their point of view. Look for opportunities to do kind things for others or to cheer them up when they need it. It doesn't take much time, but it does so much good. Cultivate the habit of being a "day brightener" for someone else.

8. Be an encourager and reinforcer. This involves openness and a willingness to get involved with others. It also includes protecting the other person's self-image. Ask yourself, "What is the most loving thing to do or say?"

These ground rules will not necessarily solve all your communication problems, but if you try to incorporate them into your everyday living, you will find positive results. Your communication level should assume a new dimension — understanding.

Summary

Communicating is more than making verbal statements. It is the conveying of feelings and attitudes by nonverbal means as well. Communication is the transmitting of messages *two* ways — sending and receiving. It is important to keep communication channels open.

There are many built-in roadblocks and gaps that stand in the way of effective communication. Areas where roadblocks are to be found involve semantics, experience, social structure, and defensive self-image.

Some of the gaps that need to be bridged are age, peer group, occupation, and social. These roadblocks can be crossed and these gaps can be bridged by the person who is willing to understand, reflect, respect, really listen, be an encourager, avoid using power destructively, and who communicates on a person-to-person level.

Terms to Define

Semantics
Communication
Nonverbal Communication

Questions:

1. What are some stereotyped barriers, besides age, that might block good communications? Can they be overcome?
2. What are some symbols that might be interpreted differently by various people? What affects one's interpretation?
3. Can gestures be both harmful and helpful in communication?
4. Are some "gaps" normal? If so, does this mean that one should not attempt to bridge them?
5. Rank the bridge-building criteria according to their importance to you. What factors affected your choices?

GROUP DISCUSSION

1. Why do parents and children seem to have communication difficulty? How can they build some bridges?
2. Discuss the causes for communication breakdown. In your opinion, what presents the biggest problem?
3. Discuss the "power play." Why do some people in authority resort to playing "Junior God?"
4. In business it is important that employees follow the "chain of command" when they have a complaint or grievance. (By this we mean that one should consult his immediate supervisor. If satisfaction is not achieved, he then goes on to the next level of authority and so forth. He does not go "straight to the top.") Why is this a good idea? What problems might arise if you bypassed the chain of command?
5. Role Play: You and your three roommates are having a lot of difficulty because you can't agree on the meaning of "keeping the apartment neat and clean." Two of you are reasonably "neat," one is pretty bad, and one is a real mess. How can you resolve this problem?

BIBLIOGRAPHY

Berne, Eric. *Games People Play: The Psychology of Human Relationships.* New York: Grove Press, Inc., 1964.

Bienvenu, Millard J., Sr., *Talking It Over at Home: Problems in Family Communication.* New York: Public Affairs Pamphlet No. 410, 1967.

Mead, Margaret. *Culture and Commitment.* New York: Doubleday & Company, Inc., 1970.

5

I Need Purpose
and Direction

Your behavior is affected by the society in which you live; within that structure there is a great deal of leeway for choice of action. However, you usually do not go through life haphazardly following one pattern of behavior one day and another the next. Your course of action is fairly predictable and your choice of behavior is fairly consistent with the value system which you have developed.

Your value system is more than just a system of rules and regulations; rather, it is a key to your way of living. Your value system is really a matter of personal ethics; it is the application of whatever you consider to be your moral principles to everyday life, work, marriage, social life, and future plans.

What's Important to Me?

Values may be defined as those thoughts and ideas, that express whatever is held to be desirable and worthwhile; "value" is said to

inher —

"Life can only be under-
stood backwards; but it
must be lived forwards." —
Soren Kierkegaard

inher in those objects and experiences that are considered desirable
and worthwhile. If an experience, object or thought is not desirable
or worthwhile from your point of view, it does not possess value for
you. That same experience, object, or thought may be of considerable value to someone else, however. You may say, "I don't care
about having a brand new car; I would rather have one that I can
easily afford and not have that big debt hanging over my head." Or
you may say, "I want that new car — it's really important to me. I
know I'll have big payments, but that doesn't scare me." In the
latter case the new car would be a very tangible example of part of
your value system. There are many other material objects which may
possess a prominent place in your value system but may be of very
little value to others.

The materialistic values which you hold are only a part of your larger *value system.* Your value system is the blueprint or guideline you have developed, based upon your values, that will help to direct your life:

> Every individual operates according to a system of values, whether it is verbalized and consistently worked out or not. In selecting goals, in choosing modes of behavior, in resolving conflicts, he is influenced at every turn by his conception of what is good and desirable for him. Although everyone's value system is in some degree unique, an individual's values are usually grounded in the core values of his culture. . . . Depending on his conception of what is desirable and good in human life, he selects certain goals over others and patterns his behavior according to standards of what he believes to be right and worthwhile. The way a man carries on his business activity, the kind of relationships he has with his wife and children and with his friends, the degree of respect he has for other individuals (and for himself), his political and religious activity – all these reflect the individual's values, though he may scarcely have thought them through. [Kluckhohn,* p. 300.]

In order to understand the formation of your value system, let us discuss some of the most influential developmental factors, such as religious beliefs, attitudes, beliefs and opinions, prejudices and stereotypes, and social class. We also will discuss the phenomenon of change in value systems. This highly personal and integral part of your life is very important in your relationship with others.

Religious Beliefs

Your religious beliefs play an important part in shaping your value system. Anthropologists have found that all cultures have established moral codes which determine the ideal – what ought to be – for that particular culture. These "codes" may be expressed differently from culture to culture, but essentially they are the same or similar. In some form, religion is and always has been part of our human experiences. Religion of one sort or another is to be found in all

*Excerpted from Chapter 7, "Value Orientations" by Florence Kluckhohn, in *Toward a Unified Theory of Human Behavior: An Introduction to General Systems Theory,* edited by Roy R. Grinker, Sr., Basic Books, Inc., Publishers, New York, 1956.

societies, despite the fact that this religious aspect of human experience does not always take the form of belief in a god, or in gods, or even in the supernatural.

Traditionally, our society has looked to religion to supply the values which give ultimate meaning to our lives. Those people who have strong religious convictions find strength and comfort in their belief in the reality of God. As Henry Maier writes:

> Religion and idealistic concepts, in addition to serving as guidelines for molding the individual, also serve him in his search for a future beyond his life's certainty. Each individual needs a clear explanation of life in the light of an intelligible theory or belief. Religion and ideology provide a needed explanation beyond the individual's limits of reason. [Maier, p. 26.]

Many young people today look for meaning and religious beliefs outside of the organized churches. Hindu ashrams, Jesus houses, mystical cults, spiritualists, astrology tables, and Zodiac charts are all part of the "new" quest for personal religious meaning.

Regardless of the nature of their beliefs, which may range from the traditional to the mystical, people with strong religious convictions view their beliefs as a major portion of the foundation for their entire value system. They look upon them both as an outward expression of their search for truth and as a source of an inner sense of well-being and security. Even those whose religious beliefs are not as strongly expressed often feel that their commitment toward a moral code helps to define their purpose in life and their goals for the future. Your religious belief, moral code, or personal commitment is an integral part of your value system.

Attitudes

Another important part of your value system is *attitudes.* You interpret, recognize, and react to the attitudes of others just as your attitudes are interpreted, recognized, and reacted to by others. Attitudes are very important in our lives.

An *attitude* may be defined as *a learned inclination or group of ideas which usually affects your actions or behavior.* You have attitudes toward specific persons (parents, teachers, friends) as well as toward groups of people (blacks, whites, the "Establishment,"

"Hippies"). You have attitudes toward objects or things – food, music (symphony or rock), job classifications, or leisure activities.

You are not born with attitudes; you learn and develop them throughout your whole life. How do people learn attitudes? As with most other types of learning, the learning of attitudes depends on the fact that you usually react favorably to situations which are pleasant or rewarding – positive situations; you learn to avoid or react unfavorably to situations which are unpleasant or disturbing – negative situations. The learning which takes place tends to carry over into later life in the form of *expectations.* You learn to expect the same or similar results from similar situations. Once you learn an attitude, it becomes very much like a habit – you rely on it without really giving it a second thought.

For example, a student may ask his advisor during registration, "Do I have to take accounting? I did a miserable job in high school, and I know I'll flunk it here." Or you may decline a blind date your best friend lined up for you because "I always get stuck with a real loser." Or you may say after your first class with a long-haired teacher wearing blue jeans, "I just couldn't believe he was the teacher; he didn't seem like one." In all of these situations the *learned* nature of the attitude expressed is very clear; it is the result of past experiences. The *expectancy* factor is also clear.

As our attitudes develop, they undergo a process of *generalization.* That is, even when we find ourselves in situations that are more or less new, attitudes formed from past experiences, which are generally similar to the new ones, come into play. For example, if you come from a home with a very strict, dominating, dictatorial father, you might find that you have a learned attitude which expects all males, not merely your own father, to have the same dominating characteristics.

Beliefs and Opinions

Beliefs and opinions are closely related to attitudes. What is the difference between a belief and an opinion? A *belief* is the *acceptance of some thought, supposition, or idea.* "It does not, by itself, necessarily imply an attitude of being for or against something. An *opinion lies between an attitude and a belief and has properties of both"* [Morgan and King, p. 510]. An opinion, we might say, is an attitude shaped by a belief. For example, if your home background taught you the *belief* that drinking any alcoholic beverage is harmful, you might have very negative *attitudes* toward those who drank any alcohol and it would be your *opinion* that drinking is wrong.

Attitudes, beliefs, and opinions overlap and influence each other to such an extent that it often seems difficult to separate them, although in most cases you can distinguish between them. It is important to recognize the interacting character of attitudes, beliefs, and opinions in developing your value system.

Prejudices and Stereotypes

Stereotypes and prejudices are also correlated with attitudes. Usually *prejudice* is thought of in terms of negative attitudes toward a minority group, and this is the accepted layman's definition. But *prejudice* may be defined more broadly, inasmuch as prejudices can be either positive or negative. For example, a mother is prejudiced about her child in the sense that her attitudes are affected by her positive feelings for the child so that she tends to see whatever he does in a good light. A prejudice, then, is any preconceived opinion, feeling, or attitude, favorable or unfavorable, which has been formed beforehand without full investigation or knowledge. A prejudice is different from an attitude in that it is not a justified attitude. Of course, most attitudes are not formed or learned with all the facts at hand either; hence most attitudes are prejudices to a greater or lesser extent.

Whenever our prejudiced attitudes lead to oversimplified generalizations categorizing an object, person, or situation, we are guilty of *stereotyping.* Most of us at one time or another have fallen into the trap of stereotyping. Do any of these statements sound familiar?

> The Democratic Party is in favor of high taxes and more government spending.
> Black people are all lazy and dirty.
> You can't even talk to that kind of teacher.
> Latin Americans are a very hot-headed race.
> The Establishment is rotten.
> Redheads have terrible tempers.
> Women always change their minds.

Unfortunately, songs, movies, and advertising often play up commonly held stereotypes: blondes have more fun; brides can't cook and they give their husbands indigestion; urban housewives are busy with laundry, housework, and chauffeuring the kids; harried business-men come home tired and cross at the end of the day; teenagers have nothing to do but talk on the phone.

One of the most disturbing aspects of stereotyping and prejudices is the polarizing effect it has. In recent years we have seen many examples of polarization where prejudiced stereotypes have been hurled back and forth across a widening gulf of mistrust. Perhaps if both ends of the pole would understand the role that prejudices and stereotypes play in their own thoughts, they could start to close that gulf and arrive at more understanding. Stereotyping is prevalent in most families, communities, and indeed in our society as a whole. No doubt it will continue, but perhaps we can lessen our tendency to display these preconceived opinions if we are conscious of them.

Why Are These Things Important to Me?

Throughout your lifetime you continue to develop new attitudes, beliefs, opinions, prejudices, and stereotypes. What factors influence this development?

Many of your attitudes have been formed through experience, and the starting point for your experience is in the home. Parental influence upon childhood attitude development is primary. Examples of this can be seen and heard by listening to children at play — they parrot the beliefs, prejudices, attitudes, opinions, and stereotypes of their parents. "My mother said I can't play with Johnny because he's dirty." "My dad gets a new car every year — your daddy can't afford it." "My mommy says it's naughty for little girls to pull up their dresses." "My dad says music is for girls."

Other subtle learning situations also occur in the home. Tone of voice and the not-so-veiled derogatory comments of parents leave their marks. Somehow parents often seem to think that children will hear only the things that they *want* them to hear, although in reality children hear everything — especially those off-guard "We-didn't-think-he-could-hear" statements.

Other forces enter the development picture with each year of growth:

During the first five years, the child's parents are clearly the primary influences on him, but, in the second half-decade of life, parental impacts become diluted by peers, teachers, and the public media. These and other outside stimuli become more influential. Acceptance or rejection by peers contributes to the child's self image and self-esteem, and the values of the majority culture are transmitted, in large measure, by the peer group. The teacher is viewed by most children as a parent [substitute]; hence, his or her nurturance and competence affect the child's tendency to model his own values upon those of the teacher's. The mass media also confront the child with models to emulate and, in so doing, may directly mold his motives and standards. All of these influences – parents, peers, teacher, and public media – are acting simultaneously in a specific social class context. But the values and motives of parents, peers, and teachers from different social class groups differ dramatically.... Middle class parents reward and encourage the development of internal standards of responsibility and self control in their children, while lower class parents tend to place greater value on obedience and a fear of authority. [Mussen, Conger, and Kagan, p. 326.]

As you entered adolescence, you probably no longer relied solely upon your parents as your source of attitudes. You were much more likely to rely upon your peer group for reassurance and direction. Most adolescents tend to hold an almost belligerent loyalty to the ideas and values of the group.

Parents have lost their roles as the essential supports and value givers, and have been replaced by the individual's peer group. Peers absorb most of the prevailing social interest and energy of the developing adolescent. They become age mates and partners.... The youth also looks to his culture's values, religion, and ideology, as a confirmed source of trust. Religion and social ideologies provide a clear perspective for man's underlying philosophy.... The youth searches for something and somebody to be true.... Such a search induces collective roles and experimentations which will combat individual inhibitions and guilt feelings. [Maier, pp. 61–63.]

Many adolescents are searching and questioning. They are "trying things out" – to see if they fit, to see if anything makes any sense. This period in a young person's development may be one of intense doubt and questioning. On the other hand, many students point out that they never have gone through a "doubt and questioning" period. "It must be rather odd," one often hears them say, "but I can talk to my parents, and I can talk to my peer group also. I really don't have any doubts about my 'identity.' I know who I am and where I'm going."

Gordon Allport, noted psychologist-author, has stated, "I just don't think it's true that every man goes through this anxiety and anguish and alienation in his effort to find meaning . . . you find a lot of personalities who live their lives without worrying about it" [Evans,* p. 84].

It is important that we point this out, for despite all the concerned attention given to the problem of the so-called "identity crisis," there are many individuals whose parental and home relationships, peer group relationships, and other experiences have been secure, open, trustworthy, and very conducive to healthy self-identity without all the anxiety and doubts that are purportedly present in the lives of so many.

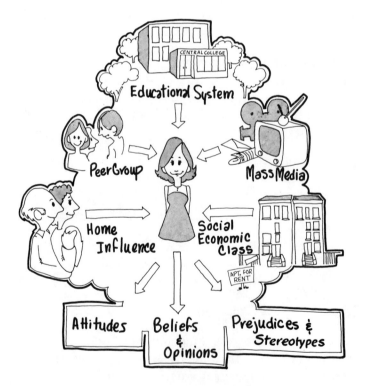

*From the book *Gordon Allport: The Man and His Ideas* by Richard I. Evans. Copyright © 1971 by Richard I. Evans. Dutton Paperback edition. Published by E. P. Dutton & Co., Inc. and used with their permission.

In addition to parents and peer groups, the *mass media* and our *educational system* are also important factors in the development of your value system. The very structure of our educational system teaches certain values — that compulsory education is necessary, for example. The subject matter that is taught and how it is presented influence the values that are formed. Students soon learn the "priority of values" held by their teachers. Some teachers feel the most important behavior trait a student can possess is quiet submission, while others welcome the questioning student. To some teachers, promptness is next to godliness, while others are more "flexible" on this matter. Some "teach" their own values regarding race, war, politics, love, — almost any topic — through the use of humor, examples cited, emphasis during a lecture, or offhand comments.

The *news* and *entertainment media* have had a tremendous effect upon the young people of your generation. Young people today have had television since they were infants, and the "instant" capacity of television news has had its effect. Saturday morning cartoons, with the commercials geared to children, have been the subject of many studies. Many parents have been bombarded by requests for certain dolls, toys, or other items which have been "sold" to the children during this prime time for youngsters. The "need" to have what "all the other kids have" has been firmly instilled in modern children.

In Alvin Toffler's remarkable book about tomorrow's life styles, *Future Shock,* he states:

> "Barbie," a twelve-inch plastic teenager, is the best-known and best-selling doll in history. Since it introduction in 1959, the Barbie doll population of the world has grown to 12,000,000 — more than the human population of Los Angeles or London or Paris. Little girls adore Barbie because she is highly realistic and eminently dress-upable. Mattel, Inc., makers of Barbie, also sells a complete wardrobe for her, including clothes for ordinary daytime wear, clothes for formal party wear, clothes for swimming and skiing.
>
> Recently Mattel announced a new improved Barbie doll. The new version has a slimmer figure, "real" eyelashes, and a twist-and-turn waist that makes her more humanoid than ever. Moreover, Mattel announced that, for the first time, any young lady wishing to purchase a new Barbie would receive a trade-in allowance for her old one.
>
> What Mattel did not announce was that by trading in her old doll for a technologically improved model, the little girl of today, citizen of tomorrow's superindustrial world, would learn a fundamental lesson

Imagine that you are th[e]
little boy: What might [be]
some of your though[ts]
about the nonpermanen[ce]
of "possessions"? Mig[ht]
some human relationshi[p]
resemble this also?

about the new society; that man's relationships with *things* are
increasingly temporary. . . . Anti-materialists tend to deride the importance of "things." Yet things are highly significant, not merely because
of their functional utility, but also because of their psychological
impact. We develop relationships with things. Things affect our sense of
continuity or discontinuity. . . . Moreover, our attitudes toward things
reflect basic value judgments. Nothing could be more dramatic than the
difference between the new breed of little girls who cheerfully turn in
their Barbies for the new improved model and those who, like their
mothers and grandmothers before them, clutch lingeringly and lovingly
to the same doll until it disintegrates from sheer age. In this difference
lies the contrast between past and future, between societies based on
permanence, and the new, fast-forming society based on transience.
[Toffler, pp. 51–52.]

Experiences such as this, stressing the nonpermanence of "things"
or possessions, are becoming more common. Some young people
tend to place less emphasis upon the traditions and rituals of the

past, while others are very "traditional" in their steadfastness to set patterns or rituals. Perhaps the biggest effect of the emphasis on the nonpermanence of "things" is the increase in the importance given to *personal* relationships. Many seem to be saying, "I can't count on permanent relationships with things, so I need secure relationships with *people* whom I can love and trust if life is going to be meaningful."

Social Class

Another factor which influences the development of value systems is the *socioeconomic class* to which an individual belongs. Our society does not formalize "class" as rigidly as some societies do, so that it is not always easy to pick out a person's social class; however, there is a class system in our society, albeit a flexible one. Rather than thinking of "social class" as a restricting or confining factor, it is better to think of it as an environmental influence. The socioeconomic nature of your neighborhood, whether it is an inner city ghetto or a suburban subdivision, is influential in determining your attitudes and values for your future.

> Class differences alone are responsible for differing views of marriage, sex, politics, education, and many other aspects of living. For example, members of the upper class tend to attach high importance to family tradition and prestige, send their children to private schools, and expect them to prepare for positions of leadership. Middle class values stress education, hard work, economic stability, professional training, and a good marriage. Lower class patterns put more values on "earthiness" and spontaneity, less on restraint and ambition. [Coleman,* p. 61.]

Although social classes are difficult to distinguish with any precision, most people *feel* that there are social class differences in our culture.

> What criteria do the members of a community use when they rate social class? The answer is never simple. The type of occupation and economic criteria are perhaps the most important, but many other

*From *Personality Dynamics and Effective Behavior* by James C. Coleman. Copyright © 1960 by Scott, Foresman and Company. Reprinted by permission of the publisher.

factors enter into the evaluation. In Yankee City, for example, people used the following yardsticks: kind of income (whether salary, commissions, dividends, or the like), moral standing, family geneology, social relationships and organization affiliations, and type of residential area. The social classes also differ, of course, in their occupational goals for their children; the higher-class parent more often wants his children to train for business and professional occupational status. The cause of this difference is partly economic. . . . (If one cannot afford to send one's son to medical school, there is little sense in thinking of becoming a doctor.) [Morgan and King, pp. 479-80.]

There is a great deal of mobility between classes in our culture. One can move from one class to another. "Originally," Pikunas writes, "class levels were based on economic assets, but personal endowment and education have since become significant in determining one's status" [Pikunas, p. 65]. Because we do not have a set class system, many "class" differences are more subjectively "felt" than objectively determined. One can't tell by looking at a person what class he belongs to, but in our daily living we sense differences, and these differences affect the formation of our attitudes.

Despite the role of class in shaping our attitudes, however, you, as a unique individual, regardless of your class background, to a large extent can determine what your value system is and will be. You can make an effort to understand your personal religious convictions, attitudes, beliefs, opinions, and the role that your social class has played in bringing you to where you are now. There must be a relationship between your goals and your value system. This chapter is not intended to delineate any "right" or "wrong" value system, for each person will make his own choices and decisions in this matter. It is intended, rather, to help you become more conscious of the options and implications of the value system you have developed and are developing.

Until you have a satisfactory system of values — satisfactory from your point of view in relation to others — you will find that you are drifting aimlessly like a kite with a broken string, subject only to the direction of the wind, with the *possibility* of floating to a safe landing or of crashing to the ground in a sudden downdraft. *Your system of values should be the anchor point or control point of your life, helping to determine the direction and course you will take.*

Personal Ethics

Clear-cut feelings about your value system are often difficult to define. You may find yourself teetertottering when you try to reconcile your theories of what *should be* with *what is.* It would be easy if your value system were nice and neat and orderly, but sometimes it gets messed up with "conditions."

The system that relates your attitudes, beliefs, prejudices, and stereotypes to the daily practice of living is called your *personal ethics.* Ethics are moral principles derived from the common human experience of desiring a better life. What that "good life" involves *for you* will be determined by your values and attitudes.

You probably will not be able to sit down and write out the contents of your value system. Your value system is not absolute; it will change just as your attitudes continue to change and develop. Portions of your value system probably will be discarded or overhauled in a few years, but an understanding of your priority of values and how they developed should help you in this process.

Summary

Much of our behavior is based on the value systems we have developed. Each individual must determine what is "right" or "wrong" for him on the basis of this value system. Religious beliefs, attitudes, beliefs, opinions, prejudices, and stereotypes are some of the factors contributing to the formation of your changing value system. The development of your value system has been influenced by many factors, such as home, peer group, educational system, mass media, and socioeconomic class. Personal ethics is a matter of attempting to reconcile what "ought to be" with "what is." Choices are available and you have the final say over the direction of your life.

Terms to Define

Attitude   Stereotype
Religion   Value
Supreme Being   Ethics
Mystic   Personal Ethics
Opinion   Value System
Prejudice

Questions:

1. What influences the changing of attitudes? Does this vary with age?
2. Do you agree that all individuals seek some belief in a Supreme Being? Why or why not?
3. How have friends influenced the formation of your values and attitudes?
4. How would you describe your personal ethics? Do you think this will change in years to come? How?

GROUP DISCUSSION

1. What are some of the differences between your "value system" of today and that of five years ago? Do you think that your value system will continue to change? If you could look *ahead* five years, what do you think would be your "priorities" in values?
2. What are some of the values that we generally accept as right or wrong? Might the "rightness" or "wrongness" be dependent upon conditions? How do you handle a change in attitude when conditions or circumstances cloud your value system?

3. Do you think establishing a value system becomes easier or more difficult as you get older? Why or why not?
4. In the past, what have been some of the factors influencing the development of your value system? Have you "tried out" your value system to see if it's "right" for you? Are there any dangers involved?
5. How does accepting responsibility for your own actions and your own values affect you personally? (For example, in the past if someone else has made your decisons for you, and those decisions were incorrect, whose "responsibility" was that?)
6. Discuss the correlation between prejudices and stereotypes? How are they similar and how are they different? What can be done to counteract the effects of prejudice and stereotyping?
7. Why do we often find it so difficult to accept another person's opinion or belief if it differs from our own? Does accepting another's belief necessarily mean that you agree with that belief?

BIBLIOGRAPHY

Coleman, James C. *Personality Dynamics and Effective Behavior.* Chicago: Scott, Foresman and Company, 1960.

Evans, Richard I. *Gordon Allport: The Man and His Ideas.* New York: E. P. Dutton & Company, Inc., 1971, excerpted in "Gordon Allport — A Conversation," *Psychology Today,* April 1971.

Kluckhohn, Florence. "Value Orientations," in *Toward a Unified Theory of Human Behavior: An Introduction to General Systems Theory,* ed. Roy R. Grinker, Sr., New York: Basic Books, Inc., Publishers, 1956.

Maier, Henry W. *Three Theories of Child Development.* New York: Harper & Row, Publishers, Inc., 1965.

Morgan, Clifford T., and Richard A. King. *Introduction to Psychology,* 4th ed. New York: McGraw-Hill Book Company, 1971.

Mussen, Paul H., John J. Conger, and Jerome Kagan, eds. *Readings in Child Development and Personality.* New York: Harper & Row, Publishers, Inc., 1965.

Pikunas, Justin. *Human Development: A Science of Growth.* New York: McGraw-Hill Book Company, 1969.

Toffler, Alvin. *Future Shock.* New York: Random House, 1970. Paperback: Bantam Books, 1971.

6

I'm Surrounded by Change

When you know what is of value to you, you will find a way to fit those values into your way of living – your life style. Your values help to determine the goals that will direct your way of life. "Life style" has become a common phrase today; with more emphasis upon individuality, with more exposure to the way of life of others, and with continued change in family structure, you are much more free to live your own life in the way you choose.

Although you may adopt a style of life which you consider to be uniquely yours, your need for group membership will in some way limit the amount of individuality which you will be willing to exert. You are probably in the center of a conflict: you feel the need to be a unique person, but you also want to belong.

"It's important to everyone to be 'one of the group,' yet it is also important for one to have a personal goal, an ideal, something to believe in and to seek after. You may never accomplish this, and maybe you should never accomplish *everything* you seek – like that never-ending road. The path is there for you to follow." That is how one student summarized her feelings about goals and their relation to her way of life.

Your way of life is very closely integrated with your values and goals. They strongly affect each other. Various factors, many of which you may share with others in your position and age group, will influence the direction of your particular life style.

What influence does the changing family structure or our affluence have upon your future life style? Does the emphasis upon youth and the development of a "youth culture" and a "generation gap" affect you? How do you reconcile your need to be a member of the group — to be included and wanted — with your need to be your own person — to be an individual? How free *are* you to make your own decisions? These are some of the questions which we will discuss. Perhaps we will not answer them fully for you, but we hope to provide the background for you to make your own decisions and answer your own questions.

Changing Life Styles

One of the most widely discussed topics in recent years has been the rapidly changing life styles which are appearing in the world today. That this is a worldwide phenomenon is evidenced by the "youth culture" which is prevalent all over the world. Young people in Tokyo, London, Melbourne, Amsterdam, and Toronto as well as all over the United States are "doing their thing." They are seeking a way of life which will be meaningful to them individually, and not one necessarily based upon the life styles of their parents or former generations. We will discuss some of the factors which have influenced the changing of life styles.

Change in Family Structure

Both through your educational experience and through your own individual family experience, you know that the structure of the family unit has changed more rapidly in the last few generations than ever before. In previous cultures, the family unit included at least three generations and changes were made very slowly. Long-standing customs, ceremonies, and rituals were unquestioningly accepted as a way of life. As Margaret Mead* explains, "Change was so slow and imperceptible that grandparents holding newborn grandchildren in their arms, could not conceive of any other future for the children than their own past lives. The past of the adults was the future of each new generation; their lives provided the ground plan" [Mead, p. 1].

In this type of home, the male was the dominant authority. There was a sense of timelessness, as though time stood still, and a strong sense of family identity. The habits of the culture were taken for granted, so that a person living in such a culture grew to accept "unquestioningly whatever was unquestioned by those around him" [Mead, p. 27].

Gradually this type of structure began to give way to the more contemporary type of family unit, where "there is a shared expectation that members of each generation will model their behavior on that of their contemporaries, especially their adolescent age mates, and that their behavior will differ from that of their parents and grandparents. Each individual, as he successfully embodies a new style, becomes to some extent a model for others of his generation" [Mead, p. 32].

Changes in families occur at different rates and in different degrees. The changes may be very small, and they may take place very slowly. Or they can occur quite rapidly, with the result that the experiences of the younger generation will be quite different from those of the older generation in their community. "Normally the first break with the parental style comes about in connection with education, when parents elect a different type of education and a new occupational goal for their children" [Mead, p. 41]. With increased mobility and differing educational and occupational skills, new ways of life follow.

In today's family unit there usually are no grandparents present in the home. Thus the authoritarian link to the three-generational family unit is broken and the relationship with grandparents becomes one of choice rather than necessity. It is no longer expected that grandparents will be models for their grandchildren, just as it is no longer expected that parents will have firm control over their adult children's marriages and/or careers.

*From *Culture and Commitment* by Margaret Mead. Copyright © 1970 by Margaret Mead. Reprinted by permission of Doubleday & Company, Inc.

Today's family unit is called the *nuclear family*. The young people who have grown up in this type of family, where there are only two generations present, know that their parents differ from their grandparents, and they also realize how different their own children will be from themselves. This type of society knows that the childhood training one receives is crucial to his social adaptability; but it also knows that this training will be only a partial preparation for his future participation in other groups besides his family.

> Taken together, living in a changing nuclear family and experiencing the effects of induction into new groups give the individual the sense of living in an ever-changing world. The more intense the experience of generational change in the family and of social change through involvement in new groups, the more brittle the social system becomes and the less secure the individual is likely to be. The idea of progress, which provides a rationale for the unstable situation, makes it bearable. [Mead, p. 59.]

Not only has family structure been altered, but *change* itself has been an influencing factor. Changes have always taken place in society, but never before at such a rapid rate.

Rapidity of Change

Margaret Mead discusses the separation between the generations from the elder point of view. She writes:

> No generation has ever known, experienced, and incorporated such rapid changes, watched the sources of power, the means of communication, the definition of humanity, the limits of their explorable universe, the certainties of a known and limited world, the fundamental imperatives of life and death — all change before their eyes. . . . Adults today know more about change than any previous generation. So [they] are set apart both from earlier generations and from the young who have rejected the past and all that their elders are making of the present. [Mead, pp. 78-79.]

That the world of today's young people is so vastly changed from what it was when today's adults were young may be illustrated in a number of ways:

It has been observed, for example, that if the last fifty thousand years of man's existence were divided into lifetimes of approximately sixty-two years each, there have been about 800 such lifetimes. Of these 800, fully 650 were spent in caves.

Only during the last seventy lifetimes has it been possible to communicate effectively from one lifetime to another – as writing made it possible to do. Only during the last six lifetimes did masses of men ever see a printed word. Only during the last four has it been possible to measure time with any precision. Only in the last two has anyone anywhere used an electric motor. And the overwhelming majority of all the material goods we use in daily life today have been developed within the present, the 800th lifetime.

This 800th lifetime marks a sharp break with all past human experience because during this lifetime man's relationship to resources has reversed itself. This is most evident in the field of economic development. Within a single lifetime, agriculture, the original basis of civilization, has lost its dominance in nation after nation. Today in a dozen major countries agriculture employs fewer than 15 percent of the economically active population. In the United States, whose farms feed 200 million Americans plus the equivalent of another 160 million people around the world, this figure is already below 6 percent and it is still shrinking rapidly.

Moreover, if agriculture is the first stage of economic development and industrialism the second, we can now see that still another stage – the third – has suddenly been reached. In about 1956 the United States became the first major power in which more than 50 percent of the nonfarm labor force ceased to wear the blue collar of factory or manual labor. Blue collar workers were outnumbered by those in the so-called white-collar occupations – in retail trade, administration, communications, research, education, and other service categories. Within the same lifetime a society for the first time in human history not only threw off the yoke of agriculture, but managed within a few brief decades to throw off the yoke of manual labor as well. The world's first service economy had been born.

Since then, one after another of the technologically advanced countries have moved in the same direction. Today, in those nations in which agriculture is down to the 15 percent level or below, white collars already outnumber blue (in Sweden, Britain, Belgium, Canada, and the Netherlands). Ten thousand years for agriculture. A century or two for industrialism. And now, opening before us – super-industrialism.

. . . We have broken irretrievably with the past. We have cut ourselves off from the old ways of thinking, of feeling, of adapting. We have set the stage for a completely new society and we are now racing toward it. This is the crux of the 800th lifetime. And it is this that calls into question man's capacity for adaptation — how will he fare in this new society? Can he adapt to its imperative? And if not, can he alter these imperatives. [Toffler, pp. 13–18.]

We have become so accustomed to rapid change that it is part of our everyday life and we take it for granted. When we stop to consider just how rapidly changes have occurred in the last few years of this 800th lifetime, we realize how important it is to have the ability to adapt while still maintaining a secure foundation. Our changing life styles reflect these challenges and possibilities.

Affluence

Another factor influencing the changing of life style has been the relative affluence our country has enjoyed in the last generation. People have more money to spend, and they spend it — either by cash or through the use of credit. This affluence extends even — perhaps especially — into the teenage market. Sellers recognize the importance of the teenage market in today's economy.

Lester Rand, head of New York's Youth Research Institute, estimates that there are 25 million youths in the United States between 13 and 19 with more than $18 billion in earnings, gifts, allowances, and family "loans" to spend pretty much as they wish. According to a market study by Scholastic Magazines, Inc., 17 percent of the teenagers owned their own TV sets, 18 percent owned tape recorders, 21 percent outboard motors, 42 percent electric razors, 68 percent cameras, and 87 percent watches.

. . . In many cases, the teenagers' spending far outweighs their numerical strength. Teenage boys, for example, are only about 12 percent of the male population but buy more than 40 percent of all sportswear sold, while teenage girls now purchase nearly a third of the nation's cosmetics output. Beyond their own purchases, they influence at least $35 billion of adults' spending, says Rand.

Market consultant Bernice Fitz-Gibbon said to 1,500 leading merchants meeting in New York, "If you haven't struck the shimmering, glimmering teenage lode, there must be something wrong with you." [Troelstrup, pp. 4–5.]

In addition to having a vast influence on the economy, the affluence of youth has influenced fashion. With this lucrative market, more and more "youth" styles appear in the shops and stores across the country. Instead of a situation where young people want to "dress up like grownups," we find that many "grownups" copy the styles which young people have popularized.

With growing abundance, people in many countries find it possible to reflect their individual tastes, and indulge their whim for novelties. Increasing leisure, as Klapp has pointed out, offers new opportunities for escape and adventures of identity.

Indeed, our seeming preoccupation with materialistic "things" has been the source of much dissatisfaction voiced by many "alienated" youth, who view it as a dehumanizing tendency. On the other hand, increased affluence and accumulation of "things" constitute the "good life" for many other youth.

Youth Culture and the Generation Gap

No discussion of the youth culture would be complete without some mention of the generation gap, for this "gap" in many ways has helped form the youth culture. We discussed the generation gap as it related to communication in Chapter 4, and will confine our comments here to its relation to that segment of the population which we call the youth culture.

Those characteristic values, activities, attitudes, and traits which we assign to youth as a separate age group make up what we call the youth culture. Actually, the characteristics of the youth culture are to be found in all sectors of our society, including not only teenagers but also many who are in their twenties and perhaps even some who are older but try to appear "youthful" by adopting those attributes and habits of the youth culture.

Increasingly we expect that youth will have a special culture of its own, with characteristics that are those of neither childhood nor adulthood. Our language reflects this: we seldom in everyday life speak of "youths" or "adolescents" — terms that implicitly suggest the transition to adulthood — but rather "teenagers," "preteen-agers," "Hippies," "kids," or other terms which belong to a world all their own.

Adults have come to expect teenagers to be different, and teenagers come to expect it of themselves also. The values and attitudes of the youth culture are not necessarily anti-adult, but they are nonadult. The average young American finds that he has to undergo two major transitions on his way to adulthood: first he moves from childhood into the youth culture, where he learns and adapts to its ways; then he either makes the second move into the "real" world of grownups or "drops out" and attempts to live in one of the "subcultures" which spring up as the need for them arises.

The majority of young men and women do not doubt that they will one day be part of our society, but they do not actively or enthusiastically *choose* to be part. Rather, they assume that they *will* be part. They wonder about *where* they will fit, but not about *whether* they will fit. They take it for granted that they will one day "settle down," and if they are troubled by their uncertainty on this matter they push it out of their minds or consider it a problem to be solved by finding a suitable husband, wife, or career. By and large they "approve" of American society if asked, though normally they do not think in these terms. Society is simply there.

At the same time, many of these same young men and women tend to show a lack of commitment to the values and goals of the adult world. Rather, they view the adult world which they expect to enter with a mild distrust, a lack of high expectations, hopes, or dreams, and often the unstated feelings that they will have to "settle" for less than they would dare to let themselves hope for. Essentially, they recognize the adult world as a cold, demanding, specialized, impersonal world where "meaningful" work is so rare that they dare not ask for it. Thus, they stay "cool" when it comes to the "real world"; and "coolness" means above all detachment, lack of emotion, absence of deep commitment, not being enthusiastic, or even rejecting adulthood.

Toward their parents, who are psychologically the most crucial examples to them of adulthood, most students in the youth culture show a similar lack of real conscious involvement. They are neither completely devoted nor completely rebellious. Many are so distant from their parents, both generationally and sometimes also affectionately, that they cannot understand the attempts of their parents to guide and advise them. Parents usually sense this distance and, fearing that they are "dated," old-fashioned, or "not with it," they hesitate to interfere by imposing their own values.

Most youths approach the world of social problems, political events, and international affairs with a comparable lack of deep commitment or involvement. To be sure, a minority becomes involved in social action movements, but most of their contemporaries are careful to avoid involvement, despite the fact that they tend to be well informed. They feel an underlying sense of powerlessness. Many see the world as too complex to comprehend or influence, and almost all see the stage of history and social changes as inhabited by vast impersonal forces which are quite beyond human control.

The focus of the youth culture is not so much on the future as on the present. Although they take courses whose ultimate goal is vocational – to become an engineer, a secretary, an accountant – most spend little time thinking about what a career will involve. They live life for the present, feeling that the future will take care of itself. [cf. Keniston, pp. 394–98.]

Some members of the youth culture want nothing to do with the adult world of the Establishment. They attempt to find an alternative way of living, which they may seek through an emphasis upon "experience" – which often means experimentation with drugs – or through communal living as a way of attempting to find a sense of identity within a group.

Communal living is not something unique to this period of history; American history has been studded with many attempts to set up utopian communities based on a sense of belonging, apart from the competition and strife of the outside world. For the most part these efforts have not succeeded, but never before have so many attempts been made all over the country concurrently. Some of the experiments in communal living seem to be very serious efforts to "bring it all together," although others appear – at least from the outside – as stopping points for those who want to stay out of the mainstream of life.

An article in *Newsweek* Magazine told of Helen and Scott Nearing's successful alternative life style, and the book they wrote about it. A portion of that article reads:

In 1954, *Living the Good Life* was first privately published; it provided an account of the creation of their self-sufficient little Walden in rural Vermont. They were opposed to profit-making, wage slavery, meat eating, pollution, and contributing to a war economy, so they just eliminated these things from their world. By means of patient organic farming they methodically restored the eroded land, and over ten years (beginning in the early 1930s) built a fine stone house with their own hands. They raised their own food and bartered, gave away, or sold the surplus; to buy clothing, tools, and the few other store goods they needed, they raised a cash crop of sugar maples. But they accepted only a subsistence return for their produce, never a profit. With very strict discipline and day-to-day and year-to-year planning, they succeeded in making their lives joyful and productive. For them, it was a solution to their searching for a life style in keeping with their value system. ["Prophets of the Good Life," *Newsweek,** September 14, 1970.]

Although the youth culture members who are attempting to develop a second society are a minority, and although their "alternative society" is full of dreams and their institutions are wobbly, the impact of these attempts is very significant. The establishment of free universities, free clinics, arts and crafts centers, and to a certain extent the currently high level of individual freedom of expression are in large part outgrowths of the emphasis upon youth and the separation of age groups.

Group Membership and Individuality

One of the conflicts which you face is your need to *belong* — to be wanted and needed. But you also need to be your own person — to be an individual. This is not a simple matter of choosing between conformity and nonconformity. Rather than being a clear-cut matter of either/or, this is a problem of *reconciliation.*

Basic Need for Inclusion in Groups

The fact of belonging to a group and feeling accepted by it affects your behavior. Groups influence your attitudes, actions, judgments, and behavior toward other people. Membership in a group entails a certain degree of conformity, which means that you tend to go along with the ideas, values, and actions of the group in most instances.

You sometimes may be surprised to realize just how powerful is the influence of other people on your behavior. It may be very

*Copyright 1970, Newsweek, Inc.

difficult for you to go against the will of the group, for you want their approval. The need to be liked and accepted may be a very strong need at this point in your life, and the group may have unwritten rules regarding habits of dress, hair style, or leisure activities. The group may expect some degree of conformity of behavior regarding drinking, cheating, shoplifting, sexual activity, and even experimentation with drugs. The fear of social disapproval by the group can be a very strong influence powerfully motivating you to go along with the wishes of the group.

Thus, it is obvious that in maintaining membership in a group you must sacrifice some of your individuality. Sometimes you might feel rather resentful of your dependence upon groups, but there are both advantages and disadvantages to group membership. Certainly if you surrender your individuality to blind conformity and to the will of others completely, you become a slave to others and lose your precious individuality. On the other hand, working in groups can result in fruitful rewards, for you can usually accomplish more cooperatively than alone. Through your associations with others you are able to meet most of your basic human needs. As we have discussed previously, it is vital to your well-being to be accepted by at least those people with whom you live and work. They allow you the interaction you need to find out "who you are."

Solitary confinement is one of the cruelest punishments known to man. But this does not mean to suggest that you should always want to be with others. There are times when you will feel the need to be alone – to be by yourself and away from others. This is very normal and healthy, for the person who is always dependent upon others is not comfortable with the person he should know best of all – himself.

Individuality

As we have pointed out previously, society today is much more concerned about self and the unique rights of the individual than in the past. Some people strongly object to this emphasis upon self, contending that it is totally self-centered and selfish. Certainly concentrating only on oneself, to the exclusion of others, would be detrimental, but on the other hand it seems natural that more emphasis is placed upon the needs of self-fulfillment and meaning at this point in history, in this country, when the satisfaction of most of our basic needs is relatively assured. Young people especially are crying out against the computerizing of human beings, and sometimes almost seem to be screaming out, whether by their manner of dress or by their behavior, "Look! I'm a person – not a statistic."

Klapp cites the instance of the bearded young man who continues to wear his beard even when he sees his boss frowning and knows that it threatens his job: "Like, it isn't the beard, Larry, it's the pressure of conformity, it's 'Who says I *can't* have a beard if I want it? Or sandals if I want to wear them?' " Klapp concludes that "wearing a beard, long hair, or whatever the symbol may be is not just deviation but public announcement of a way of life at variance with convention and assertion of a claim to the *right* to so live. The statement 'It's *my* hair. I'll cut it as I please' might be translated as: (1) 'I have a right to an identity'; and (2) 'This includes the right to make myself what I please' " [Klapp, pp. 86–87].

That one desires to be considered a person – an individual – is not really new. This desire has always been present. But what is new is the relative range of permissiveness to be found in today's society. The individual has much more freedom to express his own personality than ever before.

We look at our relationships with others with mixed feelings. We enjoy being with others, for the enrichment of our lives, for the worth and joy they add to our lives, and for the satisfaction of some of our basic needs of belonging. But we also feel a conflict when we become too dependent upon others, for it runs counter to the need we have to be our own person – to be individuals. For each person, reconciling these two needs – the need to be an individual and the need to be a part of a group – is a primary task. For most, though, the problem is not terribly difficult. The two needs can work together very well when one recognizes and allows for the expression of both.

Summary

Change has been the watchword of the past decades. Family structure has changed, we have become more affluent, and we are allowed greater freedom of personal expression. Greater emphasis is being placed upon individuality, but we still feel the strong need to belong – to be accepted and to feel wanted. As a first step toward developing a unique life style that will have true meaning, we need to understand the dynamics of change and how it affects us.

Terms to Define

Life Style	Nuclear family
Youth Culture	Communal living
Contemporary	Alternative Society
Peer Group	Reconciliation

Questions:

1. Do you think there is such a thing as a worldwide culture? Explain.
2. How has family structure affected your point of view? Will you follow the same pattern as your parents?
3. What is your attitude toward attempts at building an alternative society, especially one involving communal living? How have these attitudes been formed?
4. How has mobility affected family traditions?
5. Do you ever feel conflict between your individuality needs and your group membership needs?

GROUP DISCUSSION

1. Discuss some of the changes you have experienced in your lifetime (in your home, neighborhood, family, etc.). How do you feel about such changes? What do you "see" as changes for the future?
2. "The 'family' is dead; individuals can function on their own without the help of a family unit." Do you agree or disagree? What do you see for the "family" of the future?
3. "The family is the most basic of all human relationships." Do you agree or disagree? Do you think too much emphasis has been placed upon the importance of the family?
4. Discuss some of the effects of mobility upon a family. Have you ever moved to another community? How far? How did it affect you?

5. "Communal living is merely an attempt by the individual members to find a 'family' to which they can belong." Do you agree or disagree? Why?

6. How will changing technology affect your future? Do you feel any anxieties about your job skills in a changing job market?

7. How do you feel about becoming part of the adult society? Do you merely accept it passively or do you enthusiastically choose to become part of it?

8. Discuss the "conformity" that is present in "nonconformist" groups.

BIBLIOGRAPHY

Keniston, Kenneth. *The Uncommitted: Alienated Youth in American Society.* New York: Harcourt, Brace & Jovanovich, Inc., 1960.

Klapp, Orrin E. *Collective Search for Identity.* New York: Holt, Rinehart and Winston, Inc., 1969.

Mead, Margaret. *Culture and Commitment.* New York: Doubleday & Company, Inc., 1970.

Pikunas, Justin. *Human Development: A Science of Growth.* New York: McGraw-Hill Book Company, 1969.

"Prophets of the Good Life," *Newsweek,* September 14, 1970, pp. 100–101.

Toffler, Alvin. *Future Shock.* New York: Random House, 1970. Paperback: Bantam Books, Inc., 1971.

Troelstrup, Arch W. *The Consumer in American Society,* 4th ed. New York: McGraw-Hill Book Company, 1970.

7

How Do I
Get There from Here?

Before starting on a cross-country automobile trip you would want to get out some roadmaps and plan your trip. You might want to take some scenic side trips, or you might want to head for the nearest interstate highway so that you could get to your destination as quickly as possible. Regardless of how well you have planned, however, you may run into some unexpected difficulties: road repairs, engine trouble, flat tires, loss of your travel money, or some similar misfortune.

Setting future goals is something like planning for a trip; you will want to plan carefully so that you accomplish your goal in the manner you desire. You may want to take the direct route, or you may want to look around a bit. You probably can expect to run into some difficulties when striving to reach these goals, but if you have made adequate plans, the problems will not be insurmountable.

In this chapter we will discuss the importance of setting goals and working to achieve them. We also will point out some of the difficulties that might arise for you in the form of *Problem People*.

Climbing the Ladder toward Your Goals

If you want to take an active part in directing your future, you need a plan, an outline, or a type of structure that will direct you toward your ultimate goal. There will be many steps to follow in attaining that goal, but you must plan those steps yourself for best results. You do not leap to the top of a ladder without using any of the rungs on that ladder – although, some people, it goes without saying, are able to take the steps faster than others. Just as the rungs on the ladder lead to the top – the goal – so must our plans or goals have steps, or we will be unable to climb.

Setting Goals

Just as values help provide meaning for one's life, so *goals provide the possibilities for what one's life can be, what one might accomplish, and what kind of person one might become.* There are several factors to bear in mind when setting goals: (1) some goals will be directed at maintaining stability or equilibrium while others will be aimed at meeting challenges; (2) some goals will be short-term while others will be long-term; (3) knowledge of personal competency is a key factor in setting realistic goals; (4) goals usually will be changing in nature; they should be flexible.

1. Maintenance and Challenge Goals. The concept that the body strives to maintain certain internal conditions of stability was developed by Walter Cannon in 1939. This tendency to achieve balance is called *homeostasis,* and it involves various physiological processes of the body, such as the body's mechanism for fighting bacteria and infection and for maintaining normal blood pressure and chemistry.

Homeostasis also has a psychological dimension. Many of the goals which man develops are aimed at maintaining a feeling of stability by protecting his personal sense of worth or adequacy. Some persons spend most of their time striving to maintain their lives at a level at which most others would not be satisfied. In discussing an apparent reversal of Heirarchy of Needs (see Chapter 2), Maslow states: "In certain people the level of [goals] may be permanently deadened or lowered. That is to say . . . that the person who has experienced life at a very low level, i.e., chronic unemployment, may continue to be satisfied for the rest of his life if only he can get enough food" [Maslow p. 98].

Most people, however, constantly strive toward goals they have set for themselves:

> Man's goal is not to achieve an inactive state of reduced tension. Quite the contrary: When psychological stress is at a minimum, a person becomes bored and is likely to set out in search of excitement. . . . To regain his former zest for living the sufferer must discover some purpose for his existence, something worthwhile on which to spend himself. Rather than reduce psychological tension, he must increase it to an optimal level and employ it in the quest of some significant value. [Severin, p. 4.]

In considering the goals which we set for ourselves, we can distinguish both types of goals — those which seek to maintain stability and those which provide challenge.

2. Short-Term and Long-Term Goals. You may want to set up short-term goals in order to lead to the achievement of your long-term goals in an orderly, stepwise fashion. For example, John is competing for a special award which will go to the highest ranking student in his department. At midterm test time he knows that Joe is very close to his grade point average and that the outcome of this test will have a strong bearing on the final choice at the end of the year. But he also knows that there are other factors involved. Daily class work, practical application of his training, and extra credit work all will affect the outcome. Short-term goals in this case would involve accomplishing the desired results on all the in-between "steps" — the test, daily class work, practical work, and extra credit work — that stand between John and his long-term goal of winning the award.

In everything that you do, whether you realize it or not, you will have more success if you lay the proper groundwork by setting up short-term goals. The person who drifts along without really knowing where he is going probably will end up feeling frustrated and dissatisfied that "Luck has passed me by." Setting goals requires foresight and planning. If you think ahead and plan your future, you may not accomplish all that you have in mind, but your chances of doing so are much greater than if you let yourself become bogged down with feelings of lost opportunity — "what might have been," "if only . . ."

The pattern of one's life is often set during adolescence, with some people feeling, "I really haven't much choice," "He's just lucky," or "Some people get all the breaks," while others are busy looking ahead at their long-range goals and plans and preparing short-range goals to help themselves to overcome any obstacles that might meet them along the road.

When you set long-range goals you need to realize that the decisions you make today will affect outcomes tomorrow. You will not be content waiting for some vague "tomorrow" and the chance opportunities it brings. You will be planning for your future.

3. Knowledge of Personal Abilities.   In setting goals you must be realistic about your own abilities. Your goals must be in accord with the *possibilities* that are open to you. The easiest area to be realistic about is your physical ability to achieve your goal. If you are a very small male, being a great football star probably is not a realistic goal for you. However, if you do have the physical capabilities required, you still must keep yourself physically fit if you are to achieve your goals.

Intellectual ability is often more difficult to assess than physical ability, but you should make every effort to be reasonable and honest in evaluating yourself. If you are having a difficult time passing courses in mathematics, engineering may be an unwise occupational choice, since a strong ability in math is essential to this career.

The emotional aspect of your ability is even more difficult to determine. Generally speaking, if you are able to deal with the everyday pressures and anxieties of life, and are able to look at the world with enthusiasm, you have the ability to achieve most of the goals you are likely to set. On the other hand, if you find it difficult to work under pressure, you should set your goals accordingly.

The realistic evaluation of your abilities is necessary if the goals you set are to be rewarding. The setting of unrealistically high goals will result in frustration and discouragement; the setting of unrealistically low goals will result in boredom and apathy. Ideally, goals should be challenging enough to provide stimulation and excitement without creating too much pressure. Obviously, a healthy self-image is essential to the achievement of healthy goals. Often we find people who do not reach their goals because they think they can't, or merely because they have failed to develop the proper potentialities. Salvador de Madariaga, a Spanish diplomat and political essayist, sums up the reality of goal selection very well:

> Our eyes must be idealistic and our feet realistic. We must walk in the right direction but we must walk step by step. Our tasks are: to define what is desirable; to define what is possible at any time within the scheme of what is desirable; to carry out what is possible in the spirit of what is desirable. [Smith and Lindeman, p. 123.]

4. Changing and Flexible Goals.   As you mature and continue to grow toward your goals, you may realize that new goals are constantly replacing those you set before. Usually, it is possible for individuals to change the course of their lives and redirect their attention to new goals if the desire is strong enough and if abilities are present to fulfill the new goals. We read and know of persons who have changed their occupations and goals for life in middle age: those who are dissatisfied with the way of life as they have been living it; those who are dissatisfied with the "rat-race"; or those who desire to live in another part of the country. To think that goals are absolute once they have been set can be a very damaging mistake.

If you think back on your life over the past few years, you probably will be able to remember goals which were very important to you at one time but are no longer so. Perhaps you attained them; perhaps you failed; perhaps you redirected your goals in a new direction; or perhaps you chalked the change up to "fate." Time is constantly at work altering your goals.

If you become obsessed with one goal to the point where you are not able to change with circumstances, you are not really the "master of your destiny" as you might like to think. Destiny in the form of that obsessive goal is your master. Flexibility in dealing with goals is very important, not only in defining and redefining goals but also in the steps or methods used to achieve them. For this reason you must constantly evaluate the goals you have set and the process you are using to attain them.

Problem People Can Interfere with My Goals

Sometimes, no matter how well you have planned or worked to achieve your goals, you will run up against problems that are very difficult to handle, for they involve personality conflicts with "problem people." There is no one set way to deal with problem people, for each situation and case will be different. Most problem people can be classified into one of eight different categories: 1. Mr. Perfect 2. Miss Complainer 3. Mr. Put Down 4. Miss Jealousy 5. Mr. Cynic 6. Miss Moody 7. Mr. Phony 8. Miss Sick. (Neither sex has a monopoly on any of these categories; sexes have been alternated merely for the sake of interest.)

Mr. Perfect

When you run into Mr. Perfect, you will recognize him immediately – he's *always* right! He can be found in all occupations and social classes; every city in the United States has at least one of these lovely people. He lets you know how lucky you are even to know him and is very practiced in the art of "One-upmanship." He goes by other names also: Junior God, Bragger, Super Cool, and the Big I. He pronounces judgments and expects that his word is law. Does he sound familiar?

Miss Complainer

The room is either too hot or too cold, the weather is never just right, there's either too much to do or not enough to do, and the poor dear always gets slighted by everyone. Of course, nothing is ever *her* fault; she can find an excuse for anything! She's known for her "pickiness," negative attitude, and grumbling. Have you ever met her?

Mr. Put Down

He seems to go through life trying to build himself up at the expense of others. A kind or thoughtful word from him is very rare indeed. He enjoys cutting down people in front of others – "Nailing them to the wall," as he says. If he's in a supervisory capacity, he loves to make an example of anyone who has made an error, especially if it's in front of friends or co-workers. You never know when it will be your turn to be belittled or unfavorably compared, just to inflate his ego.

Miss Jealousy

She comes in all sizes, shapes, and ages. She may tell you that she is very happy for you, but what she says behind your back is something else. She cannot give anyone else credit for a good job, without getting in a dig or jab. She's closely related to Miss Complainer, as we can see from her comment, "Well, some of us have to work for what we have." She often becomes bitter and depressed.

Mr. Cynic

This character thinks he has a great wit, but it is actually the two-edged sword of sarcasm. He does not trust himself and he certainly does not trust others. His "wit" is often a thinly disguised put-down. "Oh, you decided to do some work today," or "If you value your life, don't eat her cooking." These cracks are often followed by "I was just kidding – boy, some people can't take a joke." As he develops this habit, his "witticisms" become more pointed and barbed, and his "humor" is often rather destructive.

Miss Moody

She fluctuates daily, like a balloon caught in the wind. One day she may be very happy and good natured, but most of the time you have to be very careful about what you say or do, for she will burst into tears, give you the silent treatment, or go off in a corner and pout. She often misinterprets your words or actions and is unduly sensitive. You feel like you're walking on eggs around this type.

Mr. Phony

When he comes up to you with a big smile saying "Hi there, honey; gee, you sure look cute today – how come you're such a doll?" you *know* he's thinking "Boy, am I snowing this chick!" You don't trust him. He is a phony out of habit; he "uses" people and you soon learn not to trust him. If he is the "knife-in-the-back" or the "win-by-any-rules" type, those around him soon recognize him for what he is — Phony Number 1.

Miss Sick

Consider yourself fortunate if you are not too familiar with this type of problem individual; she seems to *enjoy* hurting others. She takes delight in laughing at the misfortune of others and seems consciously bent on destroying any attempt at a meaningful relationship. She has a sick "sense of humor" and her whole attitude often seems warped.

Dealing with Problem People

Running into one of these types of problem people often can interfere with the accomplishment of your goals or momentarily sidetrack you. It seems that these types of people have *bent* the Golden Rule to mean "Do unto others before they do it unto you!" Unfortunately, this type of attitude is all too common, and it often begins very early.

Debbie had just gotten the grade from her last final exam and it was good enough to get her on the Dean's List. She hurried back to the dormitory to tell her roommate Carolyn. "I made the Dean's List, Carolyn," she shouted as she ran in the door. "Well, you don't have to go around bragging about it," Carolyn answered coldly. Debbie thought, "I wasn't bragging. I just wanted her to know because she's my friend." Then, two days later, Carolyn came marching proudly into Debbie's room, saying, "Hey, Debbie, I got an A in *Communications*. That puts me on the Dean's List too." Debbie hesitated, then said, "That's wonderful! Now we both made it. We must be the smartest pair of roommates in the school." After Carolyn left, Debbie realized that she had been about to "do unto Carolyn what Carolyn did unto her," but just in time she had realized how destructive that would have been.

We often find it very difficult to be charitable when dealing with problem people. We tend to react to them differently from the way we react to people who don't give us problems. We should try, however, not to forget our principles about correct behavior when dealing with problem people. There are no easy answers; each situation will be unique and must require a unique solution.

Problem People at Home

Those you live with are usually nearest and dearest to you. Often *you* may be the problem person — the events of the day might cause you to react like Mr. Perfect, Miss Moody, or one of our other examples. Your family members will not always react in the same way to you, for they, too, have been affected by the experiences of the day. Sometimes you may end up with all-out war and sometimes you may experience the kind of accepting understanding you need to help you out of your "mood."

We tend to take out our frustrations on those closest to us. For example, if your teacher has put you down unjustifiably in class, you may find yourself retaliating against those loved ones at home without realizing it.

It is not easy to be understanding, loving, or patient when you come up against a problem person in the home; your own particular situation will determine what your reactions will be. If there is mutual love, acceptance, and understanding in your home, you will find it much easier to deal with the problem people (or they with you) because the problem instances will be relatively isolated. In the home where there is an absence of love, acceptance, and understanding, however, one is more apt to find problem people and a more difficult situation to handle. When people know each other very well, they also know each other's weaknesses, so that problem people who are very close to you can become very destructive, using their knowledge of your weaknesses to hurt and to retaliate.

Problem People Socially

Problem people on a social level are a little easier to handle, for you can more readily extricate yourself from this situation and become occupied with someone else. It is much easier to stay away from a sarcastic classmate than from a sarcastic brother. If, however, the problem person is socially very important to you, you may feel that you have to "put up with it" and that you should do your best to overlook the problem or play down the intensity of your reaction.

When dealing with people socially, you are often on a relatively superficial level; consequently, you may run into more "phonies" or "perfects" for these types try hardest to impress those who don't know them well. You even may find yourself assuming the phony role, or some other problem role, without consciously realizing it. Is what you think wit really sarcasm? Examine it again. Can you think of times when you retaliated and cut someone down in response to what someone else did to you? When you recognize these weaknesses, and the tendency to use these ploys, you can better guard against becoming a problem person yourself.

Problem People at Work

Your job may be the touchiest of all areas as far as problem people are concerned. At home, you probably are dealing with people who love, accept, and understand you, and the feeling is mutual. On the social level, you have a fairly wide range of choice of friends or associates; you can avoid problem people whenever you don't want the trouble of dealing with them. But at work (or at school) you often cannot avoid the problem person. You may have to work with such an individual; indeed, he or she may be your boss.

Dealing with problem people at work calls for completely different "rules" than on the home or social level. Your job may depend upon the degree of tact, poise, and diplomacy you display with "Mr. Perfect Customer" or "Miss Moody Co-worker" or "Mr. Put Down Boss." Of course, these situations may not come up every day, but you can be sure that you will be confronted with your share of problem people on the job.

It is especially important for you to learn to control your own temper, retaliatory instincts, and tendency to complain when things get rough. The habits of problem people are easily developed, and they often tend to mushroom until they are out of proportion. They become habits that are difficult to overcome. Before you realize it, *you* may be the new Miss Complainer or Mr. Cynic.

Problem people may present more obstacles to your work goals than to other goals, but you will have to learn to handle the situation in such a way as will enable you to continue to work toward your goals. It may mean mentally ignoring Miss Complainer's grumbling, "tuning her out" while at the same time not offending her. You may have to learn to recognize your boss's "storm signals" — the furrowed brow, that certain way he stomps into the office, or his curt "Morning" may be a warning to you. Maybe your good cheer and humor can help to overcome his mood.

If your boss has had a bad day, he might put you down when you don't have it coming. Learn not to be offended; he may apologize the next day and say, "I'm sure glad you can put up with me when I'm in one of my moods."

You may have to compromise more than you think is "your share" with a co-worker; you will have to decide whether or not it is worth the price. If a co-worker is putting you down constantly or lowering morale by sarcasm or "moodiness," it may be wise for you to speak to your immediate supervisor about the situation. How you approach the subject will largely determine the outcome. If you approach with the attitude "I've been wronged — I can't stand it any longer — she's driving me nuts," you may succeed only in earning a "complainer" label for yourself. However, if you approach with a nonjudgmental attitude — "I'm concerned about the morale of the department. This is how I see it, but I may be prejudiced. Perhaps you can help me" — you will be much more apt to make your point.

Honesty, genuineness, sincerity, understanding, patience — all the virtues you can think of — are essential for dealing with problem people. A healthy sense of humor — a sense of humor that allows you to laugh with others, even sometimes at yourself — is also necessary.

Problem people may interrupt the progress you are making toward your goals, but they do not have to prevent you from accomplishing what you want to accomplish. There are no easy rules to follow when dealing with problem people, but common sense, forethought, and an understanding attitude will be a big help.

Summary

It is necessary for us to set up goals for ourselves, for they provide the possibilities for what our life can be, what we can accomplish, and what kind of person we might become.

There are maintenance/challenge goals, short-term/long-term goals, personal ability goals, and changing and flexible goals. A personal knowledge of oneself in relation to these goals is necessary if one's goals are to be realistic.

Sometimes problem people can interfere with the attainment of goals. There are many types of problem people, including Mr. Perfect, Miss Complainer, Mr. Put Down, Miss Jealousy, Mr. Cynic, Miss Moody, Mr. Phony, and Miss Sick. There is no one set way to deal with problem people. One must be as flexible, tolerant, and understanding as possible.

We tend to deal with problem people differently in various situations. At home we may be more accepting or more destructive. Socially, we can avoid problem people unless they are very "important" to us, in which case we have to work out the problem with them. At work, problem people cannot simply be avoided by choice (as they sometimes can be socially) and you often do not have the accepting relationship that is present in the home; you will have to learn the habits of tact, diplomacy, poise, and good humor, with some compromising thrown in for good measure.

Terms to Define

Homeostasis	Short-term goals
Equilibrium	Long-term goals
Maintenance goals	

Questions:

1. Compare long-term goals with short-term goals. How does one affect the other?
2. What are some of the difficulties that might interfere with the accomplishment of your goals?
3. Why is flexibility so important in setting goals?
4. Why is it necessary to have a knowledge of your own personal abilities?
5. Can you see any traces of "problem people" characteristics in yourself? What can you do about it?

GROUP DISCUSSION

1. Discuss the eight types of problem people. Which type is most troublesome for each member of your group? Try to arrive at a

consensus regarding the three most troublesome types for your whole group.

2. Discuss your reaction to a "Mr. Put Down" person. What is your first impulse? What determines what your reaction will be?

3. Discuss sarcasm. What is the difference between "wit" and "sarcasm"? Have you ever been in a situation where sarcasm was used extensively? How did you feel? When can sarcasm become destructive?

4. Discuss the "phony" male compared to the "phony" female. How are they similar? How are they different? What is your group's reaction to the "phony"?

5. Compare your handling of problem people in each of the three types of situations listed in the chapter: home, social, and work (or school). What are some of the factors which determine your reactions to various types of problem people in each of these situations?

BIBLIOGRAPHY

Maslow, A. H. *Motivation and Personality,* 2nd ed. New York: Harper & Row, Publishers, Inc., 1970.

Severin, Frank T. *Third Force Psychology: A Humanistic Orientation to the Study of Man to Supplement Morgan and King's Introduction to Psychology.* New York: McGraw-Hill Book Company, 1971.

Smith, T. V., and Eduard C. Lindeman. *Democratic Way of Life.* New York: New American Library of World Literature, Inc., 1951.

III

TIME FOR THE WORLD OF WORK

8

What's in It for Me?

"What's in it for me?" This is a very valid question for you to ask when considering your choice of jobs. There is also another side to this question. Your employer will want to know what's in it for him if he hires you. Thus the question at the head of this chapter is equally valid for both employee and employer. Both will want to know what they stand to gain by this employment and also what is expected of them. Many of the instances of job disappointment and dissatisfaction have resulted because either employee or employer did not understand that something has to be in it for both of them.

Consider this example: Sally, a young wife and mother with a second-grader, had been working in a local furniture store. She had started as a part-time office girl and had helped out on the floor occasionally when another employee was sick. Quite by accident, her "talent" for decorating had been uncovered, and she was soon noted for her flair with color and design. But the hours were longer than she wanted and the pay was less than she thought she deserved for her variety of talents.

"First I must get together with *me*." — Barry Stevens

(Courtesy of Burroughs Corp.)

When a new furniture store was being opened, she applied for the job of interior decorator. When she was interviewed, she was told "With your experience, you should be able to learn the ropes and work into a top spot rather quickly. Of course, with your family, I realize you'd like to work on a part-time basis, and after we get organized we'll see what we can work out. I'd like you to sell on the floor to begin with and then work into interior design, and perhaps help with some of our buying eventually."

Sally was delighted. She quit her other job and started to work for the new firm. "This is really great," she thought. "I'll be doing just the work that I like to do, I'll be getting paid more, and I won't have those long hours. This is just wonderful."

After three months she quit, feeling very disappointed, hurt, and "used." She said, "What a laugh! I was supposed to have the top spot in interior design, to help with the buying, and only work part-time. I ended up selling on the floor, just like all the others. I worked longer hours than before — 'just until we get organized,' he said, but how long does that take? Then, to top it all off, they went off to market without me. They didn't even consult me! I decided it wasn't worth the grief."

Her boss told his side of the story this way: "What did she expect? I told her quite explicitly what I expected: that she would have to start by selling and work into interior design. You don't do things overnight in this business. I thought with her experience she'd realize that this business means long hours and short coffee breaks if you want to get ahead. I just can't understand her. She wasn't here even long enough to learn the stock."

This is a classic example of what happens when employer and employee do not understand each other in terms of "What's in it for both of us." Sally expected all the benefits but wanted none of the drudgery. She wanted to do only what *she* thought was important and overestimated her immediate value as an employee. Her boss was also at fault for not spelling out clearly what he expected of her.

Mutual Benefit

In any job you will go through a learning period, and during this period your boss may sometimes feel, "Won't he ever learn? I wish he'd get mad and quit." For your part, you might feel, "Why in the world did I ever take this job? I want to quit." But after you have learned to do your job well, your boss might well come to wonder what he would ever do without you. Your value has increased to the point where it's worth a great deal for the employer to continue employing you.

Both employers and employees have expectations about a job. Unless they both think of the position as a chance for mutual benefit, and unless they each understand the duties and expectations of the other, their relationship will probably not be as happy as it ought to be.

Let us take a look at the mutual benefit involved in the employer-employee situation. Today's employers (management) need to produce goods or services that consumers want and need, and they need to operate at a profit in order to stay in business. With that profit, they are able to improve their business, attract new capital (investors), and hire responsible employees.

Employees need jobs to provide them with income so they can support themselves and their families. They also look for interesting jobs which will be meaningful, so that they feel their contribution to the world of work is worthwhile. If business and industry did not have responsible employees, they could not continue to exist. On the other hand, "responsible" employees need to realize that business and industry do not have unlimited resources; unless their company makes a profit, they will no longer have jobs. We have seen in recent years how the fluctuations in the job market and the financial failure of some huge corporations have affected employees. Profit, loss, income, and expenses are all part of the circle of mutual benefit which involves both employers and employees.

In this chapter we will look at the employee's side of the coin of mutual benefit – *what's in it for the employee.* We will stress the expectations of employees when looking for the ideal job. We also will discuss the importance of correlating job expectations with personal skills and will deal briefly with the techniques of job hunting.

What Am I Looking For?

You will have your own personal expectations regarding your job, but there will be some areas where most people are in general agreement. Over and above personal expectations, most young people seem to have six expectations in common: (1) monetary reward; (2) meaningful work; (3) challenging work; (4) respect for individuality; (5) satisfaction of association; (6) chance for advancement. The weight one attaches to each of these expectations will differ; for example, John might consider the chance for advancement as the prime factor when looking for a job, while Harry might be looking for challenging work as his foremost criterion when choosing his job. However, most employees seem to include all six of these criteria in their job expectations.

Monetary Reward

The economic aspect of the world of work is very basic; you are really no different from other students when you say, "I just have to find a job; I really need the money." The prospect of "cold cash" has not lost its appeal; indeed, the pay you will receive will be your compensation for the contribution you make to your company through your skills and abilities. Although many people do not feel that money is the single most important consideration in looking for a job, no one would turn down a nice raise in salary if it were offered. A good job with adequate pay is one of the factors contributing to your feelings of self-worth.

You will want to ask yourself certain questions in regard to the relative value of money when considering a job. Just how important *is* money? How much is enough? Would you go through very much inconvenience for a higher amount of money? Would you modify your goals because of higher pay?

Fringe benefits must be considered as part of monetary reward for they provide security of sorts. They always should be assessed at their actual value. For example, could you purchase health insurance cheaper yourself than the amount taken off your salary to pay for the company's policy? What about life insurance — is it convertible if you change jobs?

You will have to weigh the importance of money in relation to other job expectations.

Meaningful Work

The word "relevancy" has been used a great deal in the past few years; we want everything to have meaning, to be applicable. For example, many students feel that a lot of their school work is mere "busy work" and that it is not "relevant." A worker might feel that his job is not really relevant, that it does not have a direct bearing or connection to what he wants to achieve in his life, that it does not have meaning for him.

It is important to realize that relevance often is a matter of attitude. A student may think that taking a speech course is a waste of time: "I'm not going to be a public speaker." But when he is applying for a job, that course has real relevance in helping him organize his thoughts and express himself clearly. On the job one might sometimes feel that his work is just so much "busy work," but when seen in relation to the whole picture of the company, the job of mail clerk, or file clerk, or errand boy takes on relevance. Each job is meaningful to the company as a whole. If we remember that relevance and meaning are often a matter of attitude, it might help us through that first "learning" job and speed up the promotion possibilities.

Certainly the weight placed upon this criterion will be influenced by your definition of what is "meaningful" for you. To some people salary means more than the intrinsic meaningfulness of the job. If one thinks of his job as just a source of income, a means of support, a paycheck, then meaningfulness is mostly a matter of money. This is certainly up to the individual, but if one thinks of his job as only an unpleasant process he has to go through in order to get money, the larger paycheck often seems a sad reward for "putting up with the job." An employee is much better off if his sense of meaningfulness entails a combination of a good salary and interesting worthwhile work.

Challenging Work

Some people just seem to coast along all their lives, taking the easiest path, avoiding risks at all cost, and doing only as much as is minimally necessary. Others seem to be the extreme opposite: they always choose the most difficult path. They seem to be "born gamblers" – that is, they are always taking chances, and they use all their energy to compete and excel.

The first type of person might say, "Why should I knock myself out? I'm getting along okay," or "Why be such an eager beaver? After all, a job is a job." This type of person places little value upon the *challenging* aspect of a job. A job is merely a means to an end, something one has to do. The other person may say, "You'll never have anything if you don't take a few chances," or "Nobody remembers a loser. I intend to be remembered." This type of person is extremely competitive and seems almost driven to win. His job is also a means to an end, and the end is coming out on top. He is often characterized by a ruthless competitive drive to excel.

Challenge

Most of us are somewhere in between. We enjoy the feeling of inner pride that accompanies the accomplishment of challenging work, yet we do not feel like taking on the whole world — there are limits to the challenges which we will accept. We need to know what those limits are. Evaluation of abilities and skills is essential if we want to find work that is challenging but not over our heads. On the other hand, we need to believe in our abilities enough to accept realistic challenge and risk. We want a job that will utilize our talents and encourage us to improve and upgrade them.

Respect for Individuality

You may be number 123–45–678 to the Internal Revenue Service — thanks to your Social Security card. You may be number 894–582–003–S to your service station — thanks to your credit card. To the local department store you are number 246–380. To the telephone company you are 104–093–3069–WG and you are TX–850–JR–592 to your life insurance company. But you probably do not want to be just another number at your place of employment. You don't want to be just another cog in the wheel of the Establishment. You want to be *YOU* — a human being.

Respect for the Individual

Computers are part of modern technology. With mind-staggering capacities for storing all sorts of knowledge and statistics, they are used to print checks, issue bills, analyze data, project election results, or correct the course of moon rockets. They are part of our everyday lives. But in your relationship with your employer, you want to be more than a number on a punched card. You want to be Judy Brown, person, not Employee Number 45390.

Respect for individuality means different things to different employees. To Fred, it might mean that he can wear his hair the way *he* wants to. To another employee respect for individuality might mean the opportunity to voice his opinion and give suggestions to his supervisor. He should realize that his suggestion may not be implemented, but he wants the chance to voice it and be heard.

For you, respect for individuality may mean being recognized for your individual achievement. You may want to be consulted about working overtime, taking on new responsibilities, or changing positions. You do not want to be taken for granted.

Satisfaction of Association

It is enjoyable to associate with people you respect. Such association provides one of the ways in which you can fulfill your need for belonging and acceptance. In a sense, you want to feel that you are part of a team effort, that your job contributes to the total purpose.

Football and basketball teammates must work together to achieve their common goal. If they are working completely as individuals, they are not likely to accomplish the team goal. Members of an athletic team usually feel a bond of friendship and mutual concern because of their common purpose and interest.

Co-workers on the job also establish these close relationships. Working closely with other people on the job can be the source of many lasting and wonderful friendships. Working for the same company provides an area of common interest.

If an employee does not have respect for his company, it is bound to show in his conversation and his relationships both at work and away from work. Loyalty to one's company is the other side of acceptance or belonging to that firm. The employee who runs down his company either by action, statement, or implication probably would be better off looking for employment elsewhere.

Chance for Advancement

When you begin a new job you must have realistic expectations regarding promotions. If you expect too much, too soon, you will be disappointed and your work will show it. However, you will want to know that there is room for advancement in your company, or you may soon feel that you are wasting your time.

How much is "too much" and how soon is "too soon"? These questions vary with individuals and companies. If you feel you are not progressing as much as you want, it would be a good idea to talk with your immediate supervisor. Most large companies have a probationary period. When this period is over, you are rated by your supervisor regarding quality of work, willingness to cooperate, attitude toward job and fellow workers, plus attendance and punctuality. Your supervisor usually discusses the rating with you and offers compliments or criticism.

Being hired affords you the opportunity to prove what you can do, and then it is up to you to advance through the ranks of the business as high as you can go.

Other Factors

Ideally, all of the six expectations discussed above will be fulfilled when you land your first job. But in reality many other factors will enter the picture. To some extent the job market will determine what choices you have. You will be competing with others to land a job. Once you have the job, you still will be competing with others for the retention of your job. If you do not perform the tasks assigned to you in a satisfactory manner, you may find yourself stuck at a very low entry-level job or even looking for another job.

Your choice of a career is definitely a part of your total development as a person. No doubt, many factors have influenced you in your choice of career: an understanding of your own personal interests, abilities, needs, and values; the career opportunities available at the present time; and your knowledge of the changing aspect of careers today.

Education is no longer a preliminary preparatory stage for career development; it is a continuing, almost constant pursuit of the skilled person. Flexibility can be maintained only by constant updating of background and skills and by periodic review of the individual's goals, directions, and even values. Automation has made techniques more subject to change. A person must expect to change location, job, function or role with increasing frequency. [Dunphy, p. 12.]

Your choice of a career is one of the most important decisions you will make. Today's young person often views a "career" quite differently than his father did. His father was more apt to view a "career" as a one-time choice; he advocated as little job switching as possible. Today's graduate tends to view his future career in a different light; according to a Department of Labor report, "The average twenty-year-old man in the work force is expected to change jobs about six or seven times. . . . A new breed of working man is evolving — a man motivated by ideology, personal understanding and the need to move" ["Mental Calisthenics for the Working World Series," p. 6].

Perhaps you will be somewhere in between the extreme ends of the job-switching range. You may not consider your first job as the one and only job for the rest of your life, but you will want to have your plans and goals established well enough so that you are not always feeling the need to move on, for too much job switching can be detrimental to your record.

How Do I Rate?

It has been suggested that many people today view their jobs as a monstrous trap. Some workers feel that their jobs are trying to turn them into mindless robots, automatically reacting and performing joyless tasks, all the while hating the job and wishing to escape from it.

At the other extreme, some workers approach their jobs in the spirit of the ruthless, mercenary, selfish competitor whose only aim is to "get to the top" by any means, whose definition of success is money, whose whole life is so dominated by his need to attain materialistic wealth that his personal relationships are phony and manipulative.

Is either of these an accurate picture of the average worker today? There are those who would fit these descriptions, but many enjoy their work, feel they are contributing something worthwhile, and are aware of the mutual benefit aspect of their work. Most people would prefer to be this kind of person — truly enjoying a job that is worthwhile, rewarding, and satisfying.

Can you have any guarantees that the job you acquire will provide you with these rewards? No; there are no absolutes that can be set down to insure that you will not feel trapped by your job, but there are some steps you can take to help guide you in this matter.

Consider the person who *is* happy in his job. What makes him different from the person who feels trapped in his job? This will vary from individual to individual, but perhaps we can suggest a few differences. One individual knows his abilities and interests and has prepared himself with a marketable skill in his interest area. The other complains that someone else always "gets all the breaks," or wishes he had learned to do something else. The satisfied worker recognizes the necessity of relating and working with other people, while the other suffers from "everyone is out of step but me" feelings. The former realizes that the ideal job also calls for an ideal employee, or at least one who is willing to try to be that type of employee. The other feels that the job should adjust to him and to his abilities. Which individual fits into your idea of the trapped employee? How has he become trapped?

If we accept monetary reward, meaningful work, challenging work, respect for individuality, satisfaction of association, and chance for advancement as the criteria for the ideal job from the employee's point of view, is there any need to go further? Yes, for it is important for you to examine *yourself* and *your qualifications* in the light of these criteria. As objectively as possible, you should try to know yourself in the areas of (1) personal skill; (2) job attitudes; and (3) limitations.

Personal Skills

You will want to be as objective as you can in listing the skills which will serve as a basis for your entrance into the world of work. It is important for you to be aware of the abilities you possess, and to believe in them. This self-confidence is not something someone else gives to you; rather, it is an inner quality which you must build for yourself. Certainly, the attitude of others may help you to develop this quality, but essentially it is a matter of personal belief.

Just as you will want to know your strongest skills, so you also will need to be aware of your areas of weakness. If you are particularly deficient in one skill area, you will only be setting yourself up for defeat if you jump into a job that will stress that deficiency.

Be realistic in your evaluation. Know what your abilities and skills are, and also what your capabilities are. Dare to develop your capabilities to their fullest and add them to the list of your abilities.

It is also important that you do not place an unrealistic value upon the abilities you have. Remember the case of Sally at the beginning of this chapter? She had a great many abilities, but she valued their worth too highly. Especially in a job situation, one's value has a chance to grow and increase as experience is gained. It usually takes some time to prove your worth.

In other words, be aware of both your skills and your deficiencies; believe in your abilities, but be realistic about them. You will want a challenging job, but don't get in over your head. Positive thinking won't solve all your problems, but it is essential that you think positively and realistically when setting job goals.

Job Attitudes

Examine your true feelings regarding the career you have chosen for yourself. Have you just drifted into this field because it seemed like the easiest path? Is it merely a stopgap measure until something better comes along? Is it "just a job" — something you are doing because you have to? Is one job as good as another? Are you really suited for the field you have chosen? Have you been realistic about your expectations of what the job will entail?

Many of these questions cannot be fully answered until you have been on the job for a while and have put them to the test. But it is logical to assume that many of the "trapped" people have not realistically evaluated their personal attitudes toward the careers they have chosen.

As we will discover in Chapters 9 and 10, the intangible quality of attitude is one of the biggest "make-or-break" factors in job success. Proper attitude is not something one can fake for very long and get away with it. Your attitudes show up in so many hidden ways that it is essential for you to do some hard thinking about this matter before entering the world of work.

Limitations

There may be certain restrictions which narrow the range of jobs you want to consider. It is very wise for you to look at these restrictions and recognize their effect upon your choice of jobs. What types of limitations might there be?

1. *Physical.*   One rather obvious restriction or limitation involves physical factors. Health considerations might dictate that you work in a certain area of the country because of the climate or that you take a job that requires only a small amount of standing, carrying, or heavy strain.

2. *Type of work.*   Another restriction involves the actual *type* of work to be done. Usually, most novice employees will be happy to take almost any job within their general field of interest. But if you are certain that you definitely do not want a job as a salesman, key punch operator, or secretary, your attitude automatically limits your choice.

3. *Area of country.*   You may have some rather definite ideas regarding the area of the country or even the particular city in which

you wish to be employed. If you would not consider a job in any city but San Francisco or New York or Podunk Junction, this constitutes another restriction on your job choices.

4. *Marriage.*   If you are married or are planning to be married soon, this also will affect the choice of jobs to some extent. The main restriction here might involve geographical area, but the hours that you would want to consider also could be affected, as could the salary you would be willing to accept.

5. *Financial need.*   Your economic condition might place you in the position of allowing you to be less choosy than you would be otherwise, for if you need money right now you will have to take almost any job. This particular restriction is often more temporary in nature than any of the other limitations.

Do I Have a Plan of Action?

Your chances of finding the right job will be greatly increased if you plan your job hunting campaign carefully. After you have made your self-appraisal, you should be in a good position to begin actively seeking employment. In most instances, the jobs will not fall into your lap. You will have to take the initiative. To do this well you should: (1) consider all job sources; (2) familiarize yourself with application procedures; (3) act promptly on all leads; (4) be flexible; (5) realize the importance of the interview.

Consider All Job Sources

There are many sources to consult when trying to land a job. Your *school placement office* might be your first source. If you do not have a placement office as such, your instructors can be helpful in offering advice. Local employment agencies, newspaper ads, and personal friends are other sources. You also may want to send unsolicited resumés and application letters to any companies in which you are interested. This bit of initiative on your part may provide just the opening you need.

Familiarize Yourself with Application Procedures

It is a good idea to familiarize yourself with the mechanics of applying for employment. They vary with the field of work you are considering, but resumés, application letters, interviewing techniques, and the effect of personal appearance are some areas to consider regardless of the type of work you want. Your instructors probably are a good source of help in this matter.

Act Promptly on All Leads

When a job opening comes to your attention, you would be very wise to act on that lead as promptly as possible. The job market fluctuates yearly and you are in competition with others for any job. Too much hesitation or delay just might cost you a chance at the right job.

Be Flexible

In order to keep up with the explosion of change which seems to be occurring in our world, we need the ability to change with it. If your abilities and skills are flexible enough to adapt to change, this is a point in your favor.

Certainly we need specialists, but the overspecialized person often finds his choice of jobs rather limited. General adaptability seems to be the key factor here. When one has a wider range of choices, or is flexible enough to adapt to different job specifications, he will have a better chance of finding a satisfactory job.

Realize the Importance of the Interview

Many jobs have been lost or won on the basis of the interview. If you have a great deal of ability and skill but fail to convey your talents to the interviewer, or for some other reason do not make a good impression, you may not get the chance to show what you can do.

The mechanics of the interview will vary. Some companies will want each applicant to fill out an application blank, take tests, and have a private interview. Others will vary the procedure, but you should be familiar with all of the variations so that you can be prepared to do your best job. You tell much about yourself in the way you complete the application and take tests. Your handwriting, your thoroughness, your temperament, your accuracy, and your ability to follow directions are all in evidence, as is the speed with which you complete these tasks.

The *personal interview* is very important both to you and to your prospective employer. It is a chance for each of you to determine what the other has to offer.

It is easy to tell someone to relax and stay calm, but when you go out for your first interview it is somehow a different story. Let us set forth a few general principles to help make it a more pleasant experience.

1. *Be Prepared.*   You will want to prepare a folder to take with you. Depending upon your field of work, it might contain a data sheet, or resumé, of your skill and experience, a list of references, as well as some specific requirements such as a notebook and pen for a secretary or a sample case for an artist. It is inexcusable to be late for an interview; getting there ahead of time will assure you of being prompt and will allow you to relax a bit before the meeting.

Quite often an interviewer will open the conversation with the statement, "Tell me about yourself." Do not prepare a memorized answer to this, but try to decide ahead of time what you would like to tell him, stressing your skills, interests, and other factors that apply to your working for this firm.

Knowing something about the company you are trying to get a job with will help you a great deal in the matter of self-confidence. You should know what the company makes or what service they perform and how large their organization is. If possible, you should know something about the person who will be interviewing you. All of this information will help to put you more at ease.

2. *Appearance.*   You will feel more confident and you will show it if you know that you are presenting an attractive appearance. The first impression might be the last impression if you present a negative image. Although modern employers usually allow for individuality in dress and appearance, it would be wise to ask yourself if the possible loss of a good job is worth the self-satisfaction you might get from indulging in extreme dress styles that might be considered outside the realm of "good taste" for business.

Certainly good taste is subject to interpretation, but if you want the job you should try to think of the matter from the employer's side. The choice is yours: you do not have to dress exactly like your employer or wear your hair in the same manner, but if your appearance creates an unfavorable or distasteful impression, the chances of your getting the job are very slim.

The interviewer is called upon to make judgments about you when you apply for the job. He makes these judgments on the basis of what he sees and hears. In other words, it depends to a great extent upon the sales appeal of the product – *you*. Certainly first impressions can be very deceiving, but your creation of a favorable impression will allow you the chance to prove your abilities and skills.

3. *Communication.* The ability to express yourself clearly is definitely an asset. For most jobs you do not need to be a public speaker, but it is essential that you think before you speak. The applicant who replies with "Uh – Um – I dunno – Yeah – Nah – Kinda" may not even be asked another question.

Problems of communication resulting from a "generation gap" do not have to be present in an interview. You should not feel that you are an adolescent confronted by an adult. If you have confidence in your abilities and are prepared, you should be quite capable of speaking professionally and clearly to an interviewer who may well be a good deal older than you.

Don't worry too much about being nervous during your interview; this is rather normal and most employers will understand your mild apprehension. The interviewer is not some enemy waiting to trap you; he is looking for the right person to fill the job, and if you are that person he wants to hire you.

Let the interviewer control the interview; respond to his questions briefly but informatively. Be sure that your comments are frank and positive. Try to emphasize your strengths but admit your weaknesses if questioned directly. If questioned about previous employers, *do not* criticize or complain about them; if you do so, you will be the one who shows up in a bad light.

Watch for indications that the interview is drawing to a close. Be sure to thank the interviewer for his time but don't apologize for taking his time – there is a big difference. Remember that the interviewer is the buyer and you have something to sell – your skill and ability. With adequate preparation and self-confidence, you will be able to convince the interviewer that you are the best person for that job.

Summary

When you leave school to enter the world of work, you will find yourself faced with the problem of correlating your job expectations with your abilities and skills. Most new employees seem to have six major expectations of the right job: (1) monetary reward; (2) meaningful work; (3) challenging work; (4) respect for individuality; (5) satisfaction of association; and (6) chance for advancement. Employment should be viewed as a chance for mutual benefit rather than as a one-sided "What's-in-it-for-me?" affair.

A self-evaluation which correlates personal skills, attitudes, and limitations with job expectations is very helpful. When seeking employment, it is good to have a plan of action whereby you consider all job sources, familiarize yourself with application procedures, follow all leads promptly, are flexible, and realize the importance of the interview.

Questions:

1. Rank the six "employee expectation criteria" in the order of their importance to you. What are your reasons for this ranking? Can you add any other criteria?

2. What reason might there be for a person to stay in a job in which he felt "trapped"? Do you think that young people feel less "tied" to a job than previous generations? Support your point of view.

3. Prepare a self-analysis based upon the following items. Specify your *strength, weaknesses,* or *improvement needed* under each heading. S = strength. W = weakness. IN = improvement needed.

ABILITY

General Ability	Specific Skill	Communication Skill	Comprehension (understand meaning, direction of others)	Other
S:	S:	S:	S:	S:
W:	W:	W:	W:	W:
IN:	IN:	IN:	IN:	IN:

INTERPERSONAL

Ability to relate to others	Ability to follow others	Ability to lead others	Participation in group activities	General cooperation	Patience	Tact and Diplomacy	Poise	Other
S: W: IN:	S: W: IN:	S: W: IN:	S: W: IN:	S: W: IN:	S: W: IN:	S: W: IN:	S: W: IN:	S: W: IN:

ATTITUDE

Personal emotional stability	Self-confidence	Aggressiveness vs. Timidity	Exercise of good judgment	Positive or negative outlook	Other
S: W: IN:	S: W: IN:	S: W: IN:	S: W: IN:	S: W: IN:	S: W: IN:

LIMITATIONS

Physical	Type of work desired	Area of country desired	Marital status	Financial need	Other
S: W: IN:	S: W: IN:	S: W: IN:	S: W: IN:	S: W: IN:	S: W: IN:

SUMMARIZE: On the basis of the above information, try to arrive at some objective conclusion regarding the *type of job* you would be best suited for. Does this compare favorably with your expectations? What action should you take?

4. Secure information about three job openings in your interest area. Use any job sources available, but try not to limit yourself to just one source. Establish your plan of action: how would you apply for and land one of these jobs? Try to anticipate any problems you might run up against.

GROUP DISCUSSION. Divide into groups and choose one of the following topics for discussion. Your teacher may want you to present your conclusions to the class, so elect a recorder and a chairman.

1. Discuss the relative merits of finding a very challenging job as compared to finding a "safe" job. What factors might influence a person's decision in this respect?

2. Discuss the role of appearance and individuality as they relate to the job interview.

3. Discuss the idea of *mutual benefit* between employees and employers. Is this a realistic concept, or do you feel that each group is only "in it" for what it can get.

4. Role play for the class various interview situations – for example, an applicant with inappropriate appearance, one with poor attitude, one with poor skills (does she admit it or try to cover up), the *ideal* applicant, and so on.

BIBLIOGRAPHY

Dunphy, Philip W., ed. *Career Development for the College Student.* Cranston, R.I.: The Carroll Press, Publishers, 1969.

"Mental Calisthenics for the Working World Series," in *The Graduate.* Knoxville, Tenn: Approach 13–30 Corporation, 1971.

Also consult the following publications issued by various corporations:

Armstrong Cork Company, *Principles and Objectives.*

Beechcraft, *A Note from Hedrick.*

Burroughs, *A Career with Burroughs.*

Cessna, *Know the Ropes.*

Eastman Kodak Company, *How Kodak People Are Selected.*

Procter & Gamble, *The Development of Management from Within.*

Sherwin-Williams Company, *YOU.*

Texaco, *Texaco's Guilding Principles and Objectives.*

Texaco Topics, "Not Entirely a Man's World," Numbers 1 and 2, 1970.

Union Carbide (Linde Division), *Linde Is Looking for Some Uncertain Young Graduates.*

9

What's Expected of Me?

Students rarely concern themselves with what industry and business will expect of them until they are confronted with some of the problems involved in finding a job. We have pointed out some of the expectations of prospective employees regarding their jobs, but let us now consider the matter from the point of view of management. What does management expect from its employees?

Management expects certain things from the people who apply for and perform its jobs. Management also realizes that it has certain obligations toward its employees. Those obligations cover a wide range: they should provide safe, pleasant, and secure employment that respects individuality, rewards excellence, offers meaningful experiences, and considers the employee as a person. Over the years, many approaches have been taken to the problems of human relationships in business.

" . . . to be alive means to be productive, to use one's powers not for any purpose transcending man, but for oneself, to make sense of one's existence, to be human."
Fromm

(Courtesy of Burroughs Corp.)

Human Relations in Business

The Scientific Approach

In the early years of this century, it was generally believed that the human factor in the business equation could be solved by the application of scientific principles. This theory was based on the assumption that people naturally want to work and that their interests are virtually the same as those of the business employing them.

The idea was that the organization should be scientifically structured; that areas of responsibility and authority should be clearly defined; and that employees should be shown the right way to do their work by means of scientific time and motion studies. If these things were done, it was thought people in the organization would then be motivated to work hard and give their best to their jobs.

Unfortunately, the theory did not work very well. People do not necessarily want to work, and their personal interests are not necessarily in harmony with those of the enterprise. Furthermore, people have hopes and fears, likes and dislikes – they don't want to be treated impersonally like equipment and machinery.

Emphasis on High Morale

In the early 1920s another theory began to come into vogue. Based on assumptions almost completely opposite to those of the earlier theory, the new approach held that people find work inherently distasteful and that their interests are not the same as those of the business. In order to get the best performance from employees, it was believed supervisors should be sympathetic and understanding and should make allowances for employees' desires for security and recognition. The key idea of this theory was that *high morale equals high productivity.* For the next twenty to thirty years, all sorts of things were done to assure the happiness and high morale of employees.

In the period since World War II, however, researchers have cast doubt on the validity of the morale theory. High morale *alone* will not necessarily result in high output. A group can be very happy and contented and still not get much done. Other factors and conditions, in addition to morale, have significant effects on productivity and must be taken into account by the firm interested in satisfactory human relations with its employees.

Neither Right Nor Wrong

We now know that neither of these theories was totally right or totally wrong; both highlighted certain fundamental truths and both were guilty of fundamental misapprehensions. Business organizations do need to be properly structured, but not without regard for the people in them. Areas of responsibility and lines of authority do need to be clearly delineated, but not without considering the talents and abilities of the people involved.

Furthermore, because the interests of people are rarely identical with those of the organization, management should help people to become personally identified with the attainment of the goals of the business and thus to be motivated to give their best. At the same time, individuality, personal dignity, and self-respect must be preserved. Many of the criticisms of the "organization man" are well founded, but they stem largely from a misunderstanding of what is meant by personal involvement and identification with the goals of a business.

Essentially, industry's goal is this: to get good people; to train them well; to put the right man on the right job; to be sure he understands what is expected of him; to help him succeed; to hold him accountable for performance; and to reward him accordingly. These principles are much easier to state than to apply, but the key one is the first: *get good people,* for if good employees are not found, the rest of the points are wasted.

Employer's Expectations

What is meant by "good people"? What does industry like to see in the people it wants to employ? Generally, they are intelligent, resourceful people who can produce results. Industry probably likes to see the same characteristics in employees that teachers enjoy having in students. A student who leaves with his teachers positive impressions of success in his studies, and who has experienced pleasant, cooperative associations with those around him, probably will be acceptable to industry in some capacity.

It must be emphasized that, by and large, industry wants the well-rounded, adaptable student who can think for himself. Grades in school are just one important part of the whole picture used in evaluating a student's probability of success on a job. "People skills" are often more important than mechanical skills or the grades that one gets. Very often, however, the student who is successful in his school work is successful in his "people skills" also.

Although the requirements for any one particular job usually will be quite specific, there are quite a number of attributes that most employers expect all employees to possess. Of course, no one specific attribute can be singled out as *the* most important, for this would be a matter of personal interpretation.

Many of these attributes are closely related to each other, and the last one, attitude, affects them all. For the sake of classification, we will consider ten attributes that most employers would like all their employees to possess: (1) basic skills; (2) cooperation; (3) loyalty; (4) integrity; (5) motivation; (6) initiative; (7) performance; (8) communication; (9) appropriate appearance; and (10) proper attitude. We also will consider briefly some of the more common deficiencies of applicants who are not hired.

As was true with the expectations of employees, different employers will place differing weights of value upon these attributes. For example, performance might be the primary criterion for Company B, with appearance lowest on the list; for Company R, basic skill might be most important. Despite variations, however, these ten broad categories seem to be quite widely accepted as basic criteria for hiring employees.*

Basic Skills

There is bound to be a gap between the classroom and the job; however, employers expect their employees to have the basic skills necessary for performing the jobs they are assigned. These basic skills include skills of the mind as well as, occasionally, skills of the hands. Some jobs will put these skills to use almost immediately – as in the shops, mechanical fields, or office positions. Other jobs will require on-the-job training before the employee's basic skill can be put to use; only after this training period will the knowledge gained through courses taken in school come into play.

It is difficult to be definitive about basic skill, as requirements for each occupation will differ. For example, the basic skill expected of a legal secretary would differ from that expected of a commercial artist. The legal secretary would possess both general secretarial skills as well as the legal specialization of terminology, business law, and so forth; the artist would possess general art and design knowledge, as

---

*The supporting statements in this chapter are actual quotations from American businessmen who replied to the author's questions regarding employer-employee relationships.

well as specialization in photography, layout, and so forth. In both instances, further refinement and specialization will occur on the job.

In the competitive job market, the student who has prepared himself by acquiring more than merely adequate basic skills will tip the scale in his favor when applying for a job. The student who has acquired top skills knows he can do the job, and the boost this knowledge gives to his self-confidence just might be the deciding factor.

> — "An employee should have the basic skills (indicated by his educational background and work history) which are required of the position which he occupies. Due to our limited staffing, there is seldom time to teach an individual the basic skills required in a given position."
>
> — "In a company [of our size], it is extremely difficult to generalize about our basic skill requirements. However, we do a considerable amount of our hiring at the college campuses, and at all academic levels. Consequently, we expect from our new employees reasonable academic proficiency in the discipline studied during their college careers."
>
> — "Skills that are expected are the skills necessary to do any job that is assigned to these employees."
>
> —"We recognize that skill and initiative requirements vary with the level of the job. . . . We try to avoid employing people with various deficiencies."

Jobs for "unskilled" workers are steadily decreasing. Our complex technology demands more and more specialization, but for the student entering the world of work, specialization — and employment — begins with the basic skills. Business and industry usually cannot afford to train "unskilled" workers. Basic skill is a requirement for entry-level jobs.

Cooperation

Basic skill alone is not enough. A person with great talent and skill will not succeed on the job if he does not possess the ability to cooperate and the "people" skills necessary for getting along with others.

The person who builds up group morale is a desirable addition to any organization because he is a good teamworker. The person who will work for his company and who will work well with oth-

Cooperation

ers — even though the going may not always be smooth — is the person industry wants on the job.

— "In response to [the question about] 'most irritating faults,' these possibly have to fall into the broad scope of manifesting an inability or unwillingness to cooperate with others. Any industry, regardless of its size, is an organization very similar to the family: the larger the group, the more individual idiosyncrasies can be tolerated perhaps, but generally, personal mannerisms not acceptable in the home or family are equally not acceptable at the work site."

— "In short, we are looking for good 'team men.' As a matter of fact, using the analogy of a basketball team might be helpful. . . . Quite clearly we want a player who has the skill to do the required job. Moreover, we want a player who can play each of the positions on the team if he has to and can play most of them rather well and enjoys doing so. We are looking for a 'winning attitude'; that is, a person who wants to win and wants to do so in an *ethical* and *honest* fashion. We're also looking for the kind of individual who, like the basketball player, can sink baskets and make points by himself and yet be capable of passing the ball around so that the team as a whole benefits. Finally, we expect him to be wearing the right color uniform. I recognize that the analogy may be a rather corny oversimplification, but if you really think about it, the parallels are quite direct and highly similar."

This quotation calls to mind the broader aspects of cooperation — loyalty and integrity — which will be discussed next. It also sums up so well the importance of cooperation within a company. Cooperation means using your abilities to best advantage by working as an ethical team member, with flexibility and loyalty to the team. Working together can be a wonderful and rewarding experience, both personally and because of the results that can be achieved by group effort.

Loyalty

"We expect him to be wearing the right color uniform." When you are playing basketball, the color of your uniform distinguishes you as a member of one specific team. An employee does not necessarily wear a "uniform," but his actions, words, and deeds should show that he is loyal to his company.

Loyalty involves more than lip service. If you cannot feel pride in your company, if you do not respect it and its products, you will show this whether you are aware of it or not. In such a case, there is valid reason to question whether you should remain with the company.

Loyalty

In some cases loyalty also involves questions of company security. If a company deals in classified material or research, there is usually a standard policy regarding security. But what about the everyday "secrets" of business — those conversations, interoffice memos, or overheard comments which do not really seem to be earthshaking or "important" in content. What does loyalty have to do with such matters? Unfortunately, a lot of employees have a tendency to "leak" company information. Whether they happen inadvertently or as a result of an unconscious attempt to impress others with one's "importance," these leaks can be very misleading or damaging.

For example, Joe confides, "This really isn't for general publication yet, but I just heard from the president that the Accounting Department is going to be cut in half when that new equipment is installed." Actually, Joe only heard half the story. What he didn't know was that the company was making plans to move all those people who were no longer needed in the Accounting Department to other positions, in some cases entailing raises and increased responsibility. By spreading his half of the story, however, Joe succeeded in severely lowering department morale at a time when high morale was essential if things were to run smoothly during the changeover.

Or Lori, secretary to the Sales Manager, announces, "Boy, is old Jones a grouch today! He must have lost the Johnson contract. He really needed that to make his quota." This pure conjecture on Lori's part may start a vicious rumor.

This neurotic tendency to appear to have all the inside information and look important to others is actually a sign of lack of company loyalty. Company information should remain within the company, and the truly loyal and "important" employee — from janitor to president — does not need to impress others by "sharing" company information. This may seem like a petty point, but consider the implications of such innocent "leaks" as news of a cut in price, a merger with another company, automation, or some other policy decision. Loyalty regarding company information is an ethical matter.

> — "The attitude of new employees and to a growing degree to our older work force is that the company is only in business to provide employment for its employees and they are no longer interested in following the objectives of the company. It appears that employee loyalty is a thing of the past."

– "In short, your responsibility adds up to being loyal – to [our company], its people, and its products. As with any team, this is the ingredient that makes for a winning combination."

Working as a team member, for a company you respect, can be a great experience. Not only will you *owe* loyalty to the company, but you will *feel* loyalty to it, and your actions and words will show it.

Integrity

Many supervisors would consider honesty and truthfulness to be essential qualities in an employee. People who fake records, for example, cannot be tolerated long. Perhaps the unpardonable sin is the *hidden mistake.* It certainly is no crime to make a mistake – but to make a mistake and then try to conceal it is a very serious offense in most industries. That little error, when you make it, might seem important only in the embarrassment it can cause if it is discovered, but any form of dishonesty has a way of growing. It is far wiser and easier to admit a mistake and accept the responsibility for it than to have it catch up with you later – the proverbial mountain that has grown out of a molehill. Mistakes are common; frequently we profit from them. They are inexcusable only when they are ignored or hidden.

Even less to be tolerated is willful lack of integrity in the form of conscious dishonesty, such as padding the expense account, petty misappropriation of supplies (taking home paper, pencils, stamps, and so forth), or falsifying records. For example: a man is assigned to test crates for stress and strain. He is given twenty-five crates to test. He puts only eighteen of them — or even twenty-four — through the stress routine, but he turns in the test results as complete. However, the job is not complete *and he knows it.* He may offer all sorts of rationalizations, but the fact remains that he is lacking in integrity. He cannot be trusted.

The person who is honest with himself, his supervisor, and his associates, the person who does not attempt to pass blame on to others, who accepts and learns from his mistakes, is appreciated and sought in business.

— "The most important attribute in my opinion that a new employee can possess is one of integrity. Without it nothing much else counts."

— "We expect a person to be honest, not only with us but also with himself. By honesty, I refer to more than a description of a moral set of values that prohibits stealing pencils or habitually leaving work early (although these situations are included). Specifically, we expect a person to have a realistic appraisal of his capabilities and the willingness to apply these capabilities in his working environment. One might call this the virtue of 'hard work,' but we prefer to look at it in terms of 'not hiding one's lamp under a bushel basket.' "

Unfortunately, we often find it easier to describe integrity from the negative point of view, thinking of the person who lacks integrity, the one "you just can't trust." Our experiences with persons lacking integrity put us on guard so that we may tend to approach others with the expectation that they too lack integrity. When we meet the person with true integrity, we respond with statements like "He's almost too good to be true" or "I didn't think there were still people in the world like her." We feel trust, admiration, and warmth for such individuals. This is the type of employee who soon becomes indispensable. How do you rate on this score?

Motivation

Motivation, as it relates to an employee and a job, can be defined in many different ways. It is a desire to take action; a desire to accept challenge; a willingness to work hard; the "get-up-and-go" of one person as compared to the "I-could-care-less" attitude of another.

Most jobs will offer many opportunities for new employees to demonstrate their abilities. How you accept the challenge by taking advantage of these opportunities is pretty much up to you. If you show very little interest in progress, in the company, or in the type of work you do, your employer would rank you very low in motivation.

Industry is looking for employees who are willing to do a fair day's work for a fair day's pay. The employee who wants to "get by" doing as little as possible but who expects all the benefits is quickly spotted. So is the person who does his job — and then some — for he is quickly singled out as promotion material. The student should realize, when making the step into industry, that no one will force him to take advantage of the opportunities he finds there. Industry will supply the opportunities, but accepting the challenge is an individual responsibility. If the employee shows little interest in progress, if he does not perform his job satisfactorily, he may be passed by when promotions and wage increases are considered; he may find himself job hunting again.

> — "New applicants as well as new employees seem to lack set goals. Most outgrow this phenomena once they become acquainted with the integral working of the Company. The ones that never adjust to the philosophy and workings of the Company often show 'lackadaisical' attitudes which are reflected in the quantity and quality of their work. This attitude causes most of the problems in the Company."
>
> — " 'Are there any general areas in which new employees seem to be deficient?' has to answered affirmatively, and in the areas of human or motivational qualities. The typical Selection and Placement procedure will screen out those persons who are obviously not technically qualified: industry can readily determine, I think, if a person *can* do the job. What is more difficult to determine in the employment process is, of course, *will* he do the job. And this you truly don't know until the person has gotten a job, and in effect, the opportunity to prove himself."
>
> — "I think it is important to point out . . . that we very seldom find ourselves with a personnel problem because an employee lacks the skill to perform a job. Usually, it seems to be a question of motivation, attitude, initiative, or factors in one's personality other than his basic ability to perform a task — whether that task consists of sweeping the floor or doing chemical experimentation."

The way you apply yourself to your job is very important. In times when labor is scarce, it may be easy to get a job, but it is not always easy to keep a job and advance unless you apply yourself to the work at hand. The person who is on the job to do a full measure of work and not merely to "get by" is helping to build a better company; in the process he also builds respect for himself.

Initiative

A businessman called a placement office one day asking for some students to come and interview for a secretarial job. "I don't care if she's an A student, but I want one who can *think*. I'm tired of having to tell some of these girls how to do the same job over and over again. Some of them just don't think."

The businessman will appreciate the employee who is able to absorb instructions and work habits quickly — who is able to think for himself. Certainly you should ask questions if you don't understand, but the person who has initiative will learn to sort out important information and instructions, mentally filing them away until the next time they are needed.

Initiative

The employee who is ready and willing to accept responsibility is always welcome. He shows this willingness by his actions and his attitude. He usually has enough imagination to make routine jobs more interesting and he is willing to try new methods of doing things.

> — "To be sure, we expect to see initiative from a new employee. (Otherwise he doesn't get hired.) However, we think it is important to distinguish between initiative and a form of overaggressiveness. In other words, we hire young people expecting them to solve problems. However, in the organizational environment, it is important that the new employee not create problems either by attempting to solve them all on his own or, worse yet, by running roughshod on the sensitivities of others."
>
> — "Initiative is, of course, a desirable trait in any employee. It is not always a strong requirement for positions *lower on the job ranking scale*: however, as the position responsibilities increase, initiative becomes almost mandatory to the proper performance of most positions."
>
> — "The company expects initiative or the ability to perform a task without being told on each occasion what is necessary to perform any job."

There is a fine line between initiative and aggressiveness. The employee who is overeager, who tries too hard and appears to be too promotion conscious, is a threat to other employees and may be viewed as a disruptive influence by management. "He's just too eager to become Chairman of the Board," one hears people say about such employees. Your own good taste and judgment will help to guide you in this respect. Be sensitive to the reactions of those around you and you will be able to see if your initiative is being interpreted correctly.

Performance

The most important responsibility a new employee has is to do the best possible job on the work assigned every day. Doing a good job requires that you learn to think for yourself, ask questions when in doubt, and make constructive suggestions. It also means keeping mentally alert, using sound judgment, and being prompt in attendance.

The less supervision a person needs, the more he is worth to any firm. A man who is willing to perform consistently, whether his supervisor is present or not, is the type of person who becomes known for his dependability, a quality which has a direct bearing on his overall performance. A dependable employee is more apt to do a job *as* he is directed and *when* he is directed, even though others may take shortcuts. He continues to do this consistently, whether he likes the job or not.

For example, a young man left school before graduation because he was able to perform well in school only at the things he liked to do. This trait was discovered by his employer after he was on the job, for he attempted to apply this principle to his work. His supervisor did not feel justified in picking out only the choice jobs for him. Consequently, his lack of dependability — plus his attitude — prompted only sighs of relief when he decided to leave.

Employers usually include work attitude and habits under the heading of performance. Good work habits are *learned* as are bad work habits. An employee's ability to handle difficult situations with efficiency and flexibility is a favorable point in his boss's estimate of his performance.

One of the first questions employers often ask instructors when inquiring about students for employment, is "How is his attendance?" There is a carryover from poor school attendance to high absenteeism on the job, and the employer cannot afford to hire someone who is not going to be on the job and on time. Certainly there have been students who have had terrible attendance records in school but who have corrected this fault when they got jobs, but the problem is in getting the job in the first place, for your record is history and if that record is poor, it will not encourage employers to take a chance that you will reform.

— "One of the most irritating faults of an employee is incidental or chronic absenteeism. This employee problem has become one of the most serious facing cost-conscious industries today."

— "Some of the most irritating faults of employees are lack of interest in filling overtime vacancies, lack of respect for authority, a disinterested attitude toward the problems of the company, and a propensity for employees to be less concerned about regular attendance and tardiness."

—"We look for the kind of individual with a high ability to adapt to new and changing circumstances."

The employee who executes his tasks efficiently, accurately, and happily rates high in performance. Flexibility and adaptability are also important aspects of performance. In order to accomplish a high rating in performance, the employee also must have an attendance record which reflects his concern about his contribution to the work of the company.

Communication

We discussed problems of communication in Chapter 4, but let us here briefly consider the role of communication in employer-employee relations. Communications is a two-way street, involving the sending and receiving of messages. Too often, we tend to think of communication as merely sending – telling others what we think – and to forget that true and effective communication entails both sending and receiving.

In business and industry, as in other areas of our lives, many of our problems are the results of faulty communications. Somehow messages become garbled along the way. There is a children's game called "Gossip" or "Telephone" in which one child whispers a sentence to the person sitting next to him. That child passes it on in a whisper to the next person, and so on until the last person repeats out loud what he heard. Very rarely is that message the same as the one that started out. In the game the results can be quite hilarious, but breakdowns in communications in the business world are not very funny. They can cause anger, frustration, and mistakes, and even may be the reason for dismissal. The employer wants to hire employees who possess the ability to use verbal language that will get their point across correctly and who understand what others say.

Communications ability is not simply a matter of speaking or writing clearly. It also means the ability to *listen* – to comprehend instructions and to clarify by questions any instructions that are not clear. Listening is an *active* ability in that it takes concentrated effort; it is an ability that *can* be developed and cultivated.

> – "If I were to name one specific lack that many [employees] have it would be in English usage."
> – "One of the most irritating faults of employees is the failure to listen and absorb instructions."

The new employee who expresses himself clearly and easily and who interprets and absorbs the messages of others correctly is a real asset to any business. He remembers that communication goes both ways.

Appropriate Appearance

Individualization of dress and appearance is very much a part of each person's life style, just as appropriateness of appearance is very much a part of the "life style" of the world of work. Although attitudes toward what constitutes proper business attire have relaxed, management still holds general standards about the attire and appearance of employees.

Because employers feel that employees reflect the "company image" at work, they expect those who work for them to exercise good judgment regarding neat and orderly appearance. Most personnel policy handbooks do not establish strict dress codes; instead, they state general guidelines about "suitable dress," "moderation in styles," "cleanliness and neatness," "good taste," and "avoiding extremes."

The type of job one holds will in some instances dictate the type of clothing one should wear. Shop coats or protective clothing might be in order for some, long hair might be a definite safety hazard in some areas, there might be instances where jewelry would be discouraged for safety reasons.

Certain "high fashion" styles are acceptable in some types of work but entirely unacceptable in others; the city or part of the country in which you are located also influence the amount of leeway allowed. As an individual with good taste, you must exercise your judgment in deciding what is appropriate for you and your company.

— "Appearance of new employees is obviously a common topic in today's business world. Our attempt is to stress the value of the individual. This in essence means we rely very heavily on our employees' basic sense of responsibility [and assume] that they will dress within reasonable bounds of whatever is currently good taste. Obviously, within a company that has many different types of operations such as ours, this will vary. We have generally avoided putting out the 'Edict' kind of release to personnel that would specify you can wear this and can't wear that. We find that employee-supervisor discussions on individual problem areas are more meaningful."

    – "Appearance-wise, I personally feel that extreme styles are not appropriate on the business scene: any employee should be attired in good taste, be neat and well-groomed, and in those styles found most acceptable by other employees of the same sex."

    – "We expect a person's appearance to be appropriate for the position he or she holds. For example, a sport shirt and a pair of slacks may be entirely appropriate for some types of jobs, but would probably be considered inappropriate in a personnel office where continuous contact with the public would dictate different attire. . . . I should mention – and this holds particularly true for women – that we expect one's dress to be within the limits of contemporary and local standards of modesty."

"Local" standards of modesty vary slightly from city to city; what is "acceptable" in New York City may differ from what is acceptable in Los Angeles or in the Midwest.

One runs into all kinds of feelings when dealing with the area of personal appearance, but the employee should realize that in fact, he is representing his company in the eyes of customers and clients when he is working. Therefore, his appearance should be appropriate and in good taste if he wishes to continue in a mutually beneficial working relationship. As previously stated, most modern businesses have come a long way in recognizing that individuals want to dress as individuals; much more variance is allowed today than formerly. Your company will allow you reasonable latitude in your choice of attire but will expect you to have the courtesy and good sense to dress so that you represent the "company image" appropriately.

Proper Attitude

We have left this attribute to the last because *attitude* encompasses and affects all the rest of the attributes that management finds desirable. This nebulous, elusive term means many different things to different people, but over and over a "proper attitude" is pointed out as the single most important attribute that employers are seeking.

Employers think of attitude as overlapping all the other attributes. One's attitude will affect his performance, initiative, integrity, cooperation, and appearance. What do employers mean when they talk about "good" or "proper" attitude? Generally, we think of proper attitude *in business* as one that considers the interests of the company as well as those of the individual. An employee with proper attitude has a positive outlook, builds things up instead of tearing them down, is eager and enthusiastic, and enjoys working and living to the fullest extent. Management wants employees who care enough to do their jobs — and then some!

— "We naturally expect an attitude which will allow an employee to perform his job duties in a cheerful and efficient manner."

— "With respect to attitude, new employees should be well motivated, eager to learn and do the best job possible in whatever position they occupy, and capable of properly dealing with and cooperating with others."

— "With regard to the one most outstanding attribute an employee can possess, we might say it would be a good attitude. However, a person must also have the necessary skills and abilities, otherwise his good attitude would merely be a hollow shell."

— "The most important attribute an employee can possess is a good attitude toward his work, his management, and his company. Problems can be more easily resolved if the employee or employees concerned have cooperative and constructive attitudes."

— "I think that the two most important attributes, of course, are the proper skills for the job, plus the proper attitude which allows an employee to use those skills to the best advantage."

— "The greatest single quality that we expect from an applicant is a good attitude. If his attitude is good, we generally can follow that he has sufficient initiative, will maintain a good appearance, and if he does not possess sufficient skill for the job, would be the type of individual that you would be willing to train so that we could encourage him in becoming a permanent employee of our company."

The attitude of an applicant is evaluated by the interviewer. It is a big factor in determining who gets hired. Although attitude is intangible, it can be felt and interpreted. Let us consider some of the attitudes which have been determining factors for those applicants who were *not* hired.

— "The most frequently encountered faults of applicants would be: (1) a lack of projected enthusiasm, (2) an inability to adequately carry on a conversation, (3) an apparent unwillingness to really 'work hard' for the company, and (4) an unrealistic outlook that manifests itself in the form of wanting to start out at the vice-president level and work your way up from there. To sum up, the reason most frequently given for turning down an applicant for employment stems from a kind of *apparent* self-centeredness that exhibits itself in the form of an individual wanting to take but not contribute in either conversation or physical output."

Referring back to the definition of attitude given in Chapter 5, we may recall that *an attitude may be defined as a learned inclination or group of ideas which usually affects our actions or behavior.* We discussed the learned nature of attitudes and some of the factors which helped form them. When we now state that proper attitude is one of the most important attributes sought by employers, we must recognize that we are dealing with a complex matter involving not only *your* attitudes, but those of your employer as well. Attitude is really a relative matter; we classify attitudes as "proper" or "improper" in relation to our own standards, and those standards, like attitudes themselves, have been learned. If you want to be successful in the world of work, you would be wise to consider how your attitudes compare to those of management.

— "We think that the ability to work for, with, and through other people might be the single most important factor in determining the success of an employee's career. Obviously, this is an oversimplification since this ability is a function of an abundance of other personality traits that go into the making of an individual."

What does management look for in new employees? They look for human beings who can and will perform efficiently and enthusiastically, who possess not only the basic skills but also the "people" skills, and who realize that employment is not just a "What's-in-it-for-me?" proposition but a matter of "What's in it for both of us?"

Summary

One of the primary tasks of industry is to acquire good workers, for the success of a business depends in large part upon the quality of its workers. Industry has certain expectations regarding the qualifications of their new employees. These expectations include: (1) basic skill; (2) cooperation; (3) loyalty; (4) integrity; (5) motivation;

(6) initiative; (7) performance; (8) communication; (9) appropriate appearance; (10) proper attitude.

Although a new employee needs basic skill in order to land a job, "people skills" often carry more weight than technical skill and knowledge. Basic skill is, of course, essential, but the "attitude" traits are mentioned very often among the most important factors contributing to one's success on the job.

Questions:

1. How would you describe "a fair day's work for a fair day's pay"?
2. What are some of the qualities included in the evaluation of an employee's performance?
3. How would you react if you heard an employee criticizing or complaining about the business he works for?
4. Why are "people skills" so important not only on the job but also in your everyday relationships?
5. Can you think of a person you know who has good "people skills"? Describe that person.
6. Rate your personal qualities as they relate to the world of work by placing a check mark under the appropriate heading.

	Excellent	*Good*	*Poor*
Basic Skill			
Cooperation			
Loyalty			
Integrity			
Motivation			
Initiative			
Performance			
Communication			
Appropriate Appearance			
Proper Attitude			

SUMMARIZE: (I'm okay in _____ areas, but I need work in _____ areas. I can improve by _____.)

GROUP DISCUSSION. Break up into groups and spend five minutes on each topic. Compare your reactions to those of another group.

1. Discuss "appropriate appearance" and individuality. Does business have any "right" to tell you how to dress or wear your hair?
2. Discuss the difference between initiative and aggressiveness. Have you ever had any experience with the "eager beaver" who comes on too strong? What was your reaction?
3. "It seems that employee loyalty is a thing of the past." Discuss this statement.
4. Which of the ten traits listed in this chapter would be most important to your success in school?
5. Do you agree that proper attitude is one of the most important attributes that a new employee can have? How can you tell the difference between a sincere attitude and a phony one?
6. What would you do if some of the business practices or the products of your firm conflicted with your value system? Where does your responsibility lie – do you owe loyalty to your firm or to yourself? What are some of the alternatives available to you? What effect might your action have?

BIBLIOGRAPHY

The following publications by various corporations should be consulted:

Armstrong Cork Company, *Principles and Objectives.*

Beechcraft, *Welcome to Beechcraft.*

Burroughs, *A Career with Burroughs.*

Cessna, *Know the Ropes.*

Dow Chemical Company, *A Handbook for Salaried Employees.*

Eastman Kodak Company, *How Kodak People are Selected.*

Eastman Kodak Company, *What Industry Looks for in the High School Graduate.*

Hammermill Paper Company, *Plant and Safety Rules.*

Koracorp, *Salesman's Creed.*

Kimberly-Clark Corporation, *At Kimberly-Clark, YOU Can Make the Difference.*

Lincoln National, *YOU and Lincoln National*, and *Employment Practices.*

National Cash Register, *Welcome to NCR.*

Procter & Gamble, *The Development of Management from Within.*

Sherwin-Williams Company, *YOU.*

United Merchants and Manufacturers, Inc., *Welcome to the World of United Merchants.*

VSI Corporation, *Aerospace Group Employees Handbook.*

10

Do I Have
Promotion Potential?

New employees today probably are less inclined than formerly to think of their first employer or job in terms of a long-term career. The change-oriented generation accepts job-switching risks much more willingly than earlier generations. Young people today are much more likely to "try out" different jobs in an attempt to find one that is interesting and meaningful to them.

We have discussed both the expectations of young employees as they look for the ideal job and the expectations of employers in their search for the ideal employee. Some employers feel that the ideal employee is as hard to find as the ideal job is for the employee. Indeed, there are those in business and industry who look at young employees with fear and anxiety, feeling that any attempt to place today's youth in leadership positions in business are bound to be futile.

However, when one considers the effect that changing technology has had on business and industry, it seems more reasonable to suggest that a change-oriented generation is better equipped to cope with this situation. We have pointed out in previous chapters that your generation has been raised at a time when change has become an accepted fact of life. You have grown up with all types of change: neighborhoods have changed; people move in and out of their communities without really sinking roots; social attitudes and customs have changed; some job skills have become obsolete, making retraining programs widely accepted.

Today's employers are seasoned veterans in dealing with change; they have been in business during a period of rapidly changing times and have had to adjust to the impact of modern technology. They have had to make the necessary changes, but they also have had to maintain stability in the process. It is understandable that they feel uneasy about the future leadership of their company when they view the vast changes that have occurred in the last few decades.

The Right Man for the Right Job

How does management determine which employee is the right person for the job when a vacancy involving a responsible position occurs? How can new employees move up the ladder to those positions of responsibility? How does industry describe employees with promotion potential?

Periodic Evaluation

Many companies have a probationary status for new employees. The decision to retain or dismiss a probationary employee is based upon a progress report which is submitted at the completion of this period. This is usually not the end of progress reports, however, for they are periodically made on all employees. The evaluation is discussed by the employee and his supervisor, with attention paid to both strengths and weaknesses.

Smaller companies may not go through the same formal procedure of set periodic reviews for all employees, but an employee's performance is constantly being evaluated nonetheless. Here the employer's normal reactions to the worker's daily work and attitude replace the formal, written report. These reactions are mentally filed away and recalled when promotion time comes around. Consider the promotion potential of these employees as an employer silently makes the following evaluations:

> "Hmm, Mary's late again. I'll have to talk to her. She's always in such a dither — never on time, never organized."

> "For a young guy, that Dave is really on the ball. The customers come in asking for him now. They trust him, and his sales record shows it."

> "I can always count on Judy. Look at her now, filling in for Mary. She'll have both jobs finished by the end of the day and she won't be complaining about it either!"

> "What am I going to do with Hal? He certainly doesn't want to try anything new — just keeps plugging away at the same old job. I tried to get him interested in that new equipment, but he didn't even seem to care."

Companies have several alternatives when filling a vacancy: they may promote from within the company or they may look outside the company for a new person to come in and do the job.

In some instances, employees feel that a new procedure or new equipment is a threat to their jobs, and they react by resisting the change. The employee with promotion potential, however, tends to look at the new procedure or equipment as a challenge — an opportunity rather than a threat. "It sounds interesting; I'd like to take a crack at it," he might say, or "Could I take the operating manual home and look it over? I'm willing to give it a try."

If a company does not have this type of employee on the staff, management will be forced to look outside of the company for someone to fill the vacancy. If they try to fill a vacancy of this type with a change-resistant employee, they are almost certainly doomed to failure.

Who Will Make the Move?

What do typical personnel managers have to say about factors contributing to an employee's success and advancement on the job?

> — Significant factors in advancing on a job include job knowledge, demonstrated willingness and ability to grow with the job, and the

individual's ability to get along with others — both fellow employees and supervisors.

— Advancement factors are good attitude toward his job responsibilities and fellow employees, the skill to exercise his job properly, and the initiative to do a better job than others while preparing himself for the advancement that he is interested in.

— An individual who is enthusiastic, who can communicate well with virtually anyone, who is willing to work and try his hand at new and different things, and who can *produce* in a team atmosphere will advance in the organization.

The employee with promotion potential must demonstrate his ability and his desire to succeed. Let us consider two such employees and trace their steps along the ladder of promotion.

Janet began her career as a secretary for a large insurance company. As she gained experience, she also gained responsibility, for she had qualities that impressed her supervisor. She was enthusiastic, dependable, efficient, always ready for the unexpected. What's more, everyone liked her. No one was really very surprised when she became supervisor of her division; she seemed to "grow" with her responsibilities.

She was the logical choice for promotions all along the line, and within two years she was personnel manager. She maintained and increased the qualities that had impressed her original supervisor. There was no telling how far she would progress. She has "PP," — promotion potentiality — and it has continued to grow with each promotion.

Steve began his sales career as a shoe salesman in a local department store, working part-time while he finished his post-high school training. It was obvious that he thoroughly enjoyed selling. The customers gravitated toward him and his sales record showed it. He was sincere, happy, and honest in his approach to selling. He, too, grew with his experience and soon was assistant department manager.

When the company opened a branch store, he was asked to manage the whole menswear department. He became one of the youngest — and most successful — department managers in the company's history. He rose quickly to store manager, and his career leveled off here for a while. No one knows for sure how far he will progress — perhaps regional manager, perhaps higher. He too has "PP," and it has continued to grow with each promotion.

These are just two examples of how new employees can progress *within* a company as long as they maintain or increase their promotion potential with each move. Some companies conduct training programs within their organization to prepare future leaders. Others try to pick out employees with great potential and will help further their education while preparing them for leadership roles. The opportunities for employees with promotion potential are great; it is up to individual employees to take advantage of these opportunities. As a new employee, you may well wonder how you rate in PP. The next section is designed to help you answer your questions about yourself on this score.

Promotion Potential Criteria

Bearing in mind that the specifics for promotion will vary with each company, let us examine a few general criteria which most companies would use to evaluate an employee's promotion potential.

Achievement

Achievement may be defined as the ability to produce and to do so efficiently. An employee who has accomplished past assignments with accuracy, speed, and enthusiasm certainly would rate high in achievement. This individual can be relied upon to fulfill the assignments he has been given correctly, cheerfully, and on time. He will have work habits which are organized and efficient. He will be dependable in terms of attendance and promptness.

Most employees do an adequate job of the tasks that are assigned, but the PP employee possesses a driving insistence that every job be done more than just adequately. He has a deep sense of pride in the final achievement, and he gets the greatest possible results out of every job, regardless of the obstacles. He is characterized by persistence, concentration, and an ability to give his undivided attention to the job at hand. He sets goals and accomplishes them.

The high achiever usually can handle most situations without becoming upset or flustered. He stands up well under pressure. His supervisor may sum up his achievement evaluation in this way: "He's dependable. I know we can always count on him to do the best possible job. I never have to worry. I know that the job will be done correctly and on time."

Initiative

Initiative becomes more evident as an employee settles into the routine of the world of work. It is much more important on the promotion level than it was on the hiring level. The person with true initiative is able to anticipate needs and has the foresight to plan ahead. He also is able to anticipate results with some degree of accuracy and to envision what will happen because of his actions. He seems to be able to do the right thing at the right time.

It is sometimes difficult to draw the line between initiative and aggressiveness. The wise employee has learned early in his employment *not* to let everyone else know how much he thinks he knows. If he acts in an aggressive manner, he may be viewed as a threat to the security or tranquility of other workers. But how does the new employee let his light shine in such a way that he will be noticed and promoted? He will want to tactfully do some directing, without pushing. One of the best ways to put yourself in a good light is by focusing the light upon your boss or your co-workers so that you will shine in the reflection. The old saying "You catch more flies with honey than with vinegar" may be particularly appropriate here.

The employee with initiative is willing to do the "extras" without complaining. There will be many distasteful jobs that must be done in any type of work, and this person tries to find ways to do them without letting them become drudgery. This is the "and-then-some" worker: he does his share *and then some* without threatening others.

Adaptability and Versatility

When an employee is able to change to meet the demands of a new environment or situation, he is said to be adaptable; when he has ability in a variety of subjects and is able to turn quickly and with ease from one to another, he has versatility. The PP employee needs to have both of these qualities, for they are increasingly important in our rapidly changing world. The flexible employee is not so rigid and unbending that he cannot change a set pattern. He is able to see

Adaptability/Versatility

the advantage of keeping up with current methods and trends, yet he is able to maintain a framework of stability.

Employees with a variety of skills and aptitudes have much more PP than employees who have only one skill. The ability to perform several different functions with *equal* success and the willingness to undertake new and different responsibilities are indications of versatility. The versatile employee is able to make transitions easily and smoothly and to remain calm in any crisis.

General Attitude

General attitude is a difficult quality to define specifically, but it ranks high on the list of PP criteria. It involves the whole outlook of an employee – his approach to his work, his temperament and cheerfulness, and many of those other qualities we have mentioned in our previous discussions of attitude. The qualities associated with poise also are relevant here. Poise is the combination of humility and courageous confidence that allows the person to appear and to be in control of any situation.

Attitude is interpreted through both verbal and nonverbal responses. Thus the communications skills play a part in general attitude, for the PP employee expresses himself clearly and avoids vagueness. He listens and comprehends what he hears. His nonverbal responses show that he is keenly interested in the job he is doing.

He is aware of the feelings of others and his attitude is one of concern. He is pleasant and enjoyable — "nice to be around."

Loyalty and Integrity

Loyalty and integrity are essential for the employee with PP, who must possess the traits of honesty and trust that we discussed in the preceding chapter. Of course, at the promotion level this trait can be evaluated more objectively than when an employee is first being hired.

The most troublesome individual in this category is the person who is normally and generally productive but who will deceive with no feelings of guilt if there is any possible advantage to himself. He does not consistently lie, but is willing to do so when he can benefit from it. His stories are a mixture of truths and falsehoods, making it difficult to determine which is which. Telling "little white lies" becomes a habit which he uses whenever it is to his advantage.

The person who is lacking in integrity of this sort is a definite threat to an organization. Unfortunately, it is not unusual for him to end up in a position of power, at least for a short time, because he finds it easy to "act out" superficially the traits that are desired by management. One may fool others for a while regarding integrity, but in the long run one usually is found out.

In short, integrity deals with truth, ethics, and principle. The PP employee does not deceive himself; he does not deceive others. He is "as good as his word."

Decision-Making Ability

Decision-making ability is the ability and willingness to weigh all the facts and possibilities in a specific case, and to take the responsibility for making the right decision. The employee with good decision-making ability is able to act on his own and conceive of a course of action which will result in benefit to his company.

Decision-making Ability

The decisive person has the ability to see the alternatives and to anticipate the results of each of them. He is a good problem solver whose objectivity enables him to arrive at sound solutions.

The PP employee is noted for possessing the type of judgment that will enable him to maintain a high "batting average" in making right decisions. He has the knack for doing the right thing in his personal relationships as well as in his business dealings.

Judgment

What we are calling judgment is similar to what is often described as common sense. It is the ability to use our intelligence effectively in any situation. Judgment also may be defined as maturity and the ability to continue learning from experience. We do not mean to confuse this with intelligence; one may be extremely intelligent but lacking in judgment, as in the familiar case of the brilliant but "absent-minded professor." He has great intelligence, but his application of that intelligence is sorely lacking in some areas; his common sense skills are very minimum. We all know of persons who may not possess as much innate ability as others, but who are much more successful. They exercise good judgment and make effective use of their abilities.

If an employee wants to move up within a company, good judgment is an essential factor. A supervisor can determine an employee's judgment ability by examining his past record on such matters as these: What kind of mistakes has he made? What has been his ability to anticipate and effectively handle problems? Do others consult him or rely upon his advice? Have his decisions been wise ones?

Good judgment does *not* mean not taking any chances. On the contrary, it means knowing *when* to take a chance. The PP employee calls upon his past experience and seeks whatever new and additional knowledge is necessary to make good decisions.

Innovation

Innovation is a result of certain actions rather than a personal trait, so what we really are concerned with in this regard are the personal qualities that cause innovation. The innovative person *needs* to pursue new ideas — to take action. He is not content to just sit still; he is the opposite of the person who would not consider change or altering his actions unless forced to do so.

The innovative person is able to use his own mind and abilities to achieve maximum results. To be innovative, one needs more than just the ability to generate ideas. Innovation is an idea plus action to implement that idea. The innovator must be aware of the "climate" or point of view of his company. Some employees may get carried away with innovation to the point that the "powers that be" within a company frown upon their actions on the grounds that they are "rocking the boat" too much.

Innovative

There are two types of semi-innovators. One is the person who generates lots of new ideas but fails in the practical application of them. He soon is characterized as "all talk and no action." The second semi-innovator is the person who "picks the brain" of someone else for ideas, sorts them out, and puts them into action. He is a great action man, but cannot come up with the ideas himself.

A true innovator does both — he creates his own ideas and he takes positive action to implement them. He puts his ideas to work for himself and his company; he "tries it out." The innovator not only creates and takes action on his own ideas, but he also contributes materially to the value of the ideas of others. He has the ability to recognize "outside" ideas and can adapt them successfully to his company's benefit.

Ability to Direct the Work of Others

In order for a person to be successful in a position of leadership, he must have a genuine interest in people and an understanding that it is *people* and not *things* that are most important in almost all situations. It is *people* who accomplish goals. In our computer-run world, we must remember that people provide the input, and the output, too, depends upon the quality of the people involved.

The employee who is able to make others understand, believe, and act in such a way as to inspire their best efforts has valuable promotion potential. In order to do this, a person must have empathy with another person. By *empathy* we mean a type of "feeling with" someone else; a sort of entering into the feelings of another; an understanding that the feelings of others are as sensitive as ours. The person who feels empathy or sensitivity to other people will be aware and alert to their needs and will act accordingly.

A person with this sensitivity to others will be much more apt than someone else to motivate them to act through their own choice. He will not have to coerce or badger them into wanting to accomplish the goals or tasks they are assigned. This is not to be confused with manipulation, a term which implies the use of false or deceptive means.

The employee who has the ability to direct the work of others does so without "ruffling their feathers." His attitude is not one of inferiority or superiority, but one of respect. *How* a person is asked to do a job often will determine his attitude toward that job. Was he commanded to it, or was he asked?

A note should be added here about the bitter weapon of sarcasm. Anyone who wants to motivate others to obtain the best results would do well to bury the habit of sarcasm. Unfortunately, many people think they are being "witty," "cute," or "cool," when in essence they are merely using sarcasm — with the result that they appear crude. Sarcasm is one of the biggest obstacles to effective leadership.

Responsibility

Closely related to decision-making is the attribute of responsibility. When a decision is made, who takes the responsibility for it if it turns out wrong? Does the individual "pass the buck" to someone else, blaming the trouble on the computer, or his secretary, or her typewriter? A person with promotion potential takes the responsibility for his actions, whether they are right or wrong. Certainly no one makes the right decision all the time, so that owning up to mistakes is a true mark of maturity. What is more, learning from mistakes may be a very valuable lesson.

The PP employee welcomes added responsibility as a challenge. He is able to look at the long-range planning aspect of problems and to see the whole picture rather than individual scenes. He is able to know the difference between important and not-so-important decisions and to put first things first.

Is It Worth It?

When you are promoted, you will reap the rewards that go along with the new position, but you also will pay the price for such advancement. Undoubtedly you will receive increased pay, but you also will receive increased pressure and responsibility. Often you will be expected to put in longer hours and to perform the "extras" that someone else did before. But you also will feel the sense of accomplishment that comes from doing challenging work. Of course, it should go without saying that you must be careful not to let a promotion go to your head.

How do you rate in promotion potential? You probably will not be able to answer that question unless you are already working part-time, but when you become a full-time employee you will be better prepared in these promotion potential areas. You can set your goals and achieve any realistic aims you choose if you have true promotion potential.

If you review these criteria, you will notice that most of the qualities involve "people skills." A survey of seventy-six firms in this country recently showed that of four thousand workers who had been dismissed over a period of time, between 80 and 90 percent had lost their jobs because of lack of personal development. People were removed from their jobs for carelessness, lack of cooperation, dishonesty, lack of initiative, lack of ambition, disloyalty. The smallest percentage of all was for lack of skill. [See the pamphlet from Eastman Kodak cited in the bibliography.] To be sure, employees sometimes lose their jobs because of economic conditions which are beyond their control. But even in this case it is hard to imagine that an employer would drop his most desirable and most experienced people *first.*

How *Not* to Win Friends and Influence People

There is no one way that *every* employee can use to succeed in personal relations, but let's consider some of the irritating habits and attitudes that might stand in your way.

1. Avoid being enthusiastic. Make everything seem like a real chore. Be sure to sour everyone else's enthusiasm, too; then you can suffer together.
2. Complain constantly. Be sure that everyone knows how tough you think life is and how much better everyone else has it.
3. Cut down others at every chance. Sarcasm works wonders here; be sure to keep a mental file of cutting remarks to throw out at the slightest chance.
4. Be undecided, act on impulse all the time, and don't make up your mind without a big hassle. When you finally decide, be sure to question your decision.
5. Do only your own work; don't ever offer to help others even if they are behind in their work. After all, you were hired to do *your* job and that's all.
6. Find fault with everything. Let little things bother you. Never be satisfied with anything.
7. Cultivate the knack for passing the buck. "It's not my fault" can become your favorite line.

8. Begin and end all your conversations with "I." After all, you are so interesting that you don't have to consider the interests of others.

9. Make sure everyone realizes how important you think you are. Make sure everyone knows how hard you work.

10. Be sure to take, but don't give. Make sure others realize that they owe you a living, and they're lucky to know you.

If you want to advance on your job, you will have to prove your worth and build the people skills that are necessary for advancement. Few things are worse than a phony, so these people skills must be genuine and sincere. You can start your building program on your very first day of work.

Summary

Today's change-oriented generation may be uniquely equipped to become the future leaders of business and industry. Professional advancement is usually the goal of most new employees. Companies may promote from within or they may look outside for someone to fill a vacancy. Employees are constantly being evaluated by supervisors who are looking for those employees with *promotion potential.* The criteria for an employee with PP include: (1) achievement; (2) initiative; (3) adaptability and versatility; (4) general attitude; (5) loyalty and integrity; (6) decision-making ability; (7) judgment; (8) innovation; (9) ability to direct the work of others; and (10) responsibility.

We often can benefit from examining negative attitudes which stand in the way of promotions and toward this end we have listed a number of ways "How *not* to win friends and influence people."

Advancing on the job begins with the first day of work and continues as an individual building program. Both technical skill and "people skills" are necessary.

Questions:

1. How is an employee evaluated every day? Can you compare this to your work in school, or are these situations dissimilar?

2. If you were personnel manager of a large company, which of the

PP criteria would be most important to you? How would this vary with the job requirement?

3. What is the difference between adaptability and versatility?
4. How does initiative apply to each of the criteria?

GROUP DISCUSSION. Break into groups and choose a topic for discussion. Present your views to the class if you have time.

1. Discuss the ten points in the section entitled "How *Not* to Win Friends and Influence People." Can you add some others?
2. Is innovation more important at the promotion level than in the entry-level job? Do you think business prefers the type of employee who doesn't "rock the boat"?
3. Relate decision-making ability to responsibility. How do they differ and how are they similar?
4. Attitude has been stressed in several chapters as a very important attribute. Do you agree that it is as important as we have indicated, or do you think it is overrated? Why?
5. How would you handle a "pushy," overly aggressive new employee who has taken over and is upsetting your co-workers and you? (Role playing can be effective here.)

CASE PROBLEMS FOR DISCUSSION:

Amy Lewis is an excellent student in the computer programming field. She has received several job offers but she seems to feel that some firms, especially those offering jobs with more promising advancement, are reluctant to hire women for technical jobs. How are women discriminated against in some career fields, or isn't this a problem any more? How do you feel about women competing with men for technical jobs that have been traditionally "male only" jobs?

Jim Moore has been working as an accountant for an insurance company in Cleveland for two years. A branch office is looking for a head accountant and Jim has been given the promotion, if he wants it. However, it will mean selling his newly acquired home and moving two hundred miles away to a city where the cost of living is much higher. His wife is expecting their first child about the time they should be moving, both their parents live in Cleveland, and they thought they were "settled" for the rest of their lives. They hate to think of moving, but they realize that this is really a great opportunity for Jim. A substantial raise accompanies the move, as well as a new title. What economic factors need to be investigated before Jim comes to a decision? What personal factors will influence his decision? What would you do if you were Jim?

Sheila Wood seems to have all the ingredients for success: good education, brains, job experience, excellent grades, and a beautiful appearance. She seems popular but has had difficulty with roommates and on committees on which she has served. She is having a difficult time finding a job. She expected many offers and has been interviewed several times, but she has not been offered any jobs. What might her "problem" be? Could extreme beauty and ability be a handicap for her?

BIBLIOGRAPHY

The following publications by various corporations should be consulted:

Armstrong, *Report on Trial Employee (Salary).*

Armstrong Cork Company, *Principles and Objectives.*

Burroughs, *A Career with Burroughs.*

Dartnell Corporation, "The Art of Getting Along," *From Nine to Five or Thereabouts*, Vol. XII, Number 2 (1971).

Dartnell Corporation, "Want To Be Alone? Here's How To Get Started," *From Nine to Five or Thereabouts*, Vol. XI, Number 17 (1970).

Eastman Kodak Company, *How Kodak People Are Selected.*

General Motors, *Working with General Motors.*

Hammermill Paper Company, *Plant and Safety Rules.*

Kraftco, *Personnel Policies.*

Lincoln National, *You and Lincoln National*, and *Employment Practices.*

Procter & Gamble, *The Development of Management from Within.*

Richardson-Merrell, Inc., *You & Your Job.*

Texaco, "Not Entirely a Man's World," *Texaco Topics*, Numbers 1 and 2 (1970).

IV

TIME FOR *MY* FAMILY

11

How Do I Feel
about My Sexuality?

The man-woman relationship is fundamental to all societies. One of the most important tasks confronting you on your way to maturity is the achievement of a comfortable and healthy relationship with members of your own sex and those of the opposite sex. How you achieve this relationship will affect all areas of your life: at home, at school, at work, and socially.

Acceptance of your personal sexuality will be influenced by relationships with many different people in a complex social environment. The adjustments which you must make and the situations which arise involve your various roles as a human being. Perhaps some of your most anxious and most rewarding moments arise from your personal acceptance of your sexuality and its influence on your relationships with others.

Relationships between the sexes will be easier to understand if we examine some of the traditional sex "roles" prevalent in America, and if we examine some of the conflicts which these "roles" might present.

In this chapter we will look at some of the processes involved in establishing comfortable relationships between and within the sexes. We will consider the differences between the sexes, "typing" of sex roles, individual reactions to those roles, the meaning of sexuality, and the part played by dating in our sexual attitude formation. We also will discuss some of the standards and conflicts which arise in the dating process.

By discussing these topics, you will be better able to understand your own sexual "role" as a man or a woman, the accompanying expectations, and how they affect your relationships with others.

What Is Meant by Sexuality

One of the biggest hangups that many of us experience, even in our "enlightened" world, involves our understanding of our sexuality. Just what does it mean, *personally*, to be a man or a woman? Sexuality is more than merely classifying yourself as either male or female; your genetic inheritance (the biological sex characteristics and endowments with which you were born) is only a part of your sexuality.

Your sexuality includes all the attitudes, feelings, and characteristics which you personally identify with your maleness or femaleness. Some call this "masculinity" or "femininity," but we prefer to think of masculinity and femininity as merely two of the descriptive aspects of sexuality. If you were asked to define "masculinity" or "femininity," many factors would influence the ingredients you chose to include in your definition. It probably would include physical characteristics, but it also would include a set of attitudes or "roles" which you have assigned to each particular sex. Many of your assumptions about masculine and feminine roles are mainly the result of learning. You have come to expect certain patterns of behavior or characteristics to be either "masculine" or "feminine," despite the fact that these roles or characteristics are not clear-cut and vary from individual to individual. Many people feel upset when it is suggested that there is an overlapping of roles; they tend to give simplistic answers to questions involving sexuality, without realizing that it is a blend of inherited characteristics, learned roles, and personal expectations, and that each person views his own sexuality a little differently.

Men and women *are* different from each other — not opposite, but complementary. When something is complementary, it means that either of two parts is needed to complete the other. In this sense we may note that some of our most "complete" relationships are those resulting from man-woman interaction. Of course, no person's system of personal and social relationships can be complete if it excludes members of his own sex. We will feel more "complete" when we are able to maintain comfortable and easy relationships both with members of our own sex and with those of the opposite sex. This can more easily be accomplished when we see ourselves as complete, sexual human beings: we are sexual beings; but we are human beings first, male and female second. Understanding your individual sexuality is an integral part of understanding yourself as a human being, and of getting along with others.

Differences — More than Physical?

Physical Differences

The most obvious differences between the sexes are physical in nature. As a whole, men are larger than women. They tend to be taller and heavier, with the male skeleton being constructed in a heavier manner with larger muscles attached.

This size difference is not only a matter of common observation and fact but also one of traditional expectation. Many difficult experiences may result, especially during childhood and adolescence, if a person's size is not in keeping with sexual expectations. For example, the young boy who finds that he is the smallest child in the class may feel that his size is a very real threat to his "masculinity." The same feelings may result if a girl is "too big"; she may feel that her size undermines her "femininity." In both cases the individuals must adjust to and incorporate this difference into their own personal pictures of their sexuality. They must learn that masculinity and femininity are not dependent upon society's expectations.

Another important sex difference involves general body structure. The lines of the male body are straighter, and men are usually more stockily built, with straighter legs. Women, on the other hand, have more curvature to their bodies, with a pelvic area wider and shallower than men's, so they are better adapted for childbearing. Women's legs are more V-shaped.

The *rate of growth* between males and females varies a great deal. Girls usually experience rapid growth between the ages of ten and fifteen, whereas boys usually experience a growth spurt from ages fourteen to eighteen. Of course, there are individual differences in this general growth pattern.

Life expectancy varies, but women live longer than men as a general rule, and they display more hardiness even before birth:

> At conception, the proportion of males to females is 120 male to 100 female. There is a higher probability of miscarriage for the male fetus, and this ratio drops to approximately 105.5 males at birth. Roughly 25 percent more males than females die during the first year of life. By adulthood the sexes balance each other: but from birth to old age the advantage lies with the female. For whites, the life expectancy of the male is 67.3, of the female, 73.6; for nonwhites, it is 61.2 and 65.9 respectively. This differential longevity may be attributed to the varying rates in metabolism and other biochemical processes, to the varying resistance to disease, and to the different kinds of occupational hazard men and women encounter. [Williamson,* p. 145.]

Another major physical difference between men and women involves their *reproductive* capacity. The most significant difference here is in the number of reproductive cells produced by each sex.

> Men are capable of generating reproductive cells at [enormously] higher rates than women. A man may produce some 100 million spermatozoa daily from the mid-teens until physical decline in the mid-forties, and a man still may be [capable of producing offspring] at seventy or, in a few cases, at eighty. Women, on the other hand, ordinarily produce one ovum every 27 or 28 days within the childbearing ages of fourteen to forty-five, or in some instances a few years beyond. The beginning and end of the fertile period, the onset of menstruation and menopause, are all abrupt and dramatic in the female. [Williamson, p. 146.]

*From *Marriage and Family Relations* by Robert C. Williamson. Copyright © 1966 by John Wiley & Sons, Inc. Reprinted by permission.

Usually, a man's *sex drive* is characterized as more urgent, regular, and predictable than a woman's. A woman's sex drive may be just as strong as a man's, but she is much more influenced by indirect stimuli such as external circumstances, the setting, and gradually applied stimulation.

The *sexual threshold* of the male is lower than that of the female. He is more easily aroused and his sexual interest is more nearly constant. Women are more apt to have inhibitions regarding their sex needs. This is just one of many areas in which our attitudes towards our sexual needs are the results of learning and social conditioning. "As a group, women can get along more comfortably with less sexual release than men can," Bowman writes. "There are more women than men who have little or no interest in sexual intercourse" [Bowman, p. 12].

Men tend to *separate sex and love,* seeing them as two distinct feelings. Women, on the other hand, tend to *combine sex and love.* This is one of the most important differences between the sexes and it is especially important for young people to recognize. Males and females approach sexual behavior both before and after marriage from different points of view. Failure to understand these primary differences regarding attitudes toward sex, love, and sexual need contribute in a major way to many of the conflicts in the dating situation.

Nonphysical Differences

Many of the nonphysical differences between the sexes take the form of *learned roles.* Traditionally, men and women express their emotions differently. Women are more apt to display openly the emotions of fear, sadness, or affection, whereas men usually have learned that open display of these emotions is not "manly." A man may want to cry, or may be terribly frightened, but he has been conditioned since childhood to believe that crying or being afraid was equal to being a "sissy." In recent years, we have experienced a growing trend toward acceptance of freer expression of feelings and emotions by men as well as women. We are gradually overcoming the stereotype that men are sissies if they cry. More people realize that being masculine also involves tenderness, compassion, and showing one's feelings.

Men usually are more *aggressive* than women. Aggressiveness is often held to be a virtue in a man but is thought of as "unfeminine" in a woman. Traditionally, again, we have characterized women as submissive and men as aggressive. This tendency has decreased in recent years, especially with the growth of the Women's Liberation Movement. Women, more and more, especially those with advanced education or business skill, have struggled and won more "equality" of opportunity, and their increased "aggressiveness" has not in any way compromised their "femininity."

Nevertheless, the majority of men and women in our culture seem to accept the traditional view of aggressiveness as a male characteristic, so that a woman's "aggressiveness" must be shown, if it is to be shown at all, in more subtle ways. Thus women have learned how to get their way by indirect methods rather than by direct, aggressive means.

Interests.   Typically, there is a difference in interests and values between men and women. The Allport-Vernon test for values found that girls tend to be more concerned with beauty, religion, and social values, whereas men usually devote more interest to economic, political, and theoretical values. The Strong Vocational Interest Blank has shown that men tend to rank high in mechanical, athletic, outdoor, and mercantile areas whereas women show a corresponding interest in artistic and literary fields, as well as in the occupational fields which traditionally have been "feminine" – clerical, social work, and teaching.

These differences in interest should not be surprising when we consider the social conditioning of children. We "expect" men to be interested in sports, business, and politics, while we "expect" women to be interested in the more "artistic" or "domestic" areas. Certainly these are *learned* interests; there is nothing "natural" or inborn about them. What is more, there is considerable overlapping in the interest areas, as evidenced by the fact that we find many avid sports fans among the ranks of the women.

Another difference between the sexes concerns the value placed on rationality and logic. Men tend to be more interested in logic and facts, whereas women tend to be interested in relationships and feelings. Perhaps this is why many misunderstandings occur over "little things." A man is more apt to rely on facts when he comes up with a conclusion, but a woman sometimes may base her conclusions on "feelings," "women's intuition," or "Just because" — much to the chagrin of her "logical" husband or boy friend.

Traditional occupational roles. Traditionally, our culture has considered men as the breadwinners or supporters of their families. Men really do not have much choice in the matter; they usually do not think in terms of "if" they will have a career or job, but rather in terms of "what" that job or career will be. Women, on the other hand, traditionally have maintained the domestic role. Many feel that "a woman's place is in the home," where she is to raise the children, care for the home, and assume the main influence in domestic affairs. If she *wishes,* she may pursue a career outside the home, but necessity does not force her to do so in most instances.

Today we are finding more and more women occupying positions in the labor force, not always because of necessity but often as a matter of choice. As Bowman observes, "A man works partly . . . because of the pressure exerted by the traditional cultural pattern. He must work to prove that he is a 'real man.' A woman can be a 'real woman' and never earn a dollar" [Bowman, p. 10].

Many men and women feel very uncomfortable about the prospect of total "equality" of the sexes. They feel threatened by the modern-day departure from the traditional roles which have characterized "men" and "women" for so long. For this reason it is important that you examine your own ideas regarding your "sexuality" and just what this means in terms of "roles" or expectations, both for yourself and others. You would be wise to ask: "How do *I* feel about myself as a man/woman? Are the differences that I feel inborn or are they learned? How do I feel about the 'sexuality' of the opposite sex? What are my expectations of the opposite sex and why do I have those expectations? Even though *I* feel one way about 'masculine' or 'feminine' roles, can I accept the fact that others feel differently?"

If you answer these questions you will have a better understanding of your own sexuality, what *you* feel are the roles acceptable to you, and what you expect of the opposite sex. Such an understanding, coupled with knowledge of the very real differences between the sexes, will help you to get along better with both sexes. You can better understand why people act the way they do, what they *probably* expect of you, and also what types of action are likely to seem threatening to others.

It is doubtful that anyone will ever completely understand the "inner workings" of either sex, but this discussion should be helpful to you in your relations at school, at home, on the job, and in your social life.

Sex Typing

Each of us has learned what is considered appropriate behavior for our particular sex. The process by which we learn that behavior is called *sex typing*. This usually begins with a close identification with the parent of the same sex. Having a good model in either father or mother usually makes sex typing easier and more natural.

A male child identifies himself as a boy and likes associating with his father, whereas a female child identifies herself as a girl and becomes interested in her mother's activities. But it usually is very important that two mature sex models are available in order that the child may fashion a healthy sex identity with members of the opposite sex as well. "As compared to the family," Pikunas writes, "no other environmental contributor exerts even a comparable influence upon the formation of a child's personality. The deepest needs of the child (affection, acceptance, and security) are gratified through a dynamic interaction with his parents" [Pikunas, p. 391].

At an early age, our society exerts pressures upon its young to behave in certain "expected" ways. Parents reinforce these "expected" roles by their actions and attitudes. They become rather upset if their son plays with dolls instead of baseballs; if their daughter continues in the "tomboy" stage for too long they begin to firmly "guide" or "direct" her behavior into more "ladylike" patterns.

Children themselves reinforce these patterns through their choice of playmates and the games that are played. If a group of neighboring children get together to "play house," Billy will be "father" rather than mother, Julie will be "mother" rather than father, Mary will be "teacher" rather than fireman, and so forth.

You probably can remember some of this sex typing from your own childhood. "Timmy, don't wrestle with Judy — she's a girl!" "Mary, don't play so rough. Little girls are more fragile, you know."

"Bobby, stop crying. You don't want to be a sissy, do you?" "Oh, Debby, did you hurt yourself? Let me wipe your tears. It'll be all right." Boys and girls soon learn that boys are "supposed" to play rough and to be exuberent whereas girls are expected to be more restrained and demure.

In our society, sex typing has been more influenced by females than by males because mothers have been the decisive factor in raising children. This female influence has carried over into the schools, where teachers have been predominantly female. This trend may be modifying somewhat, but the majority of elementary teachers especially are still female.

During preadolescence most boys and girls associate almost exclusively with members of the same sex. There is almost a feeling of distaste for members of the opposite sex. Interest in the opposite sex usually begins during adolescence. Very often this is accompanied by the physical changes associated with puberty. You probably remember many of the mixed-up feelings that you had during this period in your life, for sexual growth usually has a strong effect upon a person's self-concept and personality.

Along with these sexual changes comes a whole new set of sex "roles" for the adolescent to incorporate into his or her individual "sexuality." This intensely emotional time of life often brings with it feelings of ambivalence (contradictory feelings felt at the same time, such as love and hate) directed at oneself, others, events, and things, as the individual tries to reconcile these new expectations with his or her personal performance. He knows what is "expected" of him, but often experiences many doubts and anxieties regarding fulfillment of those expectations.

Most adolescents experience some difficulty finding their own place within the "society" of their peer group, although of course this adjustment is more difficult for some than for others. It is during this part of one's life that contact with members of the opposite sex begins to assume a higher value, and the achievement of comfortable relationships with the opposite sex becomes very important.

As the adolescent moves toward maturity, he often evaluates himself in terms of successful achievement of a masculine or feminine role as well as in terms of the acceptance that he experiences from others. Now, as you are reaching maturity, you often tend to take these "roles" which you have learned for granted.

Conflicts

Many conflicts arise as a result of sex typing and roles. For example, the man who feels that "a woman's place is in the home" may suddenly find himself competing in business and professional life with a "liberated" woman. Most people can adjust to their conflicts in roles quite easily. Especially for women, it is often a matter of choosing from a variety of available culturally acceptable roles. The woman has choices ranging from "the clinging-vine type to the sport partner, from the sexual companion to the mother-sister substitute, from the languishing beauty to the fellow helper. In marriage, she may combine all of these. A young woman is especially caught in the dilemma of knowing that even the man of the twentieth century expects her to be the subservient mate on more than one occasion, and that the conception that beauty is more important than brains may still persist" [Williamson, p. 161].

We generally adopt the "roles" that we have learned through our own experience. We carry with us the habits, attitudes, values, beliefs, conditioned responses, expectations, and behavior patterns which we feel make up our own individual sexuality — our maleness or femaleness.

> An individual is born male or female, but he or she learns to be masculine or feminine, as the case may be, according to the cultural patterns of his society. Sex is genetic, but gender is acquired. . . . But masculinity and femininity are not entirely distinct; they overlap. Some individuals have more difficulty than others in living up to the standard set for their sex. . . . In some respects our society is becoming more tolerant of the overlap. Increasingly in this country we are accepting with approval — even at times expecting — either sex exhibiting characteristics and types of behavior which have been traditionally associated with the opposite sex. [Bowman, pp. 26–27.]

Our world should be one of reality; we live in the present, not the past or the future. The past has affected the present and the present is constantly changing into the future. It would be interesting to speculate what the sex roles of the year 2075 will be. No doubt they will be different from those accepted today.

The world we live in — the world of school, work, home, and society — still places a great deal of weight upon the traditional "roles" for each sex. Boys and girls, men and women have more or less been "trained" to assume certain roles that are different, yet overlapping. Understanding your own sexuality involves understanding the differences between the sexes (both inborn and learned), the complementary nature of the sexes, the traditional "roles" of each sex, as well as the changing nature of these roles. Accepting your own individual sexuality and the sexuality of others will promote more comfortable, healthy, and rewarding interpersonal relationships.

Dating as a Social Custom

Every culture has established some form of ritual or pattern of behavior which allows its young adults to pass from singleness to marriedness. In our culture the pattern or ritual is not rigidly established, but such a pattern unmistakably exists. It is to be found in the process of dating, which provides the background or the foundation for this passage.

Marriage is *not the main or only purpose for* dating; we do not normally think of marriage in connection with dating during the early teens; rather, we think of dating as a socializing process which provides the opportunity for young people to enjoy the company of a member of the opposite sex and at the same time to reinforce their own acceptance of themselves.

Often the first dating situation of many adolescents results from group activities. "All the girls" or "all the guys" may go to a game, dance, or other function. General interest in the opposite sex often develops through such group interaction.

Dating is very often a process of trial and error, where you become acquainted with and learn to be comfortable with many members of the opposite sex. Dating may be viewed as an unrealistic situation in many ways, for the individuals involved are usually more concerned about "making a good impression" than about "being themselves." Consequently, "party" manners are used and only the positive side of a person is seen. We often tend to "idealize" the other party and do not notice the flaws or defects in him or her.

Dating also serves as a gradually liberating force. Young people in essence are given the chance to be on their own in this relationship; the *individual* makes the choice of dating partner, not the parents. *A positive dating relationship usually leads to increased self-confidence.*

Dating allows individuals to become comfortable with members of the opposite sex and to better understand their own sexuality.

A negative dating relationship — or the lack of dates completely — tends to have the opposite effect. "What's wrong with me? Why don't I have dates? Why can't *I* feel comfortable on a date like my friends do?"

The tendency to allow adolescents more freedom, the ready acceptance of changing standards, the growing affluence of American society, the increased use of automobiles by teenagers, along with many other factors influence and add confusion to the dating habits of young people today. Dating success may largely depend upon the individual's ability to know what he wants, what his standards and values are, what it means to make wise decisions, how to develop a positive attitude toward sex, and how to take the responsibility for one's actions.

Casual or Random Dating

Dating usually begins at the casual level, which entails no long-range commitment. This enables the individuals to go out, have fun, and become comfortable with each other without being tied down with heavy responsibilities. This type of dating allows the individual to get to know a variety of people and helps him to become at ease with his own sexuality. Casual dating introduces a one-to-one relationship with members of the opposite sex as companions. This type of dating allows a person to date "just for fun" before "settling down."

Steady Dating

Steady dating is the first step toward "serious" dating and the frame of reference is very different from that of the casual date. Quite often, the expectations of the group play a big part in one's decision to "go steady." For some young people, steady dating is thought of as only a little more serious than casual dating, with the added benefit of a form of "social security." "I don't have to worry about having a date," a girl with a steady boyfriend says, "and I really do like him. But I'm not ready to settle down permanently!" In other words, going steady often means a short-term commitment to one person.

To others, steady dating leads to choice of a marriage partner. In this case it is hoped, either consciously or unconsciously, that this exclusive dating arrangement will lead to love and marriage.

Engagement

Engagement is the most serious form of dating, usually involving a stated commitment to marriage.

> Engagement affords added security of choice during the period prior to the wedding and provides the couple with the opportunity to make final plans and to announce their intention to marry. . . . It provides families and friends with the opportunity to make a usually much-needed contribution to the economy of the contemplated new marriage through showers, and so on. [Bowman, p. 198.]

The engagement period serves as a time during which the couple can get to know each other on a close personal level. Some of the "masks" and "party manners" of casual and steady dating can be removed, and the partners can learn more about qualities of each of them that were not evident before. (We will discuss engagements further in Chapter 12.)

Premarital Sexual Attitudes

Conflicts regarding sexual behavior may not be very prominent when one is involved in casual or random dating, but when young adults move into the relationships of going steady or engagement more conflicts often arise. The very "exclusiveness" and "commitment" involved in this type of dating often prompts a redefinition of standards of behavior. Emotional reactions often become confused, especially when the couple has to confront the intense sexual feelings connected with dating at the more serious levels of "going steady" or engagement.

We have discussed the differences between the sex drive of the male and the female. The male's sex drive is much more urgent and more easily aroused, whereas the female's drive is much more dependent upon circumstances and preparation. Her sex need is equally as strong when it is aroused, but she often tends to confuse her physical response with love. Very often, when a girl is intensely aroused, she will think, "I'm in love – this is the feeling of love," and she may be quite overwhelmed by her feelings. A boy, on the other hand, usually has had sexual reactions or feelings for some time and he is not deceived into thinking he is in love. He knows he is experiencing a sexual need.

In this context it has been said, "A girl plays at sex to get love, while a guy plays at love to get sex." Although neither may be conscious of these feelings, when we realize the different feelings that men and women have toward their sex drives, we can readily understand why people have them. Females do tend to combine sex and love, whereas males more often separate the two. For this reason you would be wise to examine your own feelings in this regard. Your sexual emotions are very powerful, but do not confuse them. Sex and love may be related, but they are *not* the same thing.

Bell's studies show that petting is the commonly accepted level of intimacy for both males and females while going steady, and that sexual intercourse is an acceptable level for a significant number of engaged couples [Bell, pp. 84–85].

A girl may "pet" and still remain a virgin, but at the same time she gains sexual experience. Thus we may have what is known as the "technical" virgin, a "role" which may be maintained as long as the girl feels that the distinction between petting and sexual intercourse is meaningful.

Traditionally we have felt that it is the girl's role to set the limits regarding sexual experimentation. However, a limit that is set mutually probably will be more satisfactory to both individuals.

In your sexual conduct you will be influenced by the degree of pressure you feel for conformity to both social and personal moral codes. You also will be influenced by the degree of "love" that you feel is present in your relationship. But you must set your own standards.

Premarital Sexual Intercourse in Perspective

"Is there a sexual revolution in progress?" "What will be the effect of 'the pill' on young people today?" "Is sexual promiscuity as widespread as some seem to think?" These questions and many many more have been discussed, written about, worried over, and perhaps "talked to death" in recent years. How would you answer them? You have had access to many modern "novels" that have explicitly described nearly every imaginable form of sexual behavior; perhaps you have seen movies that depicted everything from marathon sex orgies to the idea that it is "normal" to sleep with everyone or anyone; and your parents probably have worried about your moral "corruption" for many years. What do you think about sexual behavior, standards, and premarital intercourse in particular?

General Attitude

Many studies have been conducted regarding the premarital sexual habits of students in particular, and the findings vary. These studies have been very valuable and significant, but they are not completely conclusive in their facts.

There is evidence to support the opinion that the strongest limits one places on his or her premarital sexual behavior result from internal values rather than from values imposed from outside. One is more apt to conform to what one *feels* is right than to what someone else *says* is right or wrong.

Reiss suggests that premarital sexual attitudes may be classified into four categories:

1. *Abstinence* – premarital intercourse is wrong for both the man and the woman, regardless of circumstances.
2. *Permissible with affection* – premarital intercourse is right for both men and women under certain conditions when a stable relationship involving engagement, love, or strong affection is present.
3. *Permissible without affection* – premarital intercourse is right for both men and women regardless of the amount of affection or stability present, providing there is physical attraction.
4. *Double standard* – premarital intercourse is acceptable for men but is wrong and unacceptable for women. [Adapted from Reiss, pp. 83–84].

These four categories seem to summarize the various points of view regarding premarital intercourse. A traditional belief in the *double standard* continues to be accepted by many Americans of both sexes. The attitude of *abstinence* is still very prevalent, as is a combination of abstinence with double standard.

The attitude of *permissible without affection* emphasizes physical satisfaction without regard for stability or commitment and is accepted by a minority of individuals.

Permissible with affection seems to be increasingly popular and provides a more "equal" standard for both men and women, with emphasis placed upon stability and affection in the relationship as well as on commitment.

The question of premarital intercourse is not merely one of "should I or shouldn't I?" Rather, it is a question involving the nature of the *relationship* between the partners. "What is the meaning of our relationship? How will this affect our relationship? What is right or wrong for *us*? Do *we* realize the deeper implications of premarital intercourse, or is this merely a satisfaction of physical desire?" These are questions which the individual couple should consider.

Responsibility and Need

Many decisions regarding premarital sexual intercourse rest upon the feelings of commitment and the emotional relationship that exists between the couple. Sometimes the strength of the relationship between a couple may be very one-sided. At what point is one partner's need strong enough to dominate a relationship? We have stated that it is often the felt commitment that determines the decision for or against premarital intercourse. It seems imperative that the couple examine that commitment to see whether it is mutual or if there is a type of "psychological warfare" being waged — usually on the part of the male.

The male may very logically and "passionately" present his argument that sexual release is important to his mental and physical health. Or he may state that the girl "owes it to herself" to prove that she is a "real woman" and that this cannot be done unless she expresses herself sexually. Of course, he could use the "Prove that you love me" routine, and she could counter with the "Prove that you love me by waiting." In either case the "proving" somehow assumes rather manipulative overtones. Sometimes he may argue that "you owe it to me":

> This argument tends to center around a physical approach to sex. The male emphasizes the great strength and force of the sex drive (especially for himself, because individual males think of themselves as being well above average in sex drive) and how, if it is not satisfied, dire consequences will result for him. He sometimes goes so far as to suggest that if the girl does not provide him with sexual release, his physical health will be dangerously impaired. (There appear to be no records of males hospitalized because girls refused to provide sexual outlets.) [Bell, p. 78.]

In cases where such demands are made, the "commitment" seems to be on a very superficial and selfish level: "Commit yourself to satisfying *my* needs; I don't care about *your* needs." We must consider that what might be right for one partner might be wrong for the other. If a couple find themselves in this dilemma, they must work out the conflict together or the commitment will be one-sided.

Theoretically, one could propose that the couple should consider the questions: "What will this do to our relationship?" and "Am I merely *using* this relationship to satisfy a personal selfish need?" We say *theoretically* because it is not very realistic to assume that a couple would pause when extremely aroused to ask such questions. However, if the couple feels a deep commitment, they should be able to communicate their feelings in such a manner that they mutually arrive at a type of behavior that will not destroy their relationship, a standard that is agreeable to both and for which both are mutually responsible.

Effect upon Future Goals

No discussion of premarital intercourse would be complete without some mention of the risks involved to the couple. We have discussed the risks to the relationship, but there are also other obvious risks. There is the risk of contracting venereal disease. Statistics vary from year to year and from state to state, but in recent years VD has been reported at epidemic proportions in many areas of the country. In all but very rare instances, the *only* way that VD is spread is through sexual intercourse.

Although information about contraception is more widely available now, especially to college-age students, there always remains the risk of pregnancy. This risk affects the female more than the male, but the male also runs some risks when pregnancy is involved. Depending upon the age of the girl, he could be accused of statutory rape (if she is underage) or of "rape by force" (his word against hers); he may be named in a paternity suit or – the most obvious risk – he may be pressured into a marriage that he really does not want (and often that she really doesn't want either).

Intercourse – Deciding Yes or No

For some couples there is no decison. One or both believe firmly that intercourse should take place only within marriage. Other couples, engaged, or at least feeling they will someday marry, struggle with the question of whether to wait. Religious beliefs, family attitudes, past experiences, fears, social milieu, all these factors may enter into the decision-making process. The decision may be arrived at rationally and thoughtfully or a kind of deciding may take place in a moment of passion when, suddenly, "Yes" seems to be very right.

When a relationship is probably not permanent but still very meaningful, it is more difficult to decide confidently to say yes. We wonder how it will affect the relationship. Will it mean too great a commitment to each other? How will he or she feel about me afterward? How will I feel about me? Should I tell my parents? Will I end up being hurt or hurting? It isn't easy to manage a relationship that is emotionally and sexually intimate (sometimes a marriage in all but name) and still feel free — free to meet others, perhaps looking for *the* relationship that will be permanent. This is a serious dilemma posed by the "new morality."

There are fewer secure guidelines to follow every year. Those old, logical reasons *not* to have intercourse before marriage can be argued away and there is so much freedom of opportunity! The absence of dorm regulations is a good example of the new freedom students have — a freedom that sometimes amounts to pressure to have sex before you feel ready. The decision is all yours, and it can be very scary. One idea that seems valid to us is that no one should have intercourse just because they can't think of any reason *not* to.

The first year in college can create conflict and confusion about sexual values. Your family seems very far away and their ideas about almost everything are challenged by what you see and hear and experience on the campus. This may be the first time you realize how many people like yourself — "nice," intelligent people — believe that premarital sex is OK. You may discover that contraception is readily available to you. There may be lots of subtle pressure in favor of intercourse; pressure to prove you aren't hung-up, to prove you can be sexually responsive, pressure to get or keep a boyfriend or girlfriend, pressure to have something to talk about with your friends.

Our society really pushes the idea that repression of "instincts" is bad. We may feel guilty or abnormal about not having sex experiences. Some female students come to regard their virginity as a hang-up, the only thing standing between them and sexual "normalcy." Girls who have intercourse just to get rid of their virginity hang-ups usually seem to find it is not a pleasurable or fulfilling experience.

There is so much talk about sexual intercourse, the pros, the cons, the pleasures, the consequences, that we tend to forget sex means so much more than intercourse. Two people can have a very sexual relationship without insertion of the penis into the vagina.

Many people consider kissing to be as intimate as any act. Necking, petting, sharing the experience of mutual orgasm are obviously sexual, intimate, and satisfying experiences. It's not an all-or-nothing question. Some people feel that petting is less "natural" than having intercourse, but others feel there is a distinct moral differentiation. This is an individual matter. Each of us has to decide what seems right. [Sarrel,* pp. 40–42.]

In the final analysis, the decision to have or not have premarital sexual intercourse is an individual matter. Each of us has to decide what seems right for himself or herself. Whether or not you have premarital sexual intercourse is a very personal, complicated, and far-reaching decision. It is a matter for both males and females to consider. *Much more* is involved than a physical act or the satisfaction of a strong need or the risk of pregnancy. *A relationship is at stake.* The mature male and female must consider all the ramifications involved when determining this very important decision in human relationships.

Summary

Your sexuality includes all the attitudes, feelings, and characteristics which you personally associate or identify with your maleness or femaleness. It includes those traits which you classify as either "masculine" or "feminine" as well as your role expectations. Men and women have many differences, both physical and learned. These differences do not mean that the sexes are opposite, but rather that they are complementary in the sense that each sex serves to make the other more complete. An understanding of sex differences, as well as of personal expectations regarding roles, is necessary in order for each individual to accept his or her own personal sexuality.

Sex typing is the process by which we learn what is considered appropriate behavior for our particular sex. This begins very early in life; it changes and builds until, as adults, we take for granted certain sex roles for either men or women. Although we inherit our biological sex, we learn what is considered masculine or feminine.

---

*From *Student Guide to Sex on Campus* by Dr. Philip Sarrel. Copyright © 1971 by Dr. Philip Sarrel. Reprinted by arrangement with The New American Library, Inc., New York, New York.

Dating may present us with some conflicts as we work toward comfortable relationships with persons of the opposite sex. We may take part in casual or random dating (dating for "fun" without heavy responsibilities or commitment), steady dating (dating which involves a degree of exclusiveness and tentative commitment), and engagement (a relationship which usually involves a statement of commitment and love, with marriage as the intent).

Many conflicts may arise during the dating period as a result of sexual attitudes. Especially in the area of premarital sexual intercourse, the individuals need to be aware of the differences in arousal, need, and the meaning that is placed upon the experience by each person. Males and females tend to place different meanings upon actions and needs. Sexual intercourse is not just a physical act for most people; it involves a relationship, and the individuals must consider the impact of their actions upon that relationship.

Terms to Define

Sexuality

Masculine

Feminine

Complementary

Inhibitions

Sex typing

Sex roles

Casual dating

Going steady

Engagement

Commitment

Abstinence

Permissible with
affection

Permissible without
affection

Double standard

Questions:

1. What does being a man or a woman mean to you personally? In other words, how would you define your sexuality?
2. How have you arrived at your conception of the traits that you classify as "masculine" or "feminine"?
3. Are there any outward behavior patterns or traits accepted today by men and women as "masculine" or "feminine" that would have been completely unacceptable at another time? Why? Will this continue to change? Why or why not?

4. Think back over your life. How has sex typing affected your thinking regarding the appropriate roles for men or women?

5. How important is dating for the teenager when learning to become comfortable with the other sex? How important is it in regard to "status" in the eyes of friends? What is your reaction to the emphasis upon dating?

GROUP DISCUSSION

1. Discuss the practice of "leading someone on." Why do girls "tease" or lead a guy on and then say "I'm not *that* kind of girl!" Why do guys use words of love they don't really mean? Is this practice just "normal" and expected? What are the implications in terms of hurt feelings, misinterpretation of actions or words, and so forth?

2. How do you feel about sex roles? As a group, come up with some answers to this problem: You have just met someone from a remote mountain area who has never been exposed to the way we live. You are asked, "What's the difference between boys and girls? What is expected of girls? What do girls need to know in order to live successfully in society? How are girls supposed to act?"

3. This is the same as question 2, except substitute the word "boy" for "girl."

4. After questions 2 and 3 have been discussed, consider whether or not you would feel any differently if the words "women" and "men" had been used.

5. When considering premarital sexual intercourse, what affects your decision more — your internal values or the circumstances? Can this always be answered in a cut-and-dried manner? Does it help to understand the differences between men and women regarding their arousal, needs, and sex thresholds? Discuss this.

6. Is the "double standard" still prevalent? What is your opinion of this?

7. Do people still use the term "get caught" to describe premarital pregnancy? What is your reaction to this term? Why do so many people seem to feel that the "rightness" or "wrongness" of premarital intercourse hinges upon whether or not pregnancy occurs?

8. How do you feel about the idea that premarital intercourse is "permissible without affection"?

9. When do couples face more conflict regarding their sexual behavior and attitudes — before or after engagement? Defend your point of view.
10. Do you personally feel that premarital intercourse would affect the future relationship of most couples? Would there be any conditions under which it would or would not?

BIBLIOGRAPHY

Bell, Robert R. *Premarital Sex in a Changing Society*. Englewood Cliffs, N.J.: Prentice-Hall, Inc., 1966.

Bowman, Henry A. *Marriage for Moderns*, 6th ed. New York: McGraw-Hill Book Company, 1970.

Martinson, Floyd M. *Marriage and the American Ideal*. New York: Dodd, Mead & Company, 1960.

Pikunas, Justin. *Human Development: A Science of Growth*. New York: McGraw-Hill Book Company, 1969.

Reiss, Ira L. *Premarital Sexual Standards in America*. New York: The Macmillan Company, 1960.

Sarrel, Philip. *Student Guide to Sex on Campus*. New York: New American Library, Inc., 1971.

Williamson, Robert C. *Marriage and Family Relations*. New York: John Wiley & Sons, Inc., 1966.

12

What Do I Expect
from Marriage?

There are those who say that marriage is old-fashioned and that it is becoming obsolete, but it continues to flourish and, unfortunately, often to fail. There seems to be very little chance that this tradition will be abolished for the vast majority of individuals. In this chapter we will be considering the traditional view of marriage — as a way of life, as a personal relationship entered into by two heterosexual people, and as a matter of choice.

We will consider some of the following questions: "Why do I want to get married?" "What is the purpose of an engagement?" "Are my marriage expectations realistic?" and "Are there some fallacies prevalent about marriage?"

This discussion should be of help when you are thinking of marriage. No guarantees are offered; this is not a "Money-Back-If-Not-Satisfied" crash course in selecting the right mate. Marriage is intended for adults; we hope that you, as an adult, will be able to sort out your own attitudes, expectations, and reasons for marriage, and that you will be able to answer your own marriage questions more satisfactorily.

Why Get Married?

Although more than 90 percent of the American population eventually marries, there is a small percentage of people who do not marry. This is either by choice, lack of opportunity, or some other personal reason. We do not mean to presume that marriage is for everyone; indeed, it would be wise to ask yourself before marriage: "Should *everyone* marry? More specifically, should *I* marry?" If the answer is yes, you should also ask, "Why?"

Reasons for marriage will vary: love, companionship, happiness, sexual satisfaction, "escape," and premarital pregnancy are among those we will discuss specifically here; others include security, money, the desire to have children, physical attraction, parental pressure, prestige, and status.

Love

Perhaps the reason for marriage given by most people is love. "Love" is a very ambiguous word and people often mean different things when they say "We're in love." We discussed love as one of our basic needs in Chapter 2. We discussed the importance of being able to love and accept one's self as a person in order to love others; we also discussed the various kinds of love.

Love, in the marriage relationship, is really a combination type of love. It involves many types of love. The immature person often does not realize this and tends to think of love in terms of "What will it do for me? Will it satisfy *my* needs?" This type of love is the receiving kind of love only.

In the marriage relationship, love is sometimes *desire* − the sexual desire to experience the other person. This type of love may begin as self-satisfaction ("I need to satisfy my needs"), but in the marriage relationship the partners have the opportunity to satisfy each other's sexual needs in a complementary fashion. Love as desire is a very natural type of love, but desire alone is not enough as a basis for marriage.

Love is sometimes *companionship* or *friendship* in the marriage relationship; the marriage partners feel a mutual desire to be together and to share common interests. Marriage is a shared experience and love is part of that shared experience. This type of love is not wholly dependent upon mutual interests, but the presence of mutual interests tends to provide a setting for a "growing" relationship.

> It is not with just any desirable person of the other sex one chooses to mate, but with one with whom one finds [a natural attraction], a certain compatibility and a community of interests. Lovers in this sense of the word are "pals," companions, who enjoy being together and doing things together. [Martinson, p. 109.]

There is another kind of love that may be more rare in marriages; when it is present, it is shown by a feeling of mutuality and common concern for each other. It is more than just a matter of "my desire" or "our companionship"; it is a matter of concern and acceptance of the other person as he or she *is* and *can be*. With this acceptance comes a desire to contribute to the support and continued growth of the marriage partner. We call this the *supportive* kind of love.

The supportive kind of love *wants* to help the loved one without regard for personal needs. This is the type of love that "mellows" with a good marriage and fills the whole relationship. It does not take the place of desire or companionship, but serves to enhance them.

Is It Love or Infatuation?   Are you really in love? How do you know the difference between love and infatuation? This is often difficult to determine, for there are no set rules surrounding the definitions of *love* or *infatuation*. Romantic love is very much a part of the American way of life and many expect that some day "it" is going to hit them and they will *know* that they are in love.

What are some of the differences between love and infatuation? Genuine love is more likely to involve a process of "growing" in love rather than "falling" in love. This may sound terribly unromantic to some, who are used to hearing talk about "falling in love" or being "head over heels in love." This "falling" is often infatuation, and the sheer emotion of "falling" in love often blinds a person to the imperfections of the loved one. We tend to think of the loved one as "perfect," "ideal," or some other divine image. Real love sees the total person – both the "perfection" and the imperfection. Infatuation, then, is a sudden, emotional sense that one has discovered the "perfect" lover. On the other hand, love realizes imperfections and grows with the acceptance of those imperfections.

Love leads a person to a feeling of security and trust in the loved one. It usually involves a feeling of mutual benefit arising from the new relationship. "We are able to solve our problems together" is the feeling of love, rather than "Please love me because I *need* you."

Infatuation often entails feelings of insecurity whenever the "lovers" are separated; feelings of doubt, fickleness, uncertainty, and fear of loss often accompany infatuation. "What will I do if I lose him?" and "I wonder if she really means it when she says she loves me?" express the feelings of infatuation. In such a setting a lasting love does not have a chance to develop.

Infatuation tends to be more manipulative than love because a lasting feeling of relationship probably has not developed, so that the individuals are still concerned mainly about their own needs and satisfactions. Conversely, in love the feeling of relationship is genuine and sincere so that concern for the other person evolves naturally.

Physical attraction is an important part of both infatuation and love, but the superficial attraction is less important in love, for the couple experiencing love usually will build their relationship on a broader base than mere physical attraction.

Although genuine love is an ideal toward which a couple strives, you do not have to be *perfect* to love. True love involves a measure of self-acceptance and self-respect and a degree of self-sufficiency in order that one may accept, respect, and trust another person, but it does not require unachievable levels of these qualities.

Companionship

More and more, young people stress "the ability to communicate" and "a common interest" as the bases for a lasting marriage.

> The stress on interpersonal relationships in marriage and family has led to the current emphasis on companionship as a major test of mate relationships. Romance is the lure by which mates are drawn together, but the quality of the relationship which binds it together, if it is to be durable, is companionability. Those who not only love, but who also have enough common characteristics and interests to share each other's life as companions are the ones who are destined for the happy, durable marriage. [Landis,* p. 19.]

*From *Making the Most of Marriage,* 4th edition, by Paul H. Landis. Copyright © 1970. By permission of Appleton-Century-Crofts, Educational Division, Meredith Corporation.

A marriage relationship that is based at least in part on common interest and companionship may provide some needed stability when other insecurities threaten. It may provide the strength needed to weather other difficulties.

Happiness

The desire for happiness is listed by many as a reason for marriage: "I want a happy marriage"; "I think we can make each other happy." Happiness is a very elusive state of being which is sought by most of us today. Because of our society's prosperity, comparative luxury, and leisure, we have come to think that "happiness" is our right — that it naturally should come to us, especially in marriage.

Most of us remember some of the children's stories that we read, which ended, "and so they were married and lived happily ever after! – THE END." We often got the impression that marriage should automatically equal happiness, forever and ever.

We also tend to equate "happiness" with "the good life." How does the typical student describe happiness in marriage? Perhaps some of the following answers will match your own:

> "Well, I think it would be marrying a 'normal' type man, raising a 'normal' type family, and, well, just being happy!"

> "Happiness in marriage? That's hard to define. I guess it depends on the individual. I know, to me, it would mean communication; and caring. I mean *really* caring about me — as a person. I guess it would mean living with someone *I* could really trust and care for too — kind of, like you say, mutuality."

> "I guess I'm sort of an old-fashioned kind of guy, but I think of happiness in marriage as a good wife, a couple of nice kids, a house in the suburbs, a good job — just the kind of normal everday kind of life that everyone wants, a beer and a ballgame on Sunday afternoon."

Do these definitions seem rather one-sided, concentrating on self-satisfaction? What would you include in *your* definition of happiness in marriage? Is it just "a beer and a ballgame," or a "normal type marriage," or what?

Sexual Satisfaction

Marriage provides an approved outlet for *sexual satisfaction*; it is the only acceptable or sanctioned outlet recognized by most individuals in American society.

We have previously stated that our sexual needs are a very normal and real part of our personality. In the marriage relationship, satisfying your own sex needs and those of your partner will become an expression of love; in this case, sex and love are combined in a healthy manner.

> Sex needs are real physical needs. Their mutual expression in marriage is one of the elements in the fulfillment of one's need for feeling successful, safe, and whole. ... But the need is there and can be completely satisfied in American society in no other way as satisfactorily as in the constancy of the marriage relationship. [Landis, p. 30.]

George Bernard Shaw said that marriage is popular because it combines the maximum of opportunity with the maximum of temptation. Satisfaction of sexual needs may be *one* of the reasons for marriage.

Escape

The desire for "escape" is one of the most immature reasons cited for marriage. Some use marriage as a means of escape from an unhappy situation, although this reason is more commonly employed on an unconscious level than on a conscious level. The young person who attempts to "escape" from an unhappy home situation or from loneliness by rushing into marriage may be rushing into a situation potentially far more lonely or unhappy than the one left behind. Marriage should not be thought of as an escape route. The individuals who have such thoughts uppermost in their minds probably are not thinking very clearly about the more serious aspects of marriage.

Premarital Pregnancy

Many marriages are the result of premarital pregnancy. There seems to be growing sentiment against forcing a marriage merely because of premarital pregnancy, and certainly the individual case must be considered. Problems may arise in forced marriages that would not come up in most other marriages. This type of marriage is not doomed to failure, but the couple probably will have to work harder to achieve success, especially in the early years.

There are many other reasons for marriage that are not discussed here – such as status, money, prestige – but the ones that we have examined are fairly representative. Good reasons for marriage will help to reduce the chances of failure and may help you make a better choice of a marriage mate. *Most people will marry for a combination of reasons rather than just one reason.* In a sense, good reasoning will depend upon maturity.

What Is the Purpose of an Engagement?

Students often ask, "How long should an engagement last?" "How long should you know each other before you get married?" "Is it necessary to have an engagement?" One answer would not suffice for all these questions, for each couple is unique and their own answers must also be unique.

Length of Engagement

The most important aspect of an engagement is not its length, but what is accomplished during this period. "Getting really well acquainted is the most valuable outcome of any engagement, and in nearly all cases getting acquainted takes time" [Landis, p. 332].

How long you have known each other prior to engagement is one factor that helps determine the length of your engagement. If you have been dating or going steady for quite some time, the engagement may well be shorter than for the couple who have dated for a very short period of time.

If you have a "whirlwind" courtship and rush right into marriage, you may find that there are quite a few "surprises" in store for you after the wedding. These surprises vary in relative importance; for example, differences in food preferences would constitute a very minor "surprise." However, you may run into some major "surprises" regarding role expectations, financial matters, or sexual attitudes.

There are instances where very brief courtships and engagements have resulted in excellent marriages, but many "whirlwind" marriages end up in the divorce courts mainly because the couple did not take the time before marriage to really get to know each other.

> It is important that a couple be engaged long enough to see whether they can work out patterns of adjustment which will assure the continuing development of an ongoing companionable relationship. A long engagement, however, can do nothing for the couple who are not going in the right direction in their adjustment to each other. They should learn that they never can develop a satisfactory relationship. But a long engagement can give those who are moving in the right direction the opportunity to learn what kinds of adjustment techniques work for them. Both results are equally important — the one in blocking unwise marriages, the other in building assurance that the pair relationship has qualities that will endure in marriage. [Landis, pp. 332–33.]

The *length* of your engagement is, therefore, not as important as the process which goes on during it — the process of really getting to know each other and determining some of the adjustment techniques which you will need to make your marriage an enduring one.

Engagement Is a Time of Learning

The decision to marry is one of the most important ones you will ever make. It will affect the rest of your life either by its failure or its success. Viewed in this light, the engagement period assumes even greater importance, for it is the final preparatory step to marriage.

In taking this step, you are making a commitment; you are saying, "We are in love, and we want to be married." You probably will spend much more time together than before, and you will discover many things about your loved one. The engagement period also should serve as the time to expose many of the commonly held misconceptions and fallacies concerning marriage. In the next few pages let us examine some of the fallacies and misconceptions.

Fallacies about Marriage

We understand each other completely.
I'm marrying YOU, not your family.
Two can live as cheaply as one.

If our love is great enough, we can solve any problems.
Once we're married all of that will change.
Marriage will create common interests.
Marriage will solve all my problems.

"We understand each other completely." During the dating period, however, many couples fail to communicate honestly; they wear "masks" or play a game without really realizing it. They are making a good impression and putting their best foot forward. Sometimes we "understand" or agree with each other because we think we *should*; we mask our true feelings for fear of offending the other.

Your understanding may be more complete than most, but does it include your plans for a family? (How many children? How soon?)

Does it include the use of money? (Are you both going to work? For how long? What will happen after you start a family?) Does it include sexual agreement? (Will your marriage be based on more than sexual attraction? Do you understand each other's needs and responsiveness?)

Many people who have been married for twenty years or more say, "We still don't understand each other completely, and I sort of like it that way. I think I have him all figured out, and then he surprises me. It keeps things interesting." Understanding in the sense of "having him all figured out" probably is not possible, but understanding in the sense of agreeing on basic principles is a very helpful ingredient in a good marriage. Understanding takes time and patience, and it should continue to grow after marriage.

"I'm marrying you, not your family."   Certainly you are marrying only one person, but that person is the product of his past experiences — especially his family. He or she has been influenced by relationships in the home. (Who dominated the family — father or mother? Or was the relationship more equalitarian? What were the disciplinary methods employed in the home? What was the sibling relationship?)

You and your loved one will carry into your marriage many of the patterns each of you learned in your own families. Your expectations, your ideas of "women's work" or "men's work," and even the way you discipline your own children will be affected by the way you were raised.

In our mobile society it is very possible that you may live far away from your families, but normally you will have some family contacts. Conflict with in-laws can be a real threat to your marriage, but it need not be. One thing is quite clear, however: conflicts with in-laws or within a family do not just disappear. They will continue to fester and grow unless you understand the source of the irritation, work to adjust it, or learn to live with it.

Another problem related to family background is overdependence upon one's parents or family. If you see signs of this before marriage, recognize them as a danger sign and work the problem out *now*. Undue attachment to parents might be a symptom of a lack of individual freedom. Sometimes it might be necessary to establish some "ground rules" for interfamily relationships either before your wedding or soon thereafter. This may be especially true if you will be living quite close to each other. How do you *and* those parents feel about "dropping in" or babysitting or Sunday dinner? Find out.

In-laws and close family ties can be a wonderful part of your marriage. It is a matter of interrelationship, for you will be separate "families" yet you are still related. One of the keys to happy interrelationships within related families lies in mutual respect, which allows each to live their own lives without imposing on the other and permits them to remain close without smothering.

"Two can live as cheaply as one."   Not many people still believe that two can live as cheaply as one, but this generation has grown up in a "credit economy" in which borrowing is not frowned upon and virtually has become a way of life.

You probably came from a "middle-class" family where split-level homes, second cars, vacation retreats, and "consumeritis" were well established. If you didn't have these things, you probably wanted them. It may be a little unrealistic, then, to assume that you will be able to begin your marriage "living on love" unless you are financially sound enough to pay for that love. The young couple starting out today usually is faced with car payments, insurance payments (both life and health unless your "fringe benefits" at work cover these things), payments for furniture, stereo, and color television, in addition to the "normal" monthly expenses such as rent, utilities, telephone, food, and clothes.

Money matters are not very romantic. Statistics show that this is one of the main problems facing married people today. The *amount* of money involved may not always be the problem; perhaps more often, trouble arises because of *mismanagement* or poor spending habits. Many people absolutely shudder at the thought of making up a budget and sticking to it, but in some cases this is the only logical solution to a big headache.

When preparing for marriage, you would be wise to discuss your mutual attitudes toward money. If you both plan to work, how are you going to handle the separate incomes you earn — joint account; live on just one salary and save the other; or some other arrangement? Who is going to pay the bills? How much take-home pay will you have, and how much will you be spending for the "essentials"? Can you afford to get married?

Each of you should examine the spending habits of the other in relation to the spending habits you have been used to in your own family. How was money handled in your home? Was your mother on an "allowance" or did your parents use a joint account? Who paid the bills? How were money "problems" settled? By examining and talking over some of these questions, you may find areas of agreement or vast disagreement. Talk it out now and you will probably have fewer problems after you are married.

"If our love is great enough, we can solve any problems." What do young people really mean when they say such things? Are they saying, "If he loves me enough, he'll come around to my way of thinking," or "If she really loves me, she will understand my needs"? For example, if you know your sales job will involve traveling on the road four nights a week, your prospective wife should be aware of this. You should both discuss your feelings about the traveling and separation. If she can't adjust to it and is going to be terribly unhappy, perhaps you should look for a different job – or a different mate! But try to work it out first.

What problems do you expect love to solve all by itself? Religion? Sex? Career plans? Some problems may be just what is needed to kill love, or at least to wound it pretty badly. Engagement should be a time for you to lovingly work through some of these problems. If you have a conflict, don't assume that it will all "work out" later on. Be sure to spell out clearly what you expect and what is of real importance to you. You may be able to arrive at a very satisfactory answer, or you may discover that your problems are very great. Marriage alone, like love, alone, is not a cure-all; it takes people – loving people – to solve problems.

"Once we're married, all of that will change." If you are "putting up" with certain behavior patterns, habits, or traits until you are married, and plan to "change all that" after the wedding – forget it! If you cannot live with each other's imperfections, you are better off recognizing it *before* you get married. Don't plan to change the other person drastically after you marry; it just doesn't work. Everyone continues to change, but the changes should come about through personal desire rather than conscious manipulation.

Many conflicts have arisen after marriage because one of the marriage partners has tried to change the other. For example, Carla and Phil had only been married for six weeks when he mentioned that he would be going "out with the boys" after work. Carla said, "Oh, no, you're not. I don't want you hanging around with those fellows any more." "Why not? They were all right before we got married," he replied. "Well, that was before we were married. It's different now." You can finish the story yourself: will one marriage partner win and one lose, will they compromise, or will they have their first full-blown battle? How could this have been avoided?

If there are "pet peeves" or little irritations that really bother you, you would be well-advised to discuss these matters before you get married rather than putting them off "until we're married." Perhaps your loved one has some similar irritations that you are not aware of, and you both can get these things straightened out now.

"Marriage will create common interest." If you have widely divergent interests, your marriage is not doomed to failure, but on the other hand don't expect marriage to suddenly present you with some interest in common. Your engagement period should provide you with a time for further developing some common interests. You should ask, "Just what do we both like to do?" If one of you is an avid skier and the other hates the sport, it is likely either that one will have to give up the sport or go alone or that the other will have to tag along – either of which could mean further separation in interests.

Some difference in interests is a good thing; "togetherness" can be overdone. But how much difference do you want? Engagement is a good time for answering this question by re-evaluating your relationship with the long term in mind. Just what interests will you share over the many years that you hope to be married? You probably will want to focus most of your attention on those areas and develop them further.

"I've found the only one for me." The "one and only" mate for you in fact is yours as a result of both time and circumstance. When you discover the wonderful feeling of loving and being loved, it is difficult to realize that this "wonderful one" is only one of many possibilities for a suitable marriage mate; you both happened to be in the right place at the right time. Many "romantics" hate to acknowledge this and are afraid that they never will find another mate, so "I'll hang on to this one at any cost."

If, during your engagement, you find that you are not as "right" for each other as you thought, you might be better off canceling the whole thing and going your separate ways. Better a broken engagement than a broken marriage.

"Marriage will solve all my problems." The notion that marriage offers escape is perhaps the deadliest of all the fallacies of marriage. It may be that marriage will be a welcome and happy release from an unhappy home or a lonely life, but if you are very young, very unhappy, very lonely, or unsure of your "love" feelings, you may be setting yourself up for a real letdown. Making a marriage work requires work, patience, understanding, self-assurance, trust, love, and a host of other virtues. Don't rush into marriage unless you are *sure* that you are doing it because you really think it is right for both of you, not because you want to use it to solve some other problems.

Engagement Is a Time of Questioning

The engaged couple will want to discuss some rather obvious questions which will require mutual answers. Some of the questions that should be discussed relate to the following general areas.

Type of Wedding and Honeymoon. Are you both in agreement regarding the size, cost, and type of wedding that you want? What about the time and place for the wedding? Plans for the honeymoon also should be made together, so that both are in general agreement. Although we traditionally think of the wedding plans as the domain of the bride and the honeymoon plans as the domain of the groom, no such separation of responsibility is necessary and it is probably better if you are both in general agreement.

Finances. Financial talks are not very "romantic" but it is essential that both partners are aware of their mutual financial state. It is simply a fact of life that money will affect many things both before and after you are married – your honeymoon, where you live, furnishing your apartment, and day-to-day budgeting. Will you both work after you are married? Are you in agreement regarding how long the wife will work?

**Financial expectations may cause conflict, and these expectations
should be discussed during engagement.**

Children. When you will have your children, how many you
will have, and even *if* you will have any are all questions that should
be discussed before marriage. You should arrive at a mutual
agreement regarding family planning and the use of contraceptives.
Do you agree on these topics?

Sexual attitude. If you feel hesitant or embarrassed about discussing your sexual attitudes, you might consider mutually going to a
counselor or consulting your physician. A healthy sexual attitude
plays an important role in contributing to a successful marriage; it
should be discussed before marriage.

Parents. Your attitudes toward your parents should be discussed
openly. In-law problems are not just subjects for comic strips and
cartoons; they could be a real problem in your marriage. Of course
they need not be if you discuss your feelings before marriage to
determine if your attitudes are generally agreeable.

Careers. Do both husband and wife want careers? As Hilda Krech
reminds us, "The Women's Bureau estimates that of the girls now in
high school 8 out of 10 — whether because of widowhood, divorce,

economic need, emotional need, or psychological need – will at some period be employed" [Krech, p. 149].

How do both of you feel about the wife's working outside of the home in your marriage? How do you both feel about the husband's future occupation? Are there any conflicts present which might grow rather than diminish?

These questions, and many more, should be discussed before a couple marry; working out some of them ahead of marriage provides a great asset for the adjustment period after marriage. If seemingly insurmountable problems arise, you *might* want to consider calling off the wedding or at least postponing it for a time.

No one can ever be perfectly sure that a marriage will work. Love sometimes can be tragic and marriages all too often end in failure. If you acknowledge these possibilities, you may work harder to keep your marriage from failing. With one marriage in every four currently ending in divorce, you need all the help you can get. Prepare in advance and yours may be one of the happier statistics – a successful marriage.

Summary

More than 90 percent of all Americans eventually marry. They marry for many reasons, some of which include: love, happiness, companionship, the desire to have children, physical attraction, or the desire to escape from an unhappy situation.

The engagement period can be very valuable for the couple contemplating marriage. The length of the engagement depends upon the individuals, but it needs to be long enough for the couple to really get to know each other. The engagement period is a time for learning to recognize some of the fallacies put forth about marriage. Some of these fallacies are expressed in the following commonly heard statements: "We understand each other completely"; "I'm marrying *you,* not your family"; "Two can live as cheaply as one"; "If our love is great enough, we can solve any problems"; "Once we're married, all of that will change"; "Marriage will create common interests"; "I've found the only one for me"; and "Marriage will solve all my problems."

The engagement is also a time for questioning and understanding each other's attitudes about the future. Some of these questions involve the type of wedding and honeymoon; financial attitudes;

attitudes toward children; sexual attitudes; relationships with parents; and attitudes relating to careers for both partners.

Terms to Define

Infatuation   Engagement
Companionship   Fallacy
Maturity

Questions:

1. Why is it often difficult to distinguish between love and infatuation?
2. What are some of the types of love that are displayed in a marriage?
3. In your opinion, what would be the best and worst reasons for getting married?
4. Why is escape a rather immature reason for marriage?
5. What do you think when someone asks, "Are you mature enough to get married?"
6. What is meant by saying, "During an engagement, some of the masks are removed from the relationship"?

GROUP DISCUSSION

1. Discuss the various reasons given in this chapter for marriage. Do you think these reasons could be ranked according to their immediate importance and their long-term importance? Which reasons do you think are most important right now? Which do you think will grow in importance as the marriage continues?
2. Discuss whether or not you think the "meaning" of these reasons for marriage will change as the marriage relationship continues. (For example, will *companionship* mean the same thing now, in ten years, in twenty years? What about *love*? Do this with as many of the reasons as you can.)
3. Do you think it takes happy people to make a happy marriage? If two "unhappy" people marry each other, what would be some of the factors that determine whether or not they find happiness or just more unhappiness?
4. List some of the actions or traits of persons you consider immature. Compare your list with the lists of others in your group. How would these behavior traits affect the couple

planning to get married? Do you think these traits will be modified by marriage? Is it sometimes easier to see immaturity in others but not in oneself? Why?

5. Marcia and Mike have just become engaged. They plan to marry in six months, and as they make their marriage plans they both become aware of some of the "other" sides of their loved one. Mike is appalled at the temper tantrums and sarcastic temperament Marcia displays in her home; this is a side of her that he had not seen before. She is almost always late and he is beginning to resent her efforts to "change him." She seems to concentrate on some of his bad habits — like being careless with mone· using improper grammar, and so forth.

  Marcia is very upset over Mike's spending habits. He spends lavishly right after he gets paid, but is usually broke by the end of the month; when she mentions this, he calls her a "penny-pincher." His bad grammar embarrasses her and she intends to help him overcome his bad habits. It seems he is always complaining about her "attitude" and her habit of being late.

  In your opinion, are these two well-suited for marriage? What types of adjustments will they have to make? Is it better for them to talk these things out during their engagement, or should they wait until they are "safely" married? What would you advise them to do if you were a "best" friend?

6. When people suspect, during an engagement period, that they are incompatible, why do so many refuse to admit it or talk it over? How do you think people should handle suspected areas of incompatibility during an engagement?

7. How do you feel about the "fallacies" of marriage? Are there any that you would like to restate, defend, or reword? Why do so many people believe these fallacies are true?

BIBLIOGRAPHY

Krech, Hilda Sidney. "Housewife and Woman? The Best of Both Worlds?" in *Man and Civilization: The Family's Search for Survival,* ed. Seymour M. Farber, Piero Mustacchi, and Roger H. L. Wilson. New York: McGraw-Hill Book Company, 1965.

Landis, Paul H. *Making the Most of Marriage,* 4th ed. New York: Appleton-Century-Crofts, Inc., 1970.

Martinson, Floyd. *Marriage and the American Ideal.* New York: Dodd, Mead, & Company, 1960.

13

We Marry
and We Adjust

Weddings and honeymoons are part of our American way of life. Your wedding may involve months of detailed planning or it might be a simple private ceremony, but in either case it marks your entry into the world of the "married folk." In this chapter we will briefly discuss the wedding, the honeymoon, and some of the adjustments which are involved in making the change from singleness to marriedness.

The Wedding and Honeymoon

Preparation

Your plans will include a variety of decisions which must be made: where to live, the type of ceremony, reception, pictures, state requirements (blood tests or waiting period), premarital counseling with your clergyman in some cases, as well as the decisions involving the furnishing of your new home. Although most of the planning for the wedding itself will be done by the girl, both will want to be part of many of the decisions, so that it is not just "my" wedding or "your" wedding, but our wedding.

Plans for the honeymoon should be agreed upon by both individuals; the man usually assumes most of this responsibility, but part of the enjoyment of the honeymoon will be in planning it together. Again, cost will have to be considered; it would be unwise to jeopardize your marriage financially because you were too extravagant on your honeymoon.

The Ceremony

The ceremony you plan may be a simple service by a state official, or it may be an elaborate church wedding. Most ceremonies will be somewhere in between. Many couples today have, with the help of their clergyman, "personalized" their weddings by helping to write some of the vows and incorporating their personal philosophy into the ceremony. Others wish to follow a traditional wedding service, while some look at the wedding ceremony as merely a legal formality.

Whatever type of ceremony you decide upon, it will join you in a legal contract with each other and, even more important to the success of your marriage, it will bind you in a personal contract. That contract does not spell out all the "rights, privileges, or obligations" of each party, for this is up to you. Your contract will be one of individual responsibility and commitment – to each other and to making your marriage successful.

The Honeymoon

Although the honeymoon is not an essential part of a marriage, it has been customary in our American culture and is the "frosting on the cake" after the wedding. Very often today, the honeymoon takes the form of a "wedding trip" varying in length and distance, from a short weekend stay at a place of your choice, to an expensive, luxury trip.

The honeymoon serves to reinforce the "separateness" and the "togetherness" of your new marriage: you are a married couple beginning your life together, separated from your families and on your own. This is the beginning of intimately living together; it provides an unhurried atmosphere in which you can begin to adjust to each other's needs and desires, unpressured by time. In a sense, the honeymoon is an artificial or unreal experience; there are no deadlines, no alarm clocks, no meals to prepare, and none of the hustle and bustle of everyday living.

Back to Reality

If you have been living away from home with roommates, you already have experienced some of the kinds of problems that might arise necessitating adjustments. Whenever you bring together two or more people from different homes with different learning experiences, a period of adjustment is bound to follow. For example, if you have lived in an apartment, were the "duties" assigned or did everyone shift for himself? Who took out the garbage? When was mealtime? Who prepared the meals? Who was responsible for keeping the place clean and who defined cleanliness? When you were living with roommates, you could always move out or find another place to live with other roommates if your attempts to make adjustments did not work out. In marriage, however, your "lease" or commitment is a long-term affair and the alternative of "moving out" involves more than just finding a more compatible roommate. Adjustments in marriage are not always easy. The fact that one out of every four marriages ends in divorce seems to indicate that many couples are not prepared to cope with the adjustments necessary to make a go of their marriage.

Sometimes the big problems in your marriage can be solved more easily than the little problems, for the big problems present obstacles which *have* to be solved in order for the relationship to continue. However, many of the little problems which you both think you can overlook tend to have a compounding effect. Gradually they assume more importance until your little problem becomes a big one. You may think, "If our love is strong enough, we can solve *any* problem," but how will love affect the way you squeeze the toothpaste tube or forget to take out the garbage or leave the bathroom in a mess? *You* will have to help if "love" is going to solve your problems.

"He leaves his clothes all over the place — socks under the chairs, shoes in the middle of the floor, and his jacket is ALWAYS in a heap by the door. Sometimes I think I'm just a maid!"

"I used to think it was sort of cute that she couldn't cook — it made her seem so innocent and helpless. But I'm sick to death of eating out, or opening a can of beans or having scrambled eggs — that's all she can make! She can't even follow a recipe."

"She *never* has enough food in the apartment. At first I didn't mind going to the market for her but it's always, 'Honey, will you run out and get a loaf of bread?' or 'Oh dear, we're out of milk.' Good grief, hasn't she ever heard of a grocery list?"

"He's still going out with the boys. I thought he'd give that up because he knows I don't like it. But no — you'd think I was asking him to cut off a leg!"

These little problems can assume enormous proportions. What can be done about them?

Keep Things in Perspective

Perhaps the first commandment of all marital adjustment should be to keep things in perspective. If we try to view our problems in relation to the whole picture, they often do not seem so large. However, it is easy to lose your perspective. Have you ever noticed a billboard with a misspelled word, or a wall with a crack in it, or a piece of fabric with a flaw in it? You may not notice the misspelled word or the crack or the flaw until someone else calls your attention to it, but once you see it, that's all you see; the rest is obscured by that one small fault.

One of the biggest contributors to lack of perspective is our tendency to emphasize the "I" in marriage at the expense of the "we": "I want *you* to adjust to *my* needs because you love me!" We often enter marriage for some very selfish reasons, and although we may *say* we are concerned about the "we" relationship, we often tend to see it only through our own eyes, thinking, "What is good for me will be good for the relationship."

Keeping problems in perspective is often very difficult for the newly married couple, for they may tend to feel, "If he or she really loves me, this would be an easy way to prove it. I'm not asking so much." Whenever we begin to think in terms of "proving" love, we get on very shaky ground; the person who wants the other to *prove* love is often unconsciously saying, "*I* am important and you don't really count. Give in to me because *I* say so."

If you hold your finger up in front of your eye, you don't see much more than your finger. Little problems sometimes can be magnified in this way also, unless you keep them in perspective.

Communication as a Means of Adjustment

Married couples soon set up their own communications signals. You will develop your own meanings for facial expressions, tone of voice, or your own private words which have special meaning only for you two.

A great deal of nonverbal as well as verbal communication occurs between marriage partners, but sometimes the things communicated are different for each partner. Good communication is a continuing process in marriage; it evolves and grows out of early attempts, and when it is successful it builds a solid foundation for helping to work out mutual problems.

Unless you learn to openly communicate about irritations, worries, or problems, you will still be wearing your play acting masks, and your relationship will suffer. Building strong communication is often not easy in the marriage relationship. You still may feel unsure or afraid that what you want to say will be misunderstood or will offend, so you close up. You may have been hurt by an action or remark, but you find it less threatening to say nothing so the hurt continues to build.

There is no one sure way to establish good communication in marriage, but the right way to begin is with *loving* honesty – the type of honesty that is not destructive or judgmental. It is the type of communication that conveys feelings rather than judgments: "I feel hurt because you didn't call and tell me you were going to be late," rather than "You never think of me; I sit at home and wait and wonder and you don't even care!"

The first statement conveys honest feeling and leaves the door open for further communication, whereas the second statement signs, seals, and delivers the condemnation. Honest, loving communication in marriage needs to be mutual – it needs to go both ways. You can help your marital adjustments by mutually agreeing to communicate lovingly.

Have Realistic Expectations

Expectations will vary with each couple, but most couples share two main areas where their expectations are most likely to be out of harmony — the area of finances and the area of roles.

What About Money? A lot of couples have rather romantic notions regarding money or financial matters. Before they are married they tend to feel, "Money isn't going to be that important to us; we'll get along just fine." Michael Harrington points out in *The Other America: Poverty in the United States* that roughly one-fourth of the citizens in America have incomes considered to be inadequate for a satisfactory marital and family life. But it appears that the amount of money present is not the only factor to be considered; how the money is utilized is an equally important consideration. Williamson observes that "as many marriages appear to fail because of the spouses' inability to organize and control expenditures as are threatened by inadequate income" [Williamson, p. 385]. One does not have to look very far to see examples of people who have poor "money sense." They may have adequate incomes, but they do not manage their money effectively. People with large incomes may have to file for bankruptcy not because of business failure, but because they were unable to adequately organize and control their expenditures.

If you get married today without a sound financial foundation, you may be jeopardizing the future of your marriage. What constitutes a "sound" financial base will differ with individuals; some are able to manage very well on small incomes while others with much higher incomes are always broke. There are many questions which should be answered before you marry; if you do not discuss them at that time, they definitely will necessitate some adjustments after you marry. For example, how does your take-home pay compare to your fixed payments and expenses? Will you both be working after you marry, and if so, how will you handle two incomes? How long will the wife continue to work? Will you be able to make ends meet on one income? These are very real problems faced by all couples; various adjustments can be worked out, involving different types of budgeting.

The attitude of the couple regarding management of money often reflects their previous home experiences. The two individuals in a marriage often have learned completely different attitudes toward spending and money management, so they will have to arrive at a new pattern that will be acceptable to both.

Consider this example: Barb and Dick have been married for six weeks and already they realize that their attitudes toward spending and budgeting money are completely different. When you consider their background experiences, this is very understandable.

In Dick's home, his father always paid the bills, dispensed allowances, and managed their family's adequate but not enormous income. Dick had received a clothing allowance when he was younger to cover the "essentials," but he always had done odd jobs around the neighborhood and had worked part-time in high school to pay for his "extras" and the items which his parents considered nonessential. Except for the major items, he had been responsible for most of his clothing purchases for some time. His mother received a "household allowance" covering food, supplies, and the family's personal items. She was a very good manager, shopped the "specials," and tended to be rather conservative in the type of food she prepared. On special occasions she would splurge, but the family's food tastes were not extravagant.

Dick's father ran a "tight ship" regarding finances; saving and "getting ahead" each month was very important to the family. They all worked very hard for their money and considered their purchases carefully.

In Barb's home money was a little more plentiful and was handled quite casually compared to Dick's home. The children did not have a set clothing allowance and their parents were rather generous when asked for clothing money. Barb became accustomed to buying new clothes whenever she "needed" them. Although Barb worked part-time, she was free to use the money in any way she wished; her family took it for granted that clothing money would come from Dad, rather than from personal earnings.

A food budget or household "allowance" was unheard of, and although Barb could recall hearing her father complain occasionally about the "outrageous" cost of food, he did not restrict her mother's spending. Their food tastes were not necessarily extravagant, but they did enjoy "specialty" foods and the more choice cuts of meat. Her mother shopped whenever they needed food; she never compiled a food list or did "comparative" shopping. This was their way of life, and the family members took their spending habits for granted.

Can you imagine some of the adjustments that Barb and Dick were faced with after six weeks of marriage? They have quite different values and attitudes regarding money habits, spending, and what constitutes "essential" items. Neither is completely right or wrong in his habits – but each is completely convinced that *his* way of spending is the logical, sensible, and practical way of handling money because he is used to it that way.

Making the switch from "single" spending habits to "married" spending habits can entail quite an adjustment. This may be especially true for the wife who has not had a great deal of training regarding food purchases, comparative shopping, or stretching a given amount of money to last for a whole month. Shopping for the needs of both husband and wife can be a rather frustrating experience and may require some time before an adequate adjustment can be made.

Young "marrieds" also are confronted with the need to purchase or acquire some of the items usually described as long-term investments. Our economy has been called a "credit economy" and consumers today seem much more willing to incur debt in order to have the things they want. This is especially true of many newlyweds; credit is *so* easy – and it would be *so* nice to have a color television, a king-sized bed, a new stereo system, and so forth.

Decisions involving credit buying must be made by both marriage partners, and it is the wise couple who thoroughly weighs and investigates all aspects of credit buying before getting in over their heads. Ask yourselves: "How much will I really be paying?" (If you figure out the interest rate you may be in for a surprise.) "Will I still be paying for this when it's nearly worn out or out-of-date?" "Can we really afford it?" "Is it worth it?" If one partner has more "money sense" than the other, that person is the likely candidate to generally handle the family's finances.

All the admonishing in the world often goes unheeded, and all too often young couples sadly comment, "We were so thrilled at the prospect of having some of the things we always wanted. We were both working so we figured, 'Why not?' I guess we just got carried away, and soon we were always arguing about money. I never thought that would happen to us! We had a hard time meeting all the payments, and we had more overdrafts than I care to remember. It just got away from us." Credit can be a marvelous tool, but it also can become a tremendous burden if it is not used wisely.

Some couples have another type of "money problem" that must be evaluated: the question of where they stand on the issue of accepting "help" from parents. (Some young couples would be very happy to have that kind of "problem"!) Parental assistance is nothing new; it has been traditional in various cultures in the form of a dowry for the bride, or a parcel of land, or business assistance for the groom. Many parents say, "We can afford to help you and we want to help you. Why not let us?" What should be the young couple's answer? Inasmuch as each couple's case will be unique, the matter would have to be individually considered, but here are a few thoughts to use as guidelines: Are there any "strings" attached — either verbal or hidden? How might accepting this help affect their relationship to the other set of parents? How might parental help affect the couple's "independence" or their feeling toward those parents? Could this type of help affect the husband-wife relationship?

If parental assistance means domination, interference, or expectations of "eternal gratitude," the price may well be too high. You, as a couple, must decide for yourselves.

Try to remember one main fact regarding your financial adjustment in marriage: It is not necessarily how *much* money you have, but *how* you use it that will largely determine whether or not your marriage will be threatened by financial problems.

What About Roles?   Role expectations usually can be modified quite easily in marriage, but generally this involves a gradual and a continual process. Your parents established their "roles" over a long period of years, and when you marry you enter your relationship with your own set of ideas regarding what is "women's work" and what is "men's work"; these role expectations are based largely upon your parent's examples.

If you look at your previous family experience, you can understand why you feel certain jobs should be done by the husband or the wife: who paid the bills in your family; who mowed the lawn; who did the marketing; did your father ever help in the kitchen; who washed the car; who was the "boss"? Your answers to all of these questions and many more will help you better understand some of the role expectations you may be carrying with you into your marriage.

The roles which you take for granted as the duties of either husband or wife may conflict with those of your spouse. Look at his or her family: are their role patterns different from those of your family? Both you and your spouse will enter marriage thinking just as strongly that certain jobs belong in opposing sex categories, and you will have to work out your own particular brand of "women's work" and "men's work."

Sheila's dad always helped her mother when they were having a big family dinner party; he would arrange chairs, help with the table and carve the meat. Her mother depended on his assistance. Sheila expected that all men would do this, because her dad did.

Paul's mother wouldn't allow anyone else in her kitchen; she wanted to do things her own way and managed very well. Paul's dad would visit with the guests until dinner was ready. Paul assumed that this was the proper role for the husband.

When Sheila and Paul have their first family dinner party, are their individual expectations regarding the "roles" of husbands and wives likely to cause any conflict?

Each family will handle household chores differently; whatever the pattern, it becomes second nature to the children in the family. They "expect" mother or dad to perform certain duties, and they carry over these expectations into their own marriage.

Conflicts in role expectations also arise with regard to attitudes or actions outside of the home. For example, Bruce's father never called home if he was going to be late for dinner; the family assumed that if he wasn't there by six, he'd eat somewhere else or have something to eat when he did come home. This was the attitude they grew up with and they accepted it as the "way it was done."

Sarah's father always called if he was going to be delayed, and the family came to expect it of him. When Sarah and Bruce marry, these conflicting expectations might cause some problems. If Bruce came home at eight o'clock when he was expected for dinner at five-thirty, without a phone call or any explanation, what might Sarah's reaction be? There is likely to be trouble unless Bruce and Sarah work out their own set of expectations in this area.

Sometimes conflicts in role expectations develop with regard to career-related attitudes. How does the new wife feel about her husband's traveling job? How do they feel about a "working wife"? What are their expectations regarding a "working wife" with children at home? How involved is the wife expected to be in "helping" her husband with social obligations associated with his job?

If one or both of the marriage partners have very definite feelings regarding a wife's working, it is best that they be expressed before marriage. However, many people do not really realize their attitudes regarding women working, especially if their mothers did not work outside of the home. Some men may feel threatened by having their wives work; they feel that it reflects upon their ability to support the family.

If both partners are working when they first get married, and they get used to living on both incomes, it may be very difficult to cut back to one income when children arrive. The wife may be forced to go back to work to help support the family, and this might cause her to feel resentful about her job or her husband, and cause him to feel guilty. One of the biggest adjustments many couples have to make is living on one income after getting used to living on two.

> One of the classic confusions of expectations involves whether or not a woman should work outside the home – especially after the children come. Because there is no universal social pattern these days, many women feel guilty if they *do* work outside the home, and guilty if they *don't*. Whatever they do, they get little role satisfaction, and their equally mixed up husbands may possibly be ungrateful either way. This in itself can put a great strain on the marriage relationship. [Klemer, p. 10.]

With more women in the labor force than ever before, and more women returning to work after children are grown or partially grown, this problem is one that needs to be discussed by both marriage partners. If both husband and wife agree that the wife should work, they will be more apt to make the necessary adjustments happily; if one spouse imposes a decision upon the other, it is much more difficult for both to find the solution satisfactory.

Understanding Begets Understanding

If one expects understanding, he must give understanding in return. This is especially true in the marriage partnership. Some say that marriage is a "fifty-fifty proposition"; in other words, each partner gives and takes equally. Perhaps this is true in some cases but it seems that in most successful marriages the percentages are more like one hundred and one hundred. The couple should not be striving for equal justice so much as for whatever is best for the marriage relationship. This might mean that one partner will give 100 percent sometimes, but sometimes will receive 100 percent. The percentages are not fixed; there is no scale on which you can weigh out "marital justice." Decisions regarding one's "rights" or "needs" should be decided upon the basis of whose need is greater at that particular time.

This type of understanding, in which each individual considers the needs of the other person in relation to his own, may be rare, but it is so only because more couples have not arrived at a common concern for the satisfaction of the other partner's needs. It must be emphasized that this type of understanding is *mutual* and *common.* It is not one-sided; even though it may seem that one partner does most of the giving for quite some time, it is done willingly and lovingly. Such a couple is less concerned with keeping the giving balanced every day than with building a relationship in which both partners are mutually supportive over the long run.

In this type of "not-always-equal" justice based on the mutual understanding of each other's needs, the scale of justice may be pretty lopsided sometimes, but usually they tip back the other way at some other time. If not, the satisfaction for the partner who does more giving lies in the fact that he has helped his spouse fill a special need.

This *supportive* type of love is a matter of helping the other to become *more* than adequate as a spouse, parent, companion, or lover. We all need a little help sometimes.

> Clouds are not the cheeks of angels you know
> they're only clouds.
>   Friendly sometimes,
> but you can never be sure.
> If I had longer arms
> I'd push the clouds away
>   or make them hang above the water somewhere else,
> but I'm just a man
>   who needs and wants,
> mostly things he'll never have.
> Looking for that thing that's hardest to find—
> I've been going a long time now
> along the way I've learned some things.
> You have to make the good times yourself
> take the little times and make them into
>   big times

and save the times that are all right
for the ones that aren't so good.
I've never been able
   to push the clouds away by myself.
   Help me.
Please.
                                        —Rod McKuen,

                                *Listen To The Warm**

Sexual Adjustment Takes Time and Patience

Your understanding of the differences in needs, responsiveness, and stimulation between men and women will aid you in your sexual adjustment. We cannot separate the sexual self from other aspects of self; one's sexual behavior is affected by the rest of his personality. In human beings, sexual intercourse is more than a mere physical act; it involves emotional and psychological implications as well. If a couple have been fighting all day about money, "going out with the boys," or some other marital problem, they probably will not have very good sexual relations that night. Perhaps this is more true for women than for men, for women are much more dependent upon circumstances and conditions for sexual arousal than men. Some men may feel that sexual relations are a good way to "make up" for fighting during the day, but many women tend to feel that they cannot simply forget about fighting all day and enjoy sex.

Building a satisfactory and enjoyable sexual relationship takes time and patience for most married couples. Both men and women approach the sexual aspect of their marriage with conditioned attitudes, ideas, or inhibitions.

Communication is extremely important to the achievement of mutual sexual fulfillment; if the couple can help each other discover what is pleasing, irritating, distasteful, or stimulating, they will be better able to achieve a complementary experience.

A newly married couple are novices confronted with the problem of learning a new art and acquiring a new skill. They are almost certain to make mistakes at first. They may feel that their ignorance is stupendous and their clumsiness colossal. They need not leap to conclusions and

---

*Copyright © 1967 by Rod McKuen and Anita Kerr. Reprinted by permission of Random House, Inc.

defeat themselves. They may learn by their mistakes. With patience, understanding, intelligence, self analysis, an ample amount of love, and a liberal sprinkling of a sense of humor, errors may be corrected. To give up in defeat because sexual adjustment is not complete at the very beginning and because in their mutual experience there are mistakes is just as unnecessary and foolish as it would be to lie prone for the rest of one's life because one fell down the first time he tried to walk. Each successful act of intercourse plays a part in conditioning both husband and wife so that success in the future becomes easier. Hence, care, patience, perspective, and a will to succeed pay large dividends in terms of long-time happiness. [Bowman, p. 425.]

A couple can achieve sexual harmony if they understand the needs of the other, communicate openly, and learn from their mistakes. For the wife this involves understanding that you have married a man – with masculine impulses and needs. He may not understand your needs and impulses completely to begin with, but you can help him. Understand that he may become frustrated or angry if you arouse him or "tease" him and then deny his fulfillment. Understand that his needs may be less subject to condition or circumstances than yours. Understand that satisfaction of your sexual needs is very important to him as a man; he gains a great deal of pleasure from knowing that he has pleased you. Help him.

For the husband this involves understanding that you have married a woman – with feminine reactions and needs. She often needs tenderness, care, and adequate preparation for arousal. Understand that, because of her experience and conditioning, she is likely to have more inhibitions than you; help her to overcome them. Understand that she may have an exaggerated fear of pain connected with intercourse, so be gentle and patient.

When a couple is able to understand and accept each other's expectations and attitudes, they have taken the first step toward achieving sexual harmony. When they feel secure that they can express their feelings without rejection or humiliation, they can help each other move toward mutual satisfaction and fulfillment.

What is "good sexual adjustment" in marriage? In a sense, it is different for each couple. It involves a blending of the expectations of both partners into a pattern that is acceptable to both of them. The achievement of mutually satisfying sexual relations does not follow any set timetable; for some, it is accomplished quite rapidly, but for others it may take months or even years. Satisfying sexual relations depend upon a continual pattern of adjustment, for people change from month to month, as well as from year to year. Satisfactory adjustment depends upon both marriage partners; it is not a matter of dominance and submission, but rather of mutual acceptance and flexibility.

Handling Marital Conflicts

Tension and conflict are almost inevitable in a marriage relationship. Marriage involves two persons who supposedly become "one," but the needs of the individuals continue to exert themselves, sometimes at the expense of the marriage relationship. Marriage partners often tend to find themselves putting "what is best for me" before "what is best for our relationship."

Marriage partners do not live in complete isolation, separated from the rest of the world. They are affected by the pressures and demands of everyday living, of their job, of their community, of their spouses and children.

There may be many sources of marital conflict, for two people living together intimately are bound to disagree on some matters or to run into some conflicting desires or needs. The conflict may derive from external forces — for example, a man may want to make a success of his business, but may neglect his family to do so. Or it may arise over financial matters, as when he wants a new set of golf clubs and she wants a new coat and there is not enough money for both. Conflicts may arise from actions or lack of action — a forgotten birthday or anniversary, for example — or over differing views about methods of disciplining children, politics, home decoration, or just about anything else. The sources of marital conflict are many and varied, but one fact remains clear: marital conflict is inevitable.

Win-Lose Conflict

Win-lose conflicts can become a vicious merry-go-round for the immature or insecure couple. They cannot or will not see the other

Win or lose, conflict destroys or divides

person's point of view, so that each conflict must end up in clear-cut defeat for one party and clear-cut victory for the other.

In this type of situation, each party is determined that "I am right and you are wrong." There is no attempt at compromise or accomodation to another's point of view. Listen to an argument that is taking place at Greg and Kathy's apartment. They have been married for six months, and both are working.

GREG: I looked at a new car today and the salesman said I could really get a good deal now before the model change.

KATHY: You must be kidding! We can't afford a new car and you know it. You just bought a new fishing rod. Don't be dumb.

GREG: What do you know about cars? Look who's calling me dumb. You weren't so smart when you got that "good deal" on a dress you've worn once!

KATHY: It was *my* money and you know I needed a new dress for your office party. That has nothing to do with a dumb car anyway.

GREG: It does too; if you weren't so extravagant about all those clothes you want maybe I could have a few of the things *I* want. How come it's always *your* money when you want something for you, but it's *our* money when we're talking about *my* salary.

You can readily see the destructiveness present in this type of arguing. They use name-calling ("dumb" and "extravagant"); they make insinuations (*you* spend too much money but *I* don't); they do not define the argument (what are they arguing about — car, clothes, money, budget?); they drag up dead issues (fishing rod, dress); and they take sides instead of considering the other person's point of view.

Unfortunately, this couple is establishing some terrible ground rules for future arguments. They seem to get sidetracked into "personal" areas and are more concerned about hurting or hitting back than about solving their problems. You can almost visualize their "scoreboard" for arguments: "I scored a point when I mentioned the fishing rod, but he got two points by bringing up that dress; then I got one for getting in the fact that the dress was for the party at his office."

This very destructive type of arguing is all too common in marriage and the couple who uses it is sentenced to a life of "one-upmanship" — not a very happy prospect for marital success. They may achieve some personal "victories" but they solve few problems.

Clear-the-Air Conflict

It would be a wonderful world if all couples could calmly and rationally sit down and discuss all their problems without hurting, name-calling, and misinterpreting the other's words. Sometimes real issues become clouded because past hurts or grievances pop up: "remember when — " or "and another thing" are used to bring up old issues to be discussed anew.

One would hope that two intelligent, objective, loving people could understand each other's point of view and could discuss their problems rationally. But they are also very human and their emotions become involved sometimes rendering them less than rational and far from objective.

How can marital conflicts result in clearing of the air? You will need to establish some ground rules.

1. *Good communications go both ways.* You should allow each other to fully express his or her point of view. State feelings, not judgments. It is especially important that *both* parties be willing to listen to the other person openly, without prejudging what is said. If

you approach any conflict with a judgmental attitude, you are putting your partner in the position of having to defend himself, and you also are making a judgment or assumption that may not be accurate. "Sometimes I feel left out," would be a better expression of a certain feeling than "You really don't care about me at all."

2. *Restate your partner's point of view.*   Be sure you both understand the meaning of the words you use. Remember that what you say and what you mean are often different. Be sensitive to your partner's reactions to what you say, for they will reflect the meaning that is getting across. This should help you to define the problem and possibly to understand your partner's point of view and feelings.

3. *Define the problem.*   You may have to work through some preliminary side issues before you arrive at the real problem; it may be that the first point of view was just a smokescreen, and that the real problem will come to the surface by restating the other's point of view. "Is that what's the matter — you would like us both to go out of town this weekend instead of having me go hunting?" It is important that both partners be honest, loving, and understanding in order to establish the real problem.

4. *Stick to the issue.*   Sometimes we have a tendency to throw in some of the "old" wounds that were never completely healed ("You forgot my birthday, you know"). These side issues usually just cloud the real problem and should be tabled for the moment until the current issue is settled. "I'm sorry I forgot your birthday, but it really doesn't have anything to do with this problem. Let's talk about *that* later," would be a good way to handle a side issue.

5. *Don't hit below the belt.*   When you live intimately with another person, you soon learn his particular vulnerabilities. It may be tempting to "hit back" or hurt if you have been hurt — and you know just how to do it. Resist this temptation. You will regret lashing out in a spiteful and hurting manner, for those words can never be unsaid once they are spoken. No matter how many times you might say, "I'm sorry for what I said," if you have really struck at a vulnerable point the hurt will remain. Your words have the power to destroy and a destroyed relationship is very difficult, if not impossible, to put back together again.

6. *Be prepared to compromise.*   Some people give lip-service to the idea of compromise but watch for an opportunity to retaliate in their own way. Your compromise should represent a real willingness to meet the other person half way, not just to have "peace at any price." If both partners "compromise" but continue to feel that "I am really right," the result will be just a temporary truce and the "battle" probably will resume at a later date with new ammunition. When both parties are willing to compromise, the solution may be one of mutual acceptance and increased mutual respect.

7. *Avoid manipulative pressure.*   The man who "butters up" his wife with presents, or the wife who prepares her husband's favorite dinner *simply* to win an argument may win the battle but lose the war. Marriage partners usually see through manipulative techniques, and end up feeling resentful, especially of those techniques that involve the withholding of love or approval.

8. *Be willing to go the extra mile.*

> There are many instances in any human relationship where someone must go the second mile, and there are many second miles to be walked in a successful marriage. It will sometimes be the husband who walks them and sometimes the wife. When both are willing to do this, there is a kind of sharing that raises the marriage relationship to the highest level of happiness. [Landis, p. 421.]

Sometimes an argument or conflict will be decided on the basis of need. The husband may decide to himself, "Okay, she needs to go out of town this weekend more than I need to go hunting," or the wife may decide, "I guess he needs that new car, even if I don't think we do. I'll trust his judgment," and the argument is settled.

The ideal marriage relationship is not necessarily one where there is an absence of conflict. Conflict in marriage results from two very alive, vital, interesting people sharing a way of life and solving their problems as they arise. Some couples feel closer after they have had an argument and have reached a mutually satisfactory solution. The resolution of the conflict has served to bring them closer together and to solidify their union.

What Is a Successful Marriage?

Your definition of a "successful" marriage will depend largely upon your expectations. Some might feel that just being able to stay together for a given number of years constitutes a "successful" marriage, but most people would not be willing to settle for such a minimal definition. You may think of many other criteria that would define a "successful" marriage, but here are a few that appear to be basic.

The marriage partners help each other to continue to "grow" and to "grow up" so that both become all that they *can* possibly be. In this sort of "self-actualizing" marriage both partners realize their mutual dependence upon each other for help when needed.

The marriage partners are sensitive to each other's needs as well as to their own; they try to meet these needs through tenderness, cooperation, and love.

The marriage partners, through a loving understanding of each other's sexuality, contribute to a healthy sexual relationship. Their .sexual relationship is important to them, but it is not the only basis for their continued love and growth.

The marriage partners have developed a healthy "fighting" relationship; they are able to clear the air when conflicts arise, not through selfishness or humiliation, but through a process of mutually working through conflict to a mutually acceptable solution. Each realizes the *power* he or she has over the other – the power to destroy by words or actions, and they do not use that power in a hurtful manner.

The marriage partners have a mutual feeling of commitment to their marriage as a way of life. They share common interests but are also aware that each partner needs breathing room – some private moments of aloneness.

Perhaps these standards seem pretty high; when you look around, you probably do not see many marriages that satisfactorily fulfill all of them. Most young people, when they begin their own marriage, *assume* that theirs will be the ideal marriage, the mutually committed, totally loving relationship. Can you be sure yours will be? No; no one really can be *sure* that his marriage will even succeeed, but if both marriage partners have adequate knowledge of marriage expectations, possible sources of conflict, and the resulting adjustments, as well as an honest and loving communication system, their chances will be much better than average.

Marriages do not succeed by chance; they do not fail by chance. *People* make the difference between success and failure in marriage. *People* react and regulate their lives to changing circumstances, changing times, changing personalities, and all the other factors which interact and influence all human relationships. Marriage *may* be the most potentially satisfying or the most potentially destructive experience that two people can have together.

Summary

Preparations for the wedding and honeymoon are usually shared by the couple, with the bride concentrating on the wedding plans and the groom handling most of the honeymoon plans. The honeymoon provides a transitional period from singleness to marriedness, although the real adjustments begin after the honeymoon in the course of intimate everyday living.

Sometimes a couple's little problems get blown all out of proportion and become big problems. Couples can guard against overemphasizing little problems by: keeping things in perspective, keeping the communications channels open, having realistic expectations, handling their finances soundly, discovering their attitudes about sexual roles, and understanding each other. Sexual adjustment will take time and patience before a mutually satisfying relationship can be established.

There are two main methods of handling marital conflict: the win-lose method, and the clear-the-air method. In the win-lose method one partner must win at any cost; this is a destructive type of marital conflict, and in the end no problems are solved.

In clearing-the-air, the couples establish good ground rules. They remember that communications go both ways, they restate their partner's point of view, they define the problem, they stick to the issue, the don't hurt each other by hitting below the belt, they are prepared to compromise, they avoid manipulation, and they are each willing to go the extra mile.

A successful marriage must be built by the marriage partners. Such a marriage grows in its understanding and acceptance and allows the individuals to be all that they can be.

Questions:

1. How do marital adjustments differ from adjustments that are made when living with roommates? How are they similar?
2. Why is it so difficult to keep marital problems, especially the little gripes and pet peeves, in perspective?
3. How do people communicate in marriage without saying anything? How could a husband or wife know that the spouse was angry or hurt although nothing had been said?
4. In your opinion, what characterizes a "constructive fight" and what characterizes a "destructive fight" in a marriage relationship? Why do many fights end up being destructive?
5. Have you ever been tempted to "hit below the belt" in a fight or argument? What would prompt such a reaction? What is the person who is "hitting below the belt" really trying to do?

GROUP DISCUSSION

1. "Marital disagreements regarding money are selfish; two loving persons should not have to argue about such materialistic things." Do you agree or disagree with this statement? Why?
2. Under what conditions would you accept "help" in the form of money from parents? Do you think doing so would present any problems? What determines whether or not parental "help" harms or helps a marriage relationship? Who has to make the decision?
3. You have just gotten married; your spouse's parents want to "help" you financially but you are afraid that there will be strings attached. Will you accept their offer? If so, how will you handle the "strings"? If not, how would you refuse without hurting the parents?
4. Compile a list of ten items that your group considers to be more "women's work" than "men's work" and another list of ten "men's work" items. Were there any differences within your group? What determines your classification of "women's work" or "men's work"?
5. In your relationships with the opposite sex, what method of settling conflicts is usually used — win-lose or clear-the-air? How

do you react to these two methods? Which do you think is used most often?

6. Why is it so difficult sometimes to define the problem and stick to the issue that a couple is arguing about? Have you ever been "sidetracked" into dead issues, or issues that have not been settled in the past? What happens when a problem gets sidetracked?

7. "The healthy marriage relationship is the one that can fight well." Do you agree or disagree with this statement? Why is fighting necessary?

OUTSIDE PROJECTS

1. Find pictures in magazines showing various sex roles in the home: scrubbing the floor, washing windows, cooking, ironing, raking leaves, shoveling snow, etc. Try to find some showing alternatives to some of these roles: husband cooking, wife mowing lawn, etc. (Number each picture.) Display them around the room and have the rest of the class walk around and rank them into three categories: "women's work," "men's work," or "neutral." Then discuss the reactions. Where are there areas of agreement or disagreement? Why do students feel the way they do?

2. Using the same pictures, have the students rate these on the following scale: "I have done this," "I enjoy doing this," "I dislike doing this," "I hate doing this." Discuss the reactions. What do they tell you about each person's role expectations?

BIBLIOGRAPHY

Bowman, Henry A. *Marriage for Moderns*, 6th ed. New York: McGraw-Hill Book Company, 1970.

Klemer, Richard H. and Margaret G. *The Early Years of Marriage*. Public Affairs Pamphlet No. 424. New York: Public Affairs Committee, 1968.

Landis, Paul H. *Making the Most of Marriage*, 4th ed. New York: Appleton-Century-Crofts, Inc., 1970.

McKuen, Rod. *Listen to the Warm*. New York: Random House, 1967.

Williamson, Robert C. *Marriage and Family Relations.* New York: John Wiley & Sons, Inc., 1966.

14

How Do We Feel
about Children?

Most couples look forward to having a family and children of their own; they plan with great anticipation for the arrival of their first child. Couples usually feel that it is their "right," if not their purpose, to have children. However, more and more couples are beginning to feel that their "right" also includes planning or limiting the size of their family.

Paul Ehrlich, in *The Population Bomb,* points out the potential dangers of overpopulation, and although the birth rate has begun to stabilize in the United States, many feel that overpopulation is more than just a "national" responsibility. Emphasis has been placed not only upon the number of children per family, but also upon the quality of life desired for our survival. In the years ahead, as you begin your own family, it is not altogether unlikely that you will see more changes and restrictions regarding population control and "quality of life" standards.

Family planning is a very personal matter that must be given serious thought by each couple. If and when you decide to have children, it is essential that you view this decision in the light of the

"The natural depth of man
is the whole of creation."
— Wilson Van Dusen

many added responsibilities it entails, not only from a population standpoint but also, and even more importantly, from a personal standpoint. The birth of a child can be a wonderful and miraculous experience for most parents. Thus Paul Landis observes, "As having children becomes more of a privilege and less an inherent right, children will be a greater source of joy, and many of the burdens of having children will be removed" [P. Landis, p. 542].

In this chapter we will discuss family planning, some of the myths regarding parenthood, and the changing roles of mothers and fathers in the modern home.

Family Planning

Your decision regarding whether and when to have a child is one that should be decided mutually. It probably will be based upon many factors. You will want to ask several questions: "Do we *want* children?" "Are we mature enough to accept the responsibilities involved in raising and adequately providing for children?" "How many children are we emotionally prepared to raise?" "Can we financially care for the children we want to have?" "How real do we feel is the threat of overpopulation?"

Many methods are available for preventing conception or fertilization for couples who wish to plan for the arrival of their children. We have reached the point where it is theoretically possible for parents to have children only when they so desire. Remarkable progress has been made in recent years in the development of safe, reliable, and effective contraceptives. (*Contraception* is the term used when discussing the prevention of conception – that is, the fertilization of the egg by the sperm during sexual intercourse.) Contraception allows couples to have children by choice, not chance.

Of course, no one can tell you how many children you should have, or how soon after marriage, or how often you should have them. This is your personal choice. But if and when you marry, you probably should know something about the various methods of family planning so that your decision regarding your children can be an intelligent one. Even if your state does not require a premarital physical examination, having such an examination is *very* strongly recommended as a personal requirement. Your physician can answer any personal sexual questions you might have and is your best guide in helping you choose the contraceptive method you wish to use (if you wish to use one) in planning your family.

Just as there is no "ideal" number of children for all families, there is no one "ideal" method of birth control suitable for *all* couples. Some methods can be secured only through a doctor, while others may be purchased in a drugstore without a prescription.

The Choice Is Yours

Whether or not you "plan" your family is a personal matter which can be decided only by you as a couple. The technical know-how in the form of reliable methods is available, so that having a baby or not having a baby is entirely *your* choice. If you choose not to have a baby at this time, the method of contraception you select should be acceptable to *both* of you.

Whatever means of contraception you as a couple choose to employ, it should fulfill these requirements:

1. It should be relatively effective; no method is foolproof, but the method you choose should, if used with intelligence and care, be as nearly reliable as possible.
2. It should be relatively easy to use, simple, and readily understood.
3. It should be readily available and relatively inexpensive.
4. It should be aesthetically acceptable to both parties and distasteful to neither.
5. It should permit normal, satisfactory sexual intercourse.
6. It should have no harmful results (no serious side effects).
7. It should be temporary, so that it may be terminated at will, unless for some special reason the couple desires sterilization. [Adapted from Bowman, pp. 505-6.]

A contraceptive method meeting these standards allows each couple to decide for themselves *when* they want children, *how many* children they want, and how to *avoid pregnancy* when they so choose. It is not only for the parents benefit that many couples wish to control conception, but also for the welfare of the children, for "child spacing is considered an essential in providing the maximum social and economic advantages [for the child] " [P. Landis, p. 557].

Pregnancy as a Shared Experience

Although pregnancy is a female condition, in the course of which the mother goes through many psychological and physical changes, it is also, in a sense, a shared condition. Although the wife is the one carrying their child and the husband's biological function as such has ended, he has an indispensable function as a psychological partner. His "separateness" from their child or his physical inability to share her experiences during the prenatal period may contribute to his feelings of ineptness and being left out. Having a baby is a cooperative venture from the very beginning; the wife may contribute more physically during the nine month "waiting period," but the presence of an understanding and loving husband during those nine months is of immeasurable help to the wife's state of mind.

He can do many things to make his wife's pregnancy more enjoyable. He may help her with the housework; he may find pleasant things for them to do together during their leisure time; he may participate in prenatal classes with her, so that they will both better understand their coming role as parents. Perhaps the best thing that he can do to help his wife during these nine months is to understand that she occasionally may feel "let down," cross, or "not herself" during this time. A woman's moods may tend to intensify during her pregnancy, and they can be very changeable. Both partners will benefit if her husband accepts this and helps her through these "moods."

Adjustments are not one-sided during pregnancy. A wife cannot and should not expect that her husband will be overly solicitious to her during her pregnancy. After all, pregnancy is a normal and natural condition for women, and most emotionally well adjusted women do not "suffer" extensively during pregnancy if they take the difficult moments in stride and do not overreact to them. There may be some women who play up their discomfort, in effect using their pregnancy to gain attention, sympathy, and pity, but these are a minority.

For most women, pregnancy is a period where they reap the benefits of a healthy mental and physical attitude. It is often said that a woman is more "beautiful" during pregnancy than when she is not pregnant; she tends to show a glow and warmth that mark her enthusiasm for the life of the child she is bearing.

Adjusting to Parenthood

When your first child is born, you and your spouse will assume a completely new role – you will be parents. Half of American girls are married by the time they are twenty and half of the boys before they are twenty-three. More girls marry at age eighteen than at any other age. The trend toward earlier marriage, which grows out of the trend toward earlier dating, is a serious hazard to family life in America. Many studies have been made relating age at marriage to divorce and to happiness in marriage, and without exception the studies show that teen-age marriages are much more likely to end in divorce or to be unhappy even if they remain intact. [J. Landis, p. 176.]

Along with a trend toward earlier marriages comes an accompanying desire for couples to start their families earlier. For many couples the period of childbearing is compressed into a shorter number of years, and many women will echo the sentiment, "I want to have all my children before I'm thirty, and then I can still be young enough to enjoy them."

If your expectations regarding marriage have been somewhat realistic, you probably will find that your adjustments will be much more easily made. The same will hold true for becoming parents. Just why do you want to have children? Because it is expected? Because it will help solidify your marriage? What are your expectations regarding parenthood?

LeMasters* points out that very often we approach parenthood on the basis of folklore rather than actual fact. He lists seventeen folk beliefs about children and parents and then proceeds to analyze them:

1. That rearing children is fun.
2. That children are sweet and cute.
3. That children will turn out well if they have "good" parents.
4. That girls are harder to rear than boys.
5. That today's parents are not as good as those of yesterday.
6. That childrearing today is easier because of modern medicine, modern appliances, child psychology, and so on.
7. That children today really appreciate all the advantages their parents are able to give them.
8. That the hard work of rearing children is justified by the fact that we are going to make a better world.
9. The sex education myth: That children won't get into trouble if they have been told the facts of life.
10. That there are no bad children — only bad parents.
11. That two parents are always better than one.
12. That modern behavioral science has been helpful to parents.

---

*Reprinted with permission from LeMasters, *Parents in Modern America* (Homewood, Ill.: The Dorsey Press, 1970).

13. That love is enough to sustain good parental perform-
    ance.
14. That all married couples should have children.
15. That childless married couples are frustrated and unhap-
    py.
16. That children improve a marriage.
17. That American parents can be studied without interview-
    ing fathers. [Adapted from LeMasters, pp. 18–29.]

Sorry, but these are *all* myths! Let's rephrase and examine them
one by one.

Rearing children can *be fun*, but it is also frustrating, often
thankless, and nerve-shattering, as well as rewarding, exciting, and
stimulating. In any case, it is not necessarily *fun* in the strictest sense
of the word. This writer is reminded of her own daughters playing
"house" when they were very young; after some time, one remarked
to the other, "Let's quit. This isn't fun any more!" But you can't
quit raising children because it isn't fun any more; it is a very
responsible position which requires all the ability you can muster —
and then some!

Children may *be sweet and cute*, sometimes, but they are also
colicky, stubborn, mean, embarrassing, and sassy as well as adorable
and precious. The adjectives used to describe children could fill many
pages, but you can fill in your own from observation and experience.

Children may *turn out "well" if they have "good" parents*, but
this depends upon your definitions of "well" and "good." It seems
that parents who sacrifice for their children, show them love and
concern, and are "good" parents in the best sense of the word have
the most success in raising children. However, there are many factors
which complicate the situation and the odds may go against them.
On the other hand, we can think of examples where children from
"bad" or unfortunate homes have turned out very well, with very
little if any help from their parents.

The sex of the child does not determine its "ease" or "difficulty"
in regard to rearing. Some parents find it much easier to raise boys
than girls, and others will be just as adamant regarding the opposite
point of view. Thus it seems that parents should be equally prepared
to raise either boys or girls, and that they should be able to
realistically prepare either sex for adulthood. The "pros" or "cons"
relating to the raising of boys or girls are largely matters of personal

experience and cannot be easily generalized. Each sex will present unique problems.

Standards may well be higher for today's parents than parents of yesterday. LeMasters points out that often "it is not enough for modern parents to produce children in their own image: the children have to be reared to be not only different from their fathers and mothers but also *better*" [p. 54]. This is quite a burden to place upon new parents; perhaps many modern parents are only setting themselves up for failure and disappointment if they somehow expect their children to be "bigger and better than ever before."

Modern appliances, child psychology, and the expectations of others often set up a *vicious circle of perfection in rearing children today.* Modern communications and technology have made us more aware of standards that we expect will apply to everyone. We may feel the pressure from society to have the innate ability, somehow, to be perfect parents, and even that the caring for the first child will somehow be continuously beautiful, happy, and "full of roses." Sometimes our "perfect" expectations are a bit unrealistic, as the following anecdote illustrates:

> "A friend had her first baby, and had been home from the hospital for two days, when suddenly I heard a pounding and sobbing at my door. When I opened it, there stood Julie, tear-stained face, crying baby — they both looked a mess. I took the baby, made Julie sit down to drink some coffee, and after they both quieted down, she blurted out, 'Oh, I never thought it would be like this. I had visions of coming home from the hospital and there would be flowers, a quiet sleeping baby, an attentive husband, and I'd be wearing a long beautiful robe, and the apartment would be sparkling — and it's not like that at all. The baby is colicky and I hate to hear him cry. I have diapers all over because I haven't had time to get them folded, and Mark is working overtime, and our meals are all off kilter — and I'm just miserable!'"

Children do not necessarily "appreciate" advantages given to them, especially if they consider them to be their "right." What about you? Did you view education, freedom of religion, indoor plumbing, or a weekly allowance as "advantages" or as "rights"? If you are planning to have children just so that they can appreciate everything you can do for them, you had better re-evaluate your expectations.

Rearing children will not necessarily make the world a better place. Certainly, your children will be the hope of the future, but they may not be any braver, wiser, stronger, or happier than you are. On the occasions when rearing children becomes difficult and dreary, though, parents may need to cling to the view that these children *will* somehow make the world a better place, for this illusion makes the hard work seem worth it.

Children will not always stay "out of trouble" if they know the facts of life. Knowledge and logic often become clouded by very strong emotions. Sex education, in this writer's opinion, should begin in the home and continue through the entire school system, but knowledge alone will not determine one's sexual actions. It is to be hoped that adequate knowledge and self-respect will help young people make more realistic decisions instead of decisions based on emotions alone.

"Bad" children cannot always be blamed on "bad" parents. Our extreme emphasis upon youth may have set up parents as the "fall guys" whenever children do anything wrong. The parent who condemns himself each and every time something bad happens ("Where did I go wrong?"), may be setting himself up for too much blame. As potential parents, you will want to do everything you can to help your children succeed, but you cannot do it for them, just as your parents could not do your growing up and maturing for you.

Sometimes one parent may be better than two. The idea that two parents are always necessary to raise children properly is erroneous. It may be *easier* to have two persons to share the load and responsibilities, but it is not essential. In some cases, divorce may be the best solution to an unhappy marriage. The idea that parents should stay together "for the sake of the children" is false, for the children may be damaged psychologically by the presence of tensions, conflict, and family turmoil. In that case, one loving parent and the absence of stress may be better than two parents and constant stress.

Sometimes modern behavioral sciences have been harmful to parents, especially if they make parents feel guilty and inadequate for not being able to live up to all the "shoulds" that are put forth. Most parents have rather poor training for the job of being parents, but one does not need a degree in psychiatry to be a loving, caring, and adequate parent. Of course, not everyone can be a good parent;

it takes preparation, adequate expectations, love, concern, and all the positive attributes one can bring forth.

Love is a good beginning, but it is not enough to sustain good parental performance. If love is not accompanied by good judgment, experience, insight, and self-control, it will not be enough. Conversely, all the attributes just mentioned will not bring success if love is lacking. What is needed is a healthy combination of adequate skills and good intentions.

Parenthood is not a "club" that everyone should join. There are some couples who probably should *not* have children. If they have children just to be like everyone else, it is truly a tragedy. A couple should not feel pressured into having children, or into having *more* children than they want, just because "It's expected of us." The responsibilities of parenthood are very real and should be considered deeply before having or not having children.

Many childless married couples are very happy. The assumption that childless couples are "selfish" because they do not have children is as false as the assumption that all childless couples want children but can't have any. LeMasters points out that "It is also an interesting fact that a great many married couples *with* children are unhappy and frustrated. Thus those of us who are parents have to be somewhat careful about feeling sorry for those couples who don't have any children. They may feel the same way about us" [p. 28].

Children do not necessarily improve a marriage, nor do they provide the glue to hold a shaky marriage together. Indeed, some marriages are weakened by children and some parents have more conflict over children than over any other area in their marriage. Children can be and usually are the source of some of the greatest thrills and joys that parents can experience, but to think that children can hold together a marriage by themselves is to put the emphasis upon the wrong area. If a marriage is in trouble, it is very unlikely that children can save it.

The American father has often been the forgotten contributor in the family picture, and he is essential and important. Very often we talk only about mother in the home and stress her influence. Today's father is vastly different in role and image than the father of yesterday. Fathers today have much more leisure time and they often spend it with their families. In previous generations, fathers and sons often worked together, but today fathers camp, swim, ski, rake the leaves, take family vacations, and in general are with their wives and children – both boys and girls – much more than was formerly the case. The father in today's home is a very important force in his family's life.

Some Changing Roles

Both fathers and mothers find that their roles are changing in the modern family. In many cases, these changing roles present some conflicts, but they are not irreconcilable.

Changing Roles of the Father

The modern father is still the main provider for his family. He supports his family, spends a great deal of his time away from his home on the job, and has the responsibility for providing for his family's needs. However, he is also the partner in the home. In his childhood it may have been his mother's "job" to "raise the kids and take care of the house," but in his family he usually assumes part of this responsibility in a partnership with his wife.

Father is expected to be the "authority" in the family when it is needed, yet his children are apt to look upon him more as a buddy than as a tyrant. This is often a difficult role for him, for he must be consistently firm, yet he will want to be understanding and open to his children so that he can see their point of view.

His wife expects him to be "masculine" (whatever that means to her), but she also expects him to be tender, gentle, and considerate. She may want to be dominated *sometimes,* but she also wants him to be considerate of her feelings in a patient and loving manner.

He is expected to be assertive and strong when decisions are needed, but he also is expected to be cooperative and "equal" in the course of reaching those decisions. He no longer makes all the decisions by himself, and he seeks his wife's opinion before the two of them arrive at a mutual decision.

He is expected to be a success in his occupation, to pursue his own interests and hobbies, but still to have time to be a "family" man. Sometimes he may have to slight one of these in favor of the others, but it is expected that he will fulfill all of them to a greater or lesser degree.

Changing Roles of the Mother

Today's woman is expected to be a full-time mother, but she may feel that she wants "more" — especially after her children are grown. Society looks upon her, and she usually looks upon herself, as first and foremost a wife and mother. In addition to feeling pride and happiness in her role as a mother, she is a person in her own right, and often seeks fulfillment through a career of her own, through community service, or through personal hobbies.

Mother is expected to be the family's organizer as well as the family's improvisor. She usually takes charge of the activities of the family, assuming many "roles" as they are needed: car pool driver, nurse, peacemaker, and cook. She also needs the ability to handle situations that arise on the spur of the moment with tact, poise, and grace.

She expects to be treated as an equal partner in the family's decision-making processes, but sometimes she expects her husband to make the decisions for her.

She is expected to be her husband's companion as well as his lover, and to know when each role is necessary. She is expected to show interest, concern, and understanding for her husband's needs, and she expects the same in return.

She is expected to be a helpmate for her husband socially, but not to be his competitor. Although she may have her own "career" outside of the home, it is important that she not carry this competition with her into her home and family life. She is expected to act as her husband's hostess and his most important asset.

Summary

Family planning is a very personal matter which must be considered seriously by each couple.

For the couple who chooses to delay, plan, or space the arrival of children, there are several effective contraceptive methods available.

The couple will want to consider the advantages and disadvantages of the various methods before choosing the one that is best for them.

When children do arrive, the couple will have many adjustments to make. They would be wise to give careful consideration beforehand to their feelings regarding the advent of children in their lives, the responsibilities involved, and their expectations regarding the raising of children.

The roles of parents continue to change with each generation. Although they remain largely the same, the emphasis has shifted considerably in recent decades. The changing roles of parenthood may present some conflicts, and each couple will have to adjust their marriage in such a way that the changing roles are agreeable to both marriage partners.

Questions:

1. What are some of the differences of opinion that tend to cause disagreement between a couple with regard to family planning?
2. What are some of the adjustments that a couple must make after the arrival of children?
3. Will changing mother-father or husband-wife roles affect every marriage in the same way? Why or why not?

GROUP DISCUSSION

1. It has been determined that you and your marriage partner will not be able to have children. You decide to adopt a child. Which sex will you want to specify? Which sex do you think your spouse would specify? Why?
2. Where did you get your information about "the facts of life"? From your parents, from your friends, from school, or from some other source? Did you ever receive any faulty information? If so, how did it become clarified? What is your attitude toward sex education in the schools? Is it necessary or unnecessary?
3. Your five-year-old child has just asked you "Where do babies come from?" How would you answer? If the same question came from a nine-year-old would your answer differ? How explicit should parents be when answering their children's questions regarding sex? What factors must be taken into account here?

4. Kay and Jim have been married for two years; Jim would like Kay to stop working and have a baby, but she wants to wait a "little" longer. Inasmuch as Jim has been asking her to quit working for some time, he wonders how long "a little longer" will be? In their discussion, they finally determine that Kay does not want to have children – ever. She enjoys working, likes the things they can have and do because of the extra income, and doesn't want to get "tied down." If you were Jim, what would you do? Could this problem have been avoided or anticipated? How?

5. Sherry and Chuck have been married for ten years; they have three children, the youngest beginning first grade. Sherry wants to find a job but Chuck objects. He thinks that Sherry belongs at home with the children. Sherry replies, "But I know I'll get so bored when the children are gone all day. I've already talked to Ruth, our high school babysitter, and she would love to come after school every day to take care of the children. Oh please, I want to try it so badly." What would you advise them to do? What if the roles were reversed and Chuck wanted Sherry to go to work, but she wanted to stay home? Would this change your decision at all? What are some of the things that must be agreed upon if a mother is to go to work outside of the home while the children are in school?

OUTSIDE PROJECT. Find pictures of fathers and mothers evidently going off to work. Try to find various situations: leaving the children at home alone, leaving the children with a babysitter, leaving children at school, or the father leaving while his wife and children remain at home. Display them around the room and ask students for their reactions as to the *feelings* of the person leaving (Where is he or she going? Does he or she want to go?) and the *feelings* of the people being left behind (happy, contented, sad, unhappy, angry, etc.). Discuss the various situations. Some people will read different things into different situations. Why?

BIBLIOGRAPHY

Bowman, Henry A. *Marriage for Moderns*, 6th ed. New York: McGraw-Hill Book Company, 1970.

Landis, Judson T. "The Family and Social Change: A Positive View," in *Man and Civilization: The Family's Search for Survival*, ed. Seymour M. Farber, Piero Mustacchi, and Roger H. L. Wilson. New York: McGraw-Hill Book Company, 1965.

Landis, Paul H. *Making the Most of Marriage,* 4th ed. New York: Appleton-Century-Crofts, Inc., 1970.

LeMasters, R. E. *Parents in Modern America*. Homewood, Illinois: The Dorsey Press, 1970.

The reader also should consult the following booklets and pamphlets:

ABC's of Birth Control: How to Plan Your Family. New York: Planned Parenthood-World Population, 1969.

Getting Married: Your Quest for Intimacy. Life Cycle Center, Kimberly-Clark Corp., 1969.

Hall, Robert E. *Sex and Marriage*. New York: Planned Parenthood-World Population, 1965.

Klemer, Richard H. and Margaret G. *Sexual Adjustment in Marriage*. New York: Public Affairs Committee, Inc., 1966.

Langmyhr, Rev. George J. *Modern Methods of Birth Control*. New York: Planned Parenthood-World Population, 1970.

Your First Pregnancy: For the Young Woman Who's Contemplating or Expecting a Baby. Life Cycle Center, Kimberly-Clark Corp., 1970.

V

TIME FOR THE FUTURE

15

Take Time To Be Human

"Oh, that boss of mine; sometimes he's such a bear to get along with." "If you want to get along with Mr. Palmer, just talk about baseball." "My roommates are easy to get along with; we never have any problems." "Don't rock the boat and you'll get along just fine."

We use the words "get along" many times and for many different reasons. Although it is certainly very important for us to be able to "get along" with those with whom we live, work, or associate, human relations means more than just "getting along." Meaningful human relations are those experiences where people reach out to others with genuine care and understanding. They involve the total person, both as he sees himself and also as others see him. Meaningful human relations include the ability to "get along" with others inwardly as well as superficially.

How Does One Achieve Meaningful Human Relations?

Each person will have to work out his own pattern of human relations because each person is unique. However, there are certain ideas that can help us establish some personal guidelines. Bear in mind that it is sometimes difficult to separate some of the traits described here, for they may overlap.

Have a Healthy Self-Image

Meaningful human relations start with the individual person — *you.* Before you can accept a realistic self-image, you first need to be thoroughly familiar with the person you call "me." You may not always be happy with the picture you see, but awareness is the first step toward acceptance and/or change. There may be some aspects of yourself that really cannot be changed, in which case a healthy awareness will help you to accept the unchangeable. But there usually are many more features of yourself that *can* be changed if you have the motivation and desire to make the changes.

It is generally accepted that sound mental health is in large part dependent upon a feeling of self-worth — which is *not* to be confused with vanity or false pride. When you recognize that you have great potential and are a worthwhile person, it will show in your life. You will be more confident of yourself as an individual who has much to contribute to the world in which you live. When you begin to understand yourself, you can then begin to trust yourself and your relationships with others. You need to trust yourself and to be a trustworthy person before you can reach out and trust others.

Accept and Understand Yourself and Others

Trusting others is very closely related to trusting yourself. After you are able to accept yourself, you can then reach out and establish relationships with others on a more meaningful basis. Before this time, relationships with others may have been very hesitant, for the risk involved was often more than you dared to take; you may have felt that the threat of rejection or disappointment would be too much for you to bear.

When you can accept others and attempt to understand them, you will come to realize that it is not necessary to agree with or even to like everyone else. We are imperfect people in an imperfect world, and should not expect perfection. Accepting and understanding others is our way of trying to bridge the gap of imperfection. You will not have to agree with others in order to accept them, but you should respect the differences that make life interesting.

Accepting and understanding others, as they are, will help you to handle situations which might otherwise be intolerable. For example, you may be forced to work with someone who is very aggressive, inefficient, or defensive. Your situation may seem intolerable, for you find that you just cannot agree with this person and hostilities are constantly building. But if you take a moment, back off, and try to see the total situation, you may be able to gain more perspective. Perhaps you threaten this individual (or perhaps you feel threatened); maybe he is basically insecure and puts on his aggressive front for defensive reasons; maybe some personal problems are interfering with his work (or maybe some previously unrecognized personal problem of yours is affecting your judgment). If you try to understand *why* you have arrived at the situation in which you find yourself, you may then be able to accept or partially understand a previously intolerable situation, thereby turning it into one that is bearable or acceptable. When you are able to accept and understand others, even though you do not agree with them, your relationships will assume more meaning.

Be Genuine and Sincere

> The phony is the hollow man who can only "operate" among men rather than relate to them. It is not easy to detect him at first, for his hollowness has a smooth exterior, suave and seemingly sincere. Though he is often very intelligent, his intelligence usually is out of focus. He has more faces than Eve, is found in all professions, and infiltrates business and education. He is the despair of his wife, is despised by his children. Their love for him enables them to see through the smooth exterior to observe the hollowness and unrealized potential within. His form of communication is to broadcast two conflicting signals at the same time. [As with] the dog who growls while wagging his tail, you don't know which end to trust. [Ungersma,* p. 29.]

Maybe all of us are "phonies" once in a while. Sometimes we feel that we have to "con" or "bluff" our way, or pretend we are

*From *Escape from Phoniness* by Aaron J. Ungersma. Copyright © MCMLXIX, The Westminster Press. Used by permission.

something we are not. In meaningful human relations, however, we
do not *rely* upon these tactics and they are the exception to our
behavior, not the rule.

When we spot a phony, we gear our relationships with that person
accordingly. We find ourselves thinking, "Is this just an act?" or "I
wonder what he wants this time." Just as we resent the phony when
we are dealing with him, we should remember that others resent the
"phoniness" that may be present in us. If we want our relationships
to be meaningful, we need to *be* sincere, not merely to *act* sincere. In
order to be sincere and genuine, the next two guidelines also need to
be followed.

Be Lovingly Honest

Sometimes when someone says to you, "Now tell me the truth. What
do you really think?" he does not necessarily want the *whole* truth.
What constitutes honesty is difficult to define because conditions
and people vary, so that each situation needs to be considered
separately.

Ever since you were a child you were taught that "Honesty is the
best policy." But in practice we find so much deceit and dishonesty
that it seems difficult to separate truth from falsehood. We have
"Truth in Lending" laws to help us determine the actual true cost of
borrowing. "Honest John" the super-salesman subconsciously tries to
make the distinction between himself and other salesmen who might
not be as honest. You find yourself in the middle of all of this, trying
to determine what really is truth?

In your relationships with others you probably can think of many
occasions where you were not totally honest. It may have bothered
you, but you felt you had no alternative. The question does not
seem to be "Should I be honest?" but rather, "How do I go about
telling the truth?" Your friend asks you, "How do you like my new
coat?" and you think it is awful. But social rules tell you that you
can't say that to her. Your answer may vary from "It's beautiful" to
"It's terrible," but it probably will be somewhere in between. Using
the criteria of *"loving* honesty," you might answer, "It's really a
pretty color," or "You're lucky you can wear that style," or some
other answer that is honest but not offensive.

Many of our social, work, and home situations call for this type of

HAVE A HEALTHY SELF-IMAGE

REMEMBER, YOU HELP DETERMINE ANOTHER'S SELF-IMAGE

ACCEPT & UNDERSTAND YOURSELF & OTHERS

BE GENUINE & SINCERE

BE LOVINGLY HONEST

CULTIVATE THE "WE'RE BOTH O.K." ATTITUDE

COMMUNICATE PERSON-TO-PERSON

BE ROOTED BUT FLEXIBLE

BE RESPONSIBLE FOR YOUR DECISIONS

CONTRIBUTE TO A MEANINGFUL OCCUPATION

Can you identify the ten interrelated paths which lead to a warm, secure harbor? These ten guidelines can help you build your own meaningful human relationships.

loving honesty and do not present serious problems. But in other cases a person's dilemma about honesty may be almost insoluble. For example, your father is gravely ill with terminal cancer. When do you tell him about his "true condition"? No *one* answer can be given for all cases. You would not want to lull him into a false sense of security or to build false illusions of hope by saying "There is nothing wrong with you." On the other hand, you may feel that the "truth" would cause him to give up entirely. There are many dangers in blunt "truth-at-any-cost" answers, just as there are many dangers in "overprotecting" by withholding the truth.

In all cases, you must try to make the best judgment regarding what would be best for the other person. Try to ask yourself, "What will my answer do to the other person?" Social pressures sometimes stifle the truth; you must ask yourself "How can I be lovingly honest?"

Cultivate the "We're Both OK" Attitude

When you are able to accept yourself and others honestly you can say, "I'm OK and you're OK, too."

Not everyone arrives at this healthy point of view regarding himself and others. Dr. Thomas Harris, in his book *I'm OK — You're OK* states that this attitude is the result of a conscious expression or decision by the individual "based on thought, faith, and the wager of action" [Harris, p. 50].

Sometimes when we adopt this position we expect instant reactions in the form of acceptance by others, but it does not always happen that way. It may be that we accept someone else, open up ourselves and become vulnerable, only to be cut down. This is why Harris speaks of a "wager" of action, for there *is* risk involved in saying "I accept you."

Despite the risks, however, in the final analysis an accepting attitude will help us develop something warm and meaningful with others, remembering that we both need help in establishing a mutual relationship. When we say "We're both OK" we are saying also, "I need others in order to have a full and rewarding life; I'm willing to risk a relationship with you because you're OK — I accept you as the person you are. We don't have to agree, but let's help each other — OK?"

Be Responsible for Your Decisions

If you want to have meaningful human relationships, you cannot expect others to assume all the burdens; you have to be responsible for your own actions and to share the burdens of others.

Being responsible for your own actions also includes a knowledge of the *power* of your words and actions. We all have felt some blows to our self-image as the result of the careless, cruel, or humiliating words or actions of others, and it is only reasonable to assume that our words and actions have the same power to hurt other people. We can destroy, damage, or wound very deeply the self-image of others.

Thus, one of our responsibilities is to refrain from inflicting such pain on others. This does not mean that we should help to sustain another's faulty self-image, but it does mean that we have the responsibility to act and speak with love and concern so that we are not the cause of some unnecessary wound or scar upon the self-image of another.

Be Flexible but Rooted

We have talked about change and the effect of change many times in this book. Change will continue, and not all of it will be good. Will your human relations skills allow you to be flexible enough to change and adapt? Just as your personality will continue to change as you grow and mature, so will the personalities of others. In relating to others, you will need a continuing growth rate in flexibility also.

Flexibility will be especially helpful when adjusting to the changes of the future. You will need an accompanying measure of rootedness — something you can fall back on for stability. You can derive this from your value system, for if you have thought out your value system, if you have determined your priorities, and if you have had some success in achieving your goals, you will have developed your own warm, secure harbor — someplace where you can return, where you belong, where things "make sense." Meaningful relationships need to be based upon a deep, strong, rooted basis, as well as upon a flexible framework. The two are not incompatible; they are complementary.

Contribute to a Meaningful Occupation

When you have a realistic self-image, you will be aware of your potentialities. At this point in your life you may have decided tentatively on your future occupation; you may have set your goals and already be working to achieve them. When you leave school, you will become a part of the world of work, and your contribution to the world of work can be as meaningful as you want it to be.

If you have made good choices up to this point, you have evaluated your interests and abilities and should be fairly certain that the occupation you have chosen reflects your own choice and is one that you will be happy in. It will remain for you to "try it out," to enter the world of work and see whether or not your expectations have been realistic. You also will realize that most job skills today are somewhat changeable, so you will need to upgrade yourself continually if you wish to progress. This upgrading may take the form of seminars, in-service training programs, additional school, or perhaps even retraining.

When you contribute to a meaningful occupation of your own choice, you will find that doing so enhances your sense of self-worth. You will feel that you are a worthwhile and productive member of society. You will be a builder of the future.

Remember the Other Person's Self-Image

Other people contribute to your self-image; your relationships with them may be either positive or negative, and this will affect the way you view yourself. Conversely, you will contribute in the same way to the self-image of others. You have the power, through your words and your actions, to build up or tear down other people.

If you overcome the tendency to build yourself up at the expense of others, you will be happier with yourself and with others. If you follow the Golden Rule, and treat others in the same way you would like to be treated, you will find life much more pleasant and meaningful.

Communicate Person-to-Person

So much of our misunderstanding today is the result of misinterpretation, "getting wires crossed," or breakdowns in communications. If you remember that communication is a two-way street, you can build up good channels for both sending and receiving messages. If you are as concerned about understanding others as you are about being understood, you will be communicating person-to-person.

Remember that communication may be nonverbal also. Your physical presence – what you "say" with your eyes or with your facial expression – may be extremely meaningful. This type of communication is potentially much more personal and deep than the use of words. Person-to-person communication requires active listening, openness, loving honesty, acceptance, and sensitivity to the inner feelings of the other person. Communicating on a person-to-person level is a cooperative venture.

Everyday Relationships

Work

When we enter the world of work, much of our success is going to depend upon our "people skills" — our ability to get along with others. We have pointed out previously that proper attitude is one of the most important attributes that employers seek in a new employee; it outweighs many of the other requirements necessary for landing a job — such as skill, cooperation, and appropriate appearance.

Many factors are involved in getting along on the job — such as enthusiasm, helpfulness, and courtesy — but probably the most important is the ability to *sincerely* make the other person feel important. Again, this is a matter of protecting someone else's self-image. The person who is able to perform in a way that brings credit to the company, or that makes the boss or a co-worker look good, will look good and feel good personally, too.

Flexibility is another key to good working relationships. When you consider that the average twenty-year-old is expected to change jobs about six or seven times, you realize how important it is to remain flexible. If you accept changes as a challenge and do not resist them, you will be the winner.

Social

Living in a society that has many unwritten rules governing "acceptable" behavior can sometimes be rather frustrating. We have discussed both the need to establish meaningful relationships with others and the need to be an individual. Human relations in the social world begin with a combination of intelligent individualism ("I can stand on my own") and group spirit ("I enjoy others, too"). There is a difference between blind conformity and group membership.

Developing the arts of tact, diplomacy, poise, self-confidence, and fair play will benefit you socially, as well as in other areas of your life. These arts will help you bridge the gap between individualism and group membership. Exercising common sense, tact, and diplomacy may often save you from embarrassment or uneasiness, especially if you are aware of the emotional needs and desires of other people in relation to your own needs and desires.

Home

If you decide to marry, remember that your decision will be one of the most important decisions you will ever make. When you think of it in terms of sharing the rest of your life with one person, you can see that it is not a decision to be reached hastily.

A large portion of the success factor in marriage is dependent upon good human relations skills. Not only do you need an ability to "get along" with your spouse, but both of you also must want to help each other to be all that you can be if you are to have a truly lasting and deep relationship. You will want to establish your home on sound foundations, including financial attitudes, similar interests, a similar value system, an awareness of the problems that are going to arise from differences in backgrounds and home experiences (and a willingness to work at solving them), and healthy sexual attitudes.

If and when you have children, you will need to recognize your responsibilities. The home is one of the most crucial factors in establishing healthy attitudes in children, so that perhaps the biggest gift you can give them, besides your love, is the stability that comes from a sound marriage and home. Your home can be the warm secure harbor for those you love.

What about the Future?

People have been asking the same question for centuries: "What will the future bring?" In view of the very rapid changes which have taken place, especially in the last few generations, we can be quite sure of *one* thing the future will bring: more change. For this reason flexibility in a personal atmosphere of security is needed to help you adapt to future changes.

We know that many jobs will be obsolete in the relatively near future. Will you be prepared for this? Changing technology also will create many new jobs, and perhaps you may have to retrain for a

YESTERDAY, TODAY AND TOMORROW

I said to my friend,
  "See her leaning over his arm?
  Yesterday she leaned over my arm."
And he said:
  "Tomorrow she will lean over mine."
And I said,
  "See her sitting at his side;
  And yesterday she sat at my side."
And he said:
  "Tomorrow she will sit at mine."
And I said,
  "Don't you see her drinking from his Cup?
  And yesterday she sipped from mine."
And he said:
  "Tomorrow she will drink from mine."
And I said,
  "Look how she glances at him with eyes
  full of love!
  And with just such love, yesterday
  she glanced at me."
And he said:
  "Tomorrow she will glance at me likewise."
And I said,
  "Listen to her whispering songs of
  love in his ear.
  And yesterday she whispered the same songs
  in mine."
And he said:
  "Tomorrow she will whisper them in mine."
And I said,
  "Look at her embracing him; and
  yesterday she embraced me."
And he said:
  "Tomorrow she will lie in my arms."
And I said,
  "What a strange woman she is!"
And he said:
  "She is Life."

                              —Kahlil Gibran,

                    Thoughts and Meditations

new job that is not even in existence today. You may be quite
certain that the basic skills you now have will have to be updated in
order for you to keep up with the changing times.

What direction will your future take? What responsibility will you
take to direct your own future and that of your community? Just as

your grandfather could not envision what kind of world you would be living in, you cannot foresee the type of world that your grandchildren will be living in. In the process of living the good life yourself, can you build for the future? Will you be able to build strong human relationships? It takes time and effort and caring and love to build meaningful human relationships.

Summary

Human relations involve more than just "getting along" with others. Although it is important to get along well with others, meaningful human relations involve genuine care, concern, and understanding.

Some guidelines to more meaningful human relationships include: having a healthy self-image; accepting and understanding yourself and others; being genuine and sincere; being lovingly honest; cultivating the "We're Both OK" attitude; accepting responsibility for your decisions; being flexible but rooted; contributing to a meaningful occupation; remembering the other person's self-image; and communicating person-to-person.

We need to have meaningful human relationships with people in our work situation, in our social lives, and in our home and family circles. When one is able to achieve this, his life will be a warm, secure harbor where he can drop anchor and be "at home."

Questions:

1. How will a feeling of "I'm OK and you're OK, too" help you to get along with difficult people?
2. Do you think that everyone is a phony once in a while? How do you feel about phoniness?
3. How can flexibility and rootedness be considered together?
4. When you feel that you can't "get along" with someone else, what seems to stand in the way? Is it all one-sided?

GROUP DISCUSSION

1. Of the ten qualities listed for achieving meaningful human relations, which is most difficult for you to achieve? Compare

your answer with those of the other members of your group and discuss your differences.

2. What are some of your pet peeves regarding "getting along" with others? What are some of the traits of others that interfere with good relationships? Do you think that you have any traits that might bother someone else? Discuss them among the group.

3. What would represent a "warm, secure harbor" for you? Include things that are important to you, where you feel like you belong, where you are accepted, and what makes sense to you.

4. Where are meaningful human relationships most important – at home, in your social life, or at work? Discuss your answers and any differences within your group.

BIBLIOGRAPHY

Gibran, Kahlil. *Thoughts and Meditations.* New York: The Citadel Press, Inc., 1960. Paperback: Bantam Books, Inc., 1968.

Harris, Thomas A. *I'M OK – YOU'RE OK.* New York: Harper & Row, Publishers, Inc., 1969.

Ungersma, Aaron J. *Escape From Phoniness.* Philadelphia: Westminster Press, 1969.

Index